The Light of Roses

1·27·08

For Mary —

— A lovely Rose in the
Garden of Life —

In

To Mikaal & Ethan
My Children of Light

In the Garden of our Lives

Grows the Rose

CONTENTS

Acknowledgments

My deepest heartfelt gratitude goes to my clients who have entrusted me to bear witness to their soul journeys. I am forever inspired and humbled.

I would like to thank my teachers Evelyn Rhae and Sanford Meisner for their vision and passion, and for their indelible mark on my soul.

An enormous thank you to my family, David, Mikaal and Ethan, for their unconditional love and for the lessons they have taught me. I would especially like to thank David, my husband, for his constant belief in me and in who I am.

To my editor, Joanne Garland, who is a Cosmic gift, I am eternally grateful. Her sensitive, perceptive guidance and professional commitment to excellence have enhanced the integrity of this work. Our journey together has been a soulful one.

A special thank you to my comrade James Maynard for his helpful suggestions and support, and to Annette Warfel for her insightful comments. Thanks to you both.

To Betty Littleton, Christine Ruttmann-Disimile, and Nancy Hopwood a great big thank you for your enthusiasm, encouragement, and support. I am truly grateful. Betty, my friend, I have never known a better listener than you.

A sincere appreciation and thank you to Barbara Valocore and the Lifebridge Foundation for their generosity.

A deeply respectful thank you to my parents for the road taken.

I would like to thank my soul for the journey. I would like to thank the Master Within.

And a most profound thank you to the Cosmic for all of its intuitive guidance, Love and Light. I am graced.

From my heart, I thank you all. Namasté.

And Jesus said, We cannot look upon
a single span of life and judge of anything.
There is a law that men must recognise:
Result depends on cause.
Men are not motes to float about
within the air of one short life,
and then be lost in nothingness.
They are undying parts of the eternal whole
that come and go, lo, many times
into the air of earth and of the great beyond,
just to unfold the God-like self.
A cause may be a part of one brief life;
results may not be noted till another life.
The cause of your results cannot be found within my life,
nor can the cause of my results be found in yours.
I cannot reap except I sow
and I must reap whate'er I sow.

— *The Aquarian Gospel of Jesus the Christ*
Chapter 114, verses 26-32

Introduction

The Light of Roses is an exploration of past-life regression as a form of healing, witnessed through the fascinating case studies of my clients as well as some of my own past lives and personal, spiritual, mystical experiences—my own soul threads through time.

This book is intended for all who hunger spiritually, who seek to "know the Self," who are shifting in consciousness, and who long to live fearlessly.

It is about the unfoldment of the soul on its journey back to Oneness as seen through the transformational use of past-life regression and transpersonal hypnotherapy to resolve present issues, gain healing and insight, release us from fear and guilt, and free ourselves "to be" all that we are, realizing that we create our reality through our choices.

If fear has ever held you in its grip, wrapped in the guise of guilt, blame, shame, anger, anxiety, if you have ever longed for "something more," if you have issues that you can't seemingly resolve with the tools you have at your disposal—issues that keep you from living your life at your highest potential—if you have ever felt spiritually isolated and alone . . .

If you have "memories" not of this life and time, if you have ever experienced a déjà vu, if the idea of reincarnation fascinates you, if you've ever wondered if this is all there is . . .

If you suffer from anxiety, phobias, or emotional blocks, if you have ever felt disempowered, if you want to know more about the karmic residue of the past, the Higher Self, the Inner Guide, the Soul's purpose, if you want to gain insight through the shared stories of others on their journey back to Oneness . . .

If you are a spiritual seeker, if you are on a journey of self-discovery, if you are aware of the speed at which life is moving, if you are learning to listen and heed your intuition, if you have experienced the synchronicity of life, if you are learning to love unconditionally, if you long for "Home," you will find resonance here . . . insight . . . perhaps answers.

The Light of Roses is about taking responsibility for your choices, recognizing that you do indeed create your own reality, leaving judgment in the past, loving and forgiving yourself, and realizing that you are worthy—that YOU are a part of God. All that is ever expected of you is simply *To Be Who You Are*. You are not in competition with anyone. You are all sacred beings of Light—Roses in the Garden. As your petals open to the Light, as your Soul unfolds, you reveal, unveil, the Light Within. Then comes the realization—It is One and the Same—*You Open As "I Am."* The Master Within is God.

The material esoterically embraces the Oneness of humanity and its evolvement metaphorically as a Garden of Roses. The Light of Roses is the aura around each soul, or "rose," as it unfolds in its evolution on the cross of matter—life, this incarnation. We, as a humanity, are a garden of roses here on planet Earth—in our garden of lives—to learn our lessons so that we may evolve into a state of Oneness, where the garden is simply Light.

The Light of Roses is a mystical journal of my work and a spiritual journey of my soul. In the evolution of this book, I've shared more of myself than I ever intended. In the beginning of this endeavor, I simply wanted to share with others the past-life regression work of my clients, knowing that if more people were merely aware of the profound healing that emerges through this process, humankind would benefit greatly.

Somehow, along the way, it became more than that. I found myself sharing parts of my life and I really didn't know if I wanted to do that. It certainly wasn't my intention. But when I sat down to write, that was what kept happening. So, I've let it be what it is. I've shared some of my most sacred and psychic experiences, as well as some of the most painful. They are the kinds of life experiences that we each have, and they stand out in all their vibrant color and avow the defining moments of our journey.

Pseudonyms have been used and some identifying details have

been changed to protect the privacy of my clients and others who have been mentioned.

In over twenty-nine years of work in the metaphysical field, it has been my experience that the most common malady of humanity is a lack of self-love, a feeling of unworthiness. In practical and immediate terms I hope this book will empower you, feed the flames of your spiritual fire, and help you to further your personal journey of self-realization.

Opening

This book is a story of Grace. Among the characters are pioneers, initiates, knights, nuns, and barmaids. On the pages of time travel the wicked, the innocent, the trapped, the deceived, the victims, the perpetrators—you and me. We have all been there at one time or another. We are all traveling the same road. We are all going to the same place. We are all headed Home. We are soul threads weaving our way through time. Some may get there sooner, but that may only be in how you look at it. Perhaps, it's all happening Now . . . *all of it*.

The mystery of our lives is the best part. Here anything is possible and yet most of us have forsaken our mystery without even knowing it. Now it's time to don our mantle of power, create our sacred circle, be the priestesses and priests we truly are, and remember what we have forgotten.

These are stories of good and evil—of humanity. Tales of intense pain and soul-deep sorrow, of extremes in suffering and moral degradation, which in their retelling have opened the doors to great insights, resolution, and profound healing. Through these journeys of past lives, these explorers have found peace, understanding, forgiveness, and self-acceptance, because of their willingness to follow the cause of their present pain back to its source. They invite us to share their journeys with an open mind and an open heart. Their journeys are unique to them, but they are not unlike our own.

As roses upon the cross of physical manifestation, our souls unfold as we evolve, each in its own rhythm of vibration, each according to the amount of light received of the sun, illumination from the moon, the amount of nurturance given and water received. We are in charge of the process. The purpose is the same for all who dwell in the garden of lives—to become One. The journey to this ultimate destination differs for all, but the result remains constant. We are on this journey to come into pure knowledge of the Self so that we may live our lives in unconditional Love, as aptly demonstrated by the Master Jesus.

We are Divine. The spark of Divinity resides in each of us, no matter how deeply it may be buried by layers of illusion brought about through poor choice. We have free will. We can choose our reality. Most of us don't remember this either, as evidenced by the current state of our world. Nonetheless, the truth is that we, in conjunction with God, the Cosmic, Spirit, create our reality. For this process we must bear the responsibility, but also the exhilaration. We as a people have the power and the spiritual responsibility to create sacred community, a living garden.

In this reality called Earth, our energy expression has been sorely limited, bound in its physical vehicle. Yet, this vehicle is dual in nature, for it is, indeed, the temple of our souls, and only by honoring it as such are we able to move beyond the limitations of the body.

Good and evil are but two aspects of a single quality. The forces of both are present in all situations. We have within ourselves the Divine and the infinite potential to be all that we are. The choice lies within each of us. The power and the karma—in other words, what is to come based on what has gone before—lie in our choices. Sometimes our choices have enriched the lives of others; at other times we have been the bearers of darkness. It is the Earth experience.

An exploration of our past lives is a form of healing that is much needed by many of us at this juncture of our journey. Resolving the past frees us for the present moment and allows the future to unfold in the embryonic, yet ancient-seeded, wisdom of today. We are the totality of our experiences. The seeds of tomorrow lie in the actions of today. Through past-life recall, we have the opportunity to return to the cause of a present problem and gain the insight and resolution to allow ourselves to be whole again. We must ready ourselves for the amazing journey that lies ahead. We must treat each moment as if it were our last so that we do not lose, through our procrastination, the opportunity presented in the Now.

We *are* intuitive psychic beings. The true measure of a person might be how aware she, or he, is of their spiritual path. We all have intuitive promptings and psychic impressions that are available to guide us. We have only to practice listening. When our awareness is in an active state, we experience the synchronicities that affirm our life process, our ever-evolving transformation into Light Beings.

In this time in which we are now living, the potentiality of transformative evolution is higher than perhaps ever before. We are at a point humanity has never before reached. Atlantis possibly could have reached such a point, but it strayed too far away from the heart. However, we are at a stepping-off point. A shift in consciousness is upon us. It has already begun. It is time for the rose to manifest solely as Light—open, moving, transmuting beyond its cross of matter into Spirit. All the roses whose petals have opened as the "I Am" consciousness are in readiness to merge as ONE.

Our life experiences here on the Earth plane are determined by our choices. The more we choose the positive, the lighter we grow with each decision. Here to guide us is that still small voice within, the voice that we need to heed every moment. It's simply conscious living. In learning to listen to our intuition, our inner promptings, we are guided to make the wisest choice in all things. Making choices is what life is all about. We are merely a compilation of our choices throughout eternity. Our being able to attune with the positive, while not giving in to the negative, constitutes true self-mastery. At some point ideally, and hopefully, in the not too distant future, we—all souls—will function as One, and the Divine Harmony of that music will be the Grand Transmutation.

Until then, as we struggle along, or skip along, we must continue the effort to choose the positive, thus absolving the negative. We are children of the future hierarchy, those spiritual beings who form the bridge between God, the Cosmic, and Humanity. We must each tread our path through the garden of our lives. We must each reflect all that we are, moment to moment. In each moment, depending upon where our choices have taken us, we can reach illumination. Sometimes it is but a brief glance; other times, it is a blissful bath. Most times this illumination is fleeting, but as our rose continues to *Open As I Am,* the unfoldment becomes the journey, and each moment is All.

We have all had our moments in the Sun, in the rivers of life, in the dark caves of the Soul. We each, at some time, have our turn as teacher, student, marauder, peasant, nobleman, artisan, priest. And we have all known Grace . . . *Amazing Grace.*

PART ONE

The Spiritual Journey of a Soul

I

In the Beginning . . .

Simplicity of character is the natural
result of profound thought.
— Chinese Proverb

Sitting at the foot of the Sphinx I knew I had been there before. I had come with the Sphinx. Its roots were mine. The energies moving through my body and the Cosmos were one and the same. I was one with the Cosmic. There was no doubt. The Cosmic lived and breathed within the center of my being, and I lived out in the Cosmic unfettered and unafraid. I knew my role—deep within the depths of my beingness. I was a Guardian—a Guardian of the Truth, of this sacred energy and the sacred space wherein humanity can leap. I knew my place. I was that place. There, with the serene face of the Goddess luminescent in the moonlight, I felt the Oneness of All Things, and I understood that I was doing all that was ever expected of me. I was simply being who I am—and that was why I had come to Egypt that first time . . . to find out *Who I am*. And there between the paws of the Great Sphinx—I knew.

Many times since, I have reached back into the past to recreate for myself that feeling, so that all is right with the world, at least from my perspective—that feeling of wholeness and total connectedness to Life, to Spirit, to the Cosmic . . . to the Earth . . . to *ALL*.

I felt calmer there, nestled between the paws of the Sphinx on the soft, soft sand, calmer than I had ever been in my life. I became more alert, aware, focused, and serenely alive. The serenity of being in my place . . . the absolute peace . . . the absolute understanding . . . *I am that I am* . . . the Absolute.

"I am going to Egypt to remember who I am." That was what I had found myself writing in the front of my journal of violet cloth, as I had started this journey for which I had hungered my entire life. I had always had memories, even as a young girl. Those memories I now believe were bits and pieces of my past that had spontaneously filtered up through the prism of my present life. I had always known that I had lived before, that this life was not *it*. This present lifetime formed only a piece of my quilt. All the other pieces, from all the other times lived, made up other colorful, lively, somber pieces of my quilt of lives. My present life was but a step on my soul's path, and with all the other steps taken before, formed my spiritual journey.

Growing up in a Southern Baptist environment had made it all the more evident to me that reincarnation was a more natural way of looking at life. I once wrote a college paper with the creative juices finally starting to flow at the eleventh hour, when I gratefully, and I might add desperately, shifted into "hyper focus." There, in that space, I heard the words of my opening sentence: "Socrates said *Know Thyself.*" And I'll never forget the feeling I experienced with the power of those words, as their revealment of inner truth reverberated throughout my being, from the deepest recesses of my soul, all the way out to the outer reaches of my auric field. I felt electrified with recognition. I knew, as I sat there sobbing, writing those words, that they meant more than I could possibly comprehend at that moment. And, so it has been. These words of Socrates have echoed throughout my life at insightful moments, taking me deeper into myself and closer to my destination—Home.

Here on Earth, Egypt is the closest energy to home that I have ever felt. Meditating between the paws of the Sphinx, with the moonlight striking just her face, I knew a peace that I had never felt before—not here, not on this planet. It was a sense of my place in the cosmic scheme of things. I knew that I had come here with the same energy as the Sphinx. Through that portal of light I, too, had descended. In doing so, I had left my true home for which I have been longing all these many years. Sometimes when I let myself realize how terribly lonely it can be here on Earth, this loneliness more than saddens my heart. It could shatter my soul if I did not force myself to remember why I came. We are guardians here. We are here to hold the energy. When I am in that consciousness of the *I Am*, I feel my connectedness to the Cosmic, my true home, and I know . . . I know myself. *I am that I am*. All that is ever expected of me is to *BE* all that I am, and I am free . . . I must remember to remember.

Upon first arriving in Egypt, stepping off the plane in Cairo, I found that the smell of smoke in the air was so acrid that it burned the back of my throat, making Los Angeles, my home of nearly twenty years, seem a fair-aired city in comparison. This, I knew, was just a passing ground. Our group boarded a private plane almost immediately, en route to the South of Egypt, to the Temple of Abu-Simbel, an architectural feat that left me cold because it felt dead. This temple carried more energy of a man's ego than that of a spiritual journey. The structure itself was an amazing edifice built by an egomaniac to make of himself a god. It didn't work.

The Temple of Philae, however, carried a much different energy. Here I was a young girl with the breeze rustling my skirts as I communed with my feminine side. Touching the temple walls with my hand made me weak-kneed. Once I entered the "holy of holies" my tears began to flow as I began to feel myself here in this place. Even though the temple had been moved to higher ground in more recent times, I responded not to the placement of the structure here, but to the energy of Isis. The goddess energy within swam through tears of joy in recognition of itself. Even my very first glimpse of the Temple of Philae from the felucca, an Egyptian sailboat, had made me gasp, for I knew this place. I *did* remember . . . and I *continued* to remember as we journeyed down the Nile heading north.

Being on a boat on the Nile, moving from sacred site to sacred site, is the only way to travel in Egypt. It envelops you in a web of sacred time wherein to create and contemplate your own journey of the soul, to journal your feelings and simply be with the water and the Land. For someone whose roots lie in Egypt, there is nothing like a sunset from the top deck as you watch the land take on its cloak of night. Impregnated with memories, I wept for a long time. I have always experienced spiritual realities through my emotional body. It is the key that opens the locked door into my own Cosmic attunement.

Having known this emotional expression of Spirit all my life made our final night at the Sphinx that much more intriguing, for at the Sphinx I felt no welling up of emotion. This lack of emotion was such a strange sensation for me. There was an utter calmness to my being, and an incredibly vast expanse of tranquil space within me. Thank God, earlier that afternoon, my longing to be closer to the Sphinx and to spend some quality time with her ultimately drove me back there. A day or two earlier, we had simply been let off the bus at the bottom of the hill to take pictures of ourselves with the Sphinx in the background, as if that was somehow supposed to be enough. Well, it wasn't. Since I had no earthly interest in learning how perfume or papyrus were made, I soon struck out on my own up the hill leading to the Giza Plateau.

When I reached the top of the plateau, having already dealt with the Egyptian men calling to me, trying to persuade me to give them some "baksheesh," an Egyptian word for a small gratuity, or alms, I wished I had not come. Our group's pristine journey before sunrise to the Great Pyramid that very morning was a total dichotomy to what my eyes now beheld. There were Egyptian children everywhere, hundreds of them climbing all over the bottom of the Great Pyramid, oblivious to the signs "Do Not Climb" that were incongruously written in English. The camel and horse men yelled at me, trying to force me to get up on one of their animals, while the smell of hot dung hung thick in the air. I chose finally to ignore them, bringing forth the calling of names such as "Bitch" or "Queen." Some English they *did* know! Yet a part of me wanted to scream, "You are not the people who built this. You have no respect, no lineage here! How dare you desecrate this space!" But . . . they would not have understood.

So I pushed forward, up and around the back of the Great Pyramid, to where I could see the Sphinx, raised up out of the sands of time, off in the distance further down the hill. Her back was to me, but that didn't matter. It didn't matter that she seemed so small and unassuming from this direction. My heart had already begun to pound. Her vibrations drew me closer, as if I were being pulled by a magnet. I wanted to run to her and embrace her. Once I reached her I sat as close as allowed until they closed. It was not close enough, but at least I enjoyed some time alone with her, feeling a tremendous connection. The guards motioned for me to leave, so that the area could be made ready for the farcical sound and light show later that evening.

As I started back up the hill, an Egyptian man approached me, and asked if I meditated. I did not respond. He followed me, putting very little distance between our bodies. With his face very close to mine, he asked the same question again. I turned to face him and slowly said yes, and continued on. Then he asked the golden question, "Would I be interested in meditating between the paws of the Sphinx tonight?" Of course, I stopped. There was no way I could not stop. He proceeded to pull me over to a stone, where we sat as he negotiated with himself. He started at two hundred dollars a person. When I laughed uproariously, he gradually talked himself down to fifty dollars a person. At this I paused and then responded by saying that the price was still too high, since this was the last night we would be here, but I would see what I could do. We decided where and when to meet. As I walked away I knew this was why I had come back to the Sphinx. The Cosmic works in mysterious ways. Upon returning to The Mena House, a gorgeous hotel in Cairo that sits right at the base of the Giza Plateau, I talked with a few people from our group and it was set. Five of us would go.

I still felt no emotion. Nothing. How could that be? I always emote. Early that evening in the shower I had pondered this lack of emotion, wondering what it meant. I also couldn't help wondering if tonight would be much like adventures I had taken in college, often bringing others with me who weren't necessarily as daring as I. Well, that was a thought. I didn't want others to put themselves at risk by taking my lead. But enchantment reigned.

As Greg (one of the two men going) and I were leaving our building at The Mena House, we ran into our tour director, who always seemed to have a glint in his eye. There was the moment needed. I told him I had met a man named Said, who for a price had offered to take us to meditate inside the paws of the Sphinx. Our tour director's eyes were dancing as he said, "Great!" He had done that himself. "It happens. Go for it." Aha . . . a clear path.

There being only five of us, Said was not a happy camper. When he heard we were willing to pay only twenty-five dollars a person, he balked. Still it was American money. Soon his never-ending zest for bargaining had Said trying to entice our jewelry off our bodies. At this new effort, Greg gallantly offered his watch, said that was it, and the deal was struck. Having a male energy helped us to deal with Said in this obviously male-dominated society.

Soon we were off, first in two little cars moving with our headlights turned off down an alley, then on foot up across the desert, slinking across the sands as if we were fugitives. The guards did carry guns, big ones, and these guards were not friendly. They spoke a foreign language, this was a third world country, and terrorists had been killing tourists. But, so what. This was the Sphinx! And, it did seem as if we moved outside of time, as if in a state of grace.

As we approached the Sphinx, we moved in pairs. Greg walked ahead and conversed with Said. Diana—a sister in spirit from Santa Cruz—and I walked arm in arm and felt perfect. As we drew closer to the Sphinx I said to Diana, "Isn't she beautiful?" Diana inquired, "She?" I immediately responded with, "Of course!" Diana then said, "Well, I know that. But you are the only other person I know who has ever referred to her as a 'she.'" I replied, "Really? I thought everyone knew that." I realized then that I had never thought of her otherwise. Behind us came Christine and Mark.

As we drew nearer to the Sphinx, we heard a shout, followed by muffled quick exchanges between Said and one of the guards. Finally we were there. We took turns going inside a little dug-out portion at the base of the Sphinx behind the stela—an upright stone that had been placed there at a later date—only because Said seemed to think it was a big deal. We accommodated him, entering in pairs because the space was so small. Diana and I—who both knew this was not why we were here—entered first, then Christine and Mark, followed by Greg, who asked me to accompany him, since there was an uneven number of us.

There in the darkness, feeling nothing—which was so unusual for me of the "faucet eyes"—I asked Greg what he was feeling. As he later told me, in that very instant he began to have a transformative inner experience of initiation. When he started his descent entering the Sphinx, I asked if this were a steep descent, to which he answered affirmatively. Some moments later I found myself without any conscious thought placing my left hand on his forehead, which felt wet and clammy. My three fingers formed a triangle on his third eye.

As Greg's experience within himself deepened, he found himself moving mentally from the Sphinx into the pit of the Great Pyramid. This initiatory climb to the King's chamber was laborious, as it took place long before there were railings to help in the ascent. Once inside the King's chamber, Greg saw himself lowered into the sarcophagus for his initiation. At this point, we moved out into the night air of the desert, with Greg continuing his experience on the inner planes of his own awareness.

We each found our place between the paws of the Sphinx. I sat down in front of the Sphinx left of center and stared up at the moonlit face and knew I could stay there virtually forever. Diana positioned herself to my right and Mark and Christine sat behind us. Greg sprawled in the sand in front of us, still wrapped in his own transmutative experience, while the four of us, each in his or her own way, realized our guardianship of this place, of this moment. We were here to perform group ritual in a state of "I am" consciousness, connected to the Earth and the Hierarchy, the Celestial Hierarchy, those nine orders of spiritual entities that serve as intermediaries between God—the Cosmic—and man. That was our role. It is still.

Afterward, back at the hotel, we sat until three in the morning sharing our individual experiences and relishing the time we had just spent together—a time of intense clarity, transmutation, and vision. It was the perfect way to leave Egypt, having found what I had come to find . . . *myself.*

II

To Know Thyself

God has placed in each soul
an apostle to lead us
upon the illumined path.
Yet many seek life from without,
unaware that it is within them.
— Kahlil Gibran

Socrates said *"Know Thyself."* Therein lies the key to our journey here. We are committed to realizing our true selves. Ancient wisdom teaches that we are all gods in the making. We just don't know it yet, or more rightly we've just forgotten. The pineal gland, referred to by mystics as a bridge between the higher planes of consciousness and the physical plane of expression, is pretty much atrophied in most of humanity due to a lack of use. However, once we begin this journey, at some point we start to know who we truly are—a part of God—a part of the Cosmic Whole. Of course, some people would regard such a statement as blasphemous. They just don't know yet. They haven't traveled far enough on their journey. Some inhabitants of this planet seem to be on an express train, while others are taking the slow boat to who knows where. Ultimately, eventually, we are all to reach the same place—self-realization.

Much to our chagrin, it's doubtful that at this point in the history of human life there is enough linear time to reach this goal, as it is not of peak concern to millions. Huge numbers of humanity are not even aware of their sojourn. Needless to say the trip is happening anyway.

However, it's quite obvious to countless observers at this time that the pace at which life is moving has speeded up. Time, though an illusion in the real scheme of things, is moving quickly. A definite but subtle shift occurred in the early eighties, an increase in rate of vibration. At least that is when I became aware of it. From that juncture onward, the horse had started to gallop and humanity had begun to lose its grip. Many people felt as if they were holding on by the slimmest of threads. That feeling has accelerated through the last two decades, and so a deadening of the spirit has settled in. Seldom is time taken to nurture the soul. In the morning, these people hit the floor running. They remind me of a caricature of a person holding on to the back of a trolley while her body flaps helplessly behind in the wind. This spiritually debilitating state is one of denial hounded and kept in motion by Fear. Somehow money and what it can buy have become more important than spending time with our children or simply slowing down to take in the beauty of life. We can never realize the full nature of Self if we continue to be constantly preoccupied with external matters. Humanity, in order to survive the leap into a new millennium, has to remember its own identity. It's difficult because there are so many layers to maneuver through—layers of fear, doubt, misplaced values, spiritual disempowerment, and misinformation, often fed to us by those whom we are taught to trust—our government, our clergy, and our doctors. Unfortunately for all of us, but especially devastating for our children, our society has become one whose bottom line is money and assumed status rather than love and self-realization. But in the same breath there *is* grace—Amazing Grace, bearing the possibility of transmutation.

The Road into Ourselves

The interesting thing about this time on Planet Earth is that while many are overwhelmed by life and the speed at which it is moving, many are also breaking forth who are aware of the light in their own consciousness, who sense the changes that Earth and humanity are to endure, and who know they can no longer continue as they were. People are seeking answers. People are hungering for a more spiritual life. They sincerely want to move beyond fear and denial and once again get in touch with themselves and their purpose for being.

We have all taken many paths, some very painful, some quite honorable, lives of great spiritual growth and lives of deprivation and abuse. But through it all there has always been a reason, a purpose to our being. *"To be, or not to be,"* as the great bard had his famous character, Hamlet, say in his despair. We, too, must ask ourselves this question. To be or not to be? Which is it? The choice is ours. The road into ourselves is *the* experience we each are here to have.

We are indeed here on this Mother Earth, Gaia, to experience the full gamut of human emotion so that, at some point in our evolutionary cycle, we learn to live Love unconditionally. Until that time we travel upon the wheel of life and live under the Law of Karma—the Law of Cause and Effect—the law that says that for every action there is a reaction, that we must be responsible for what we say and do and think. Whatever we sow, so shall we reap.

This pattern is interesting to observe in working with past-life regression because one is able to see quite clearly how this law works in the lives of all of us. Simplistically, it is to say that if you are abused in this life, you have abused in the past. If a particular person is treating you badly in the present life, a reason for their behavior can be found in the past. If someone is asthmatic in the present, they may have drowned, suffocated, or in some way been asphyxiated in the past. Eating disorders, such as obesity, bulimia, and anorexia can be reactions to poverty, starvation, or strong feelings of never having had enough in an earlier time.

In other words, we bring with us the karmic residue of the past. All of this does embrace the idea of reincarnation—that we have lived before in other bodies, at other places and points in time as we know it, and in different circumstances.

Many of us have experienced a déjà vu. You meet someone and they are so familiar to you, it's as if you've always known them. Or, you've gone somewhere you've never been before and yet you know your way around. Or, you start studying something, such as music, and it quickly becomes more of a remembering than a learning of something new. That's the way it was with me when I first studied astrology. I felt as though I were opening doors in my mind, doors that had simply been closed for a while. The same thing is true of my beginning to work with past-life regression. It felt so natural and comfortable—like an old shoe, like coming home.

A major aspect of my service in this life is to facilitate this recognition of Self, to guide my clients toward self-knowledge, as Socrates said, and self-empowerment, thus self-healing. A part of my service is to bear witness to the transformations of the Soul, as you will see the energies of the mountains of my Appalachian childhood bore witness for me.

Unworthiness Rears Its Head

In many cases, one past-life regression does wonders to eliminate a problem in the present life. For example, Amber came to me because she wanted to lose weight. As she spoke of her problem, she said, "To be thin is a treat. I'm not worthy. I don't deserve it." She expressed an inability to love herself "all the way," saying that she was not perfect. I promptly responded, "None of us are. If we were, we wouldn't still be here." Amber also suffered from low self-esteem. In my work over the years, I have come to believe that the greatest affliction of humanity is a lack of self-worth. People sincerely and deeply believe they are not worthy.

Going back to the cause lifetime, Amber found herself in Egypt, as a man named Hunza. Hunza was being chased by warriors because he had stolen some food to feed his starving family. He died at the hands of these warriors, feeling helpless and "not good enough" to even feed, let alone save, his family. He experienced rage at his death, because he couldn't offer anything but himself, and it wasn't *good enough*. The soldiers found his family and killed them anyway. During the session, Amber spontaneously realized why she ate compulsively, wanting to eat it all now because she couldn't get enough then. Her craving for salt now, she also realized, came from this prior lifetime because salt had been scarce in Egypt.

After her transition, Amber entered the white light and immediately moved into another lifetime, again in Egypt. Only this time she became a vain, well-to-do Egyptian woman who loved rubies, silver, and diamonds, but only the "powerful ones." She remained haughty and mean, and enjoyed spending lots of time at the goldsmith's house. At the end of her life she found herself old, unmarried, and lonely, her beauty long since gone. She felt terrible as she saw that she had done nothing with her life. All she had cared about were herself and her looks.

These two prior lifetimes did, in a very real sense, haunt Amber during her present life. Obviously, she did not feel that she deserved to be thin or loved. She believed that it had been her fault that her family had died. Her own death had not been enough to save them.

During the prenatal period of Amber's present life, we discovered that she chose a mother who did not want her. While pregnant, her mother beat her own stomach and said that she hated the baby. This made Amber feel unwelcomed and angry and reinforced her feeling of not being good enough. Amber said she didn't feel good enough to get a good mom, and she felt rage that this mother was never nice enough to let Amber love her.

At Amber's birth, the doctor described her as ugly, which bothered her, but which she believed to be her just desert after her life as the vain Egyptian woman. Here she was born into an unloving, technical atmosphere. Her mother was given drugs and was not present for her. Amber described her birth as "real ugly and undignified." As the doctor handed her to the nurse, he said, "You can have her." Amber regarded his words as a value judgment. She was then put into a box, alone; in actuality it was an incubator.

The first food substance she received was a sweet liquid. It was sugar water. At first she didn't like it, but then started to crave

it. She was breast-fed for one month and weighed after every feed-
ing, because she continuously threw up the milk, refusing to be
nourished by this woman who hated her. Her body weight remained frighteningly low. Here her being so skinny carried the
threat of death. Amber realized that she was always hungry during
this period because she never got enough. Once she was put on
formula, she fattened up and made everybody happy.

Another interesting connection to her past life as the vain
Egyptian woman occurred when she reached age thirteen and started
to blossom. Her mother considered this change to be a threat and
so Amber gained twenty pounds. Up to this point, Amber's mother
had forced her to wear unfashionable homemade clothes. The other
kids made fun of her, again playing out her theme of not being
good enough. By fourteen she had become a drug addict. By age
sixteen Amber was a runaway and a prostitute and ended up in a
hospital mental ward, where some of the other female inmates
beat her up. This beating also played into Amber's not-good-
enough syndrome. She now understands that she did these things
to keep herself from being happy; she believed that she didn't
deserve happiness due to these two past lives.

When Amber came to see me she was clean, sober, and married with two children. I impressed upon her how far she had
come. However, she described herself as a person who failed to
take action, ate, and apologized. At the end of our session, Amber
knew that she was the one who had to love herself *all the way*. The
weight then dropped off quickly as Amber learned to honor herself.

In such cases of past-life recall, it's as if the veil has been lifted
and we have been allowed to see, to know. Then, it's up to us to
take it, process it, and let it go, gaining the insights and understanding, and releasing the guilt, judgment, blame, or shame. We
must take this knowledge and integrate it into our whole being
and allow the growth. Many times it seems that people can much
more easily look at themselves as victims of malice, violence, or
cruelty, than to see themselves as perpetrators. We must remember that each of us has lived many lives. Did you really think you

were experiencing lives only as nice, compassionate, totally together people? Of course not. We've been there, done that, on both ends of the spectrum, as well as many in between.

We have each had many opportunities for learning. Just think of the incredible gift given by those souls who come in for a very short time only to leave through crib death, or due to an illness or accident, or perhaps even to be stillborn. Those parents, and others involved in the loss, receive a gift of experience that they had needed. Truly there are no accidents. You needed to learn something or you wouldn't have had the experience. Thank such souls. They must love you very much to have chosen to use that incarnation in such a limited expression of time. But then again, karmically they also needed to do that, to experience that particular lesson.

What is important now is not to feel guilty about something we did hundreds, or thousands of years ago, but to see the connections, forgive ourselves and be able to detach ourselves from our ongoing pattern, so that we can live our lives to our fullest potential.

As you'll see from the various case studies and examples herein, no matter what the circumstance or the part we played in it, we are each learning to love and honor and accept ourselves as being who we are. We are each evolving in our own time. We are each opening as a Rose of Light in the garden of humanity.

The Process of Transformation

The work of my clients is a living testimony to the benefits of past-life regression work and transpersonal hypnotherapy. I am constantly fascinated as I watch the process unfold. I am, however, no longer amazed at the results, but I am still awed by the resilience of the human spirit.

One might ask when does a person do a past-life regression? If you have a problem in your present life and you seemingly cannot get to the bottom of it with the tools you have to work with, past-life regression is a major consideration. What happens in a past-life regression is that you go back and reexperience the cause lifetime—the root of your current problem in the present life.

Past-life regression is one of the most powerful transformational tools we have to work with as we leap into the new millennium. It is a directed and extremely focused access to the real reasons behind an issue. It goes to the cause, to the source, to the root of the problem.

Regression therapy has been proven to be successful in helping to free us of our fears, phobias, and deep-seated anxieties. It appears that the patterns of a present problem are rooted in the past. Thus a resolving of that particular past life or lives can alleviate or lessen the emotional or physical problems that a person may encounter in the present. The results to be gained are a resolution of the issue, as well as a greater insight and awareness. This combination leads to self-realization and a healing.

It is evident from my work, and from the work of many others in this field, that regression therapy offers a wide-open area of exploration. Because of its results, past-life regression has become an area that traditional ways of therapy are having to look at. It has proven itself to be a much faster way of work than many other therapies. Often in a single session a client is able to explore one or more past lives. Through such exploration, the sources of a problem can be seen by the client spontaneously, rather than through years of traditional therapy that might reach the same conclusion. The client is able to make conscious connections and experience spontaneous revelations during the course of such a regression. More insight and further awareness often surface during the days that follow a regression.

One of the first things I tell my clients is that it is very common to feel as if they are making it up. I tell them that if that thought occurs, just let it, and then let it go. The main reason for taking the time to get a person deeply relaxed is so that the conscious mind feels relaxed enough and safe enough to step aside. Then the subconscious can come forward with the pertinent memories, which are right there pleading to be accessed. In order to experience a successful regression, a client needs simply to be willing to allow the images, the impressions, to emerge without judging them, but just allowing the process.

People often ask where these images come from. There are two "schools" of thought here. One says that the images are indeed from past lives. The other tends to think they are metaphors that the subconscious has created to help a person get in touch with the cause of a problem. In a practical sense, it doesn't really matter what we name an image, or what people think or feel about it, as long as they remain open to the *process*.

Every person who comes to me wants to resolve a problem that is manifesting in his or her life. Some believe in reincarnation. Others don't. Some don't know how they feel about the idea, while others are quite skeptical. Interestingly enough, those who are skeptical are often the best subjects. It doesn't matter what a person believes, as long as he or she is willing to do the work. Whatever makes a person the most comfortable is fine.

From my own experience of working with my clients, I tend to believe that images of past lives are indeed, for the most part, past-life experiences. However, sometimes these images are metaphors that the subconscious mind develops to help the client reach a needed understanding. Most often I can tell the difference. A metaphor is uncovered differently. The tone and feeling are not the same as in a past-life regression. A metaphor sounds and feels more like the telling of a story rather than a profound emotional reexperiencing. Nonetheless, metaphors can also be of immense value for a client. What is really important is that after just one session, some clients can rid themselves of problem situations in their lives and experience a great sense of release and resolution, as well as greater insight and revelation in the days that follow.

Past-life regression has shown clearly that physical pain in the present can be the result of past experiences. It's a matter of holding onto the past-life traumatic injury or death that occurred in that particular body part. Past-life death by violence will certainly lock into the actual tissues of the body where the fatal blow took place. This we will see in the case study in which a client experienced problems in a particular area of his back. He found pronounced improvement to his back once he had relived lifetimes of being crushed, whacked with a sword, trampled, and attacked from behind, all to the same area of the back. That specific part of his body had carried the past-life traumas.

Once a person relives the life, he or she relieves or removes the pain. When we carry it in a part of our body, as cellular memory, it will manifest psychosomatically. For instance, if migraine headaches manifest in the physical vehicle during the current lifetime, that person could have been beheaded in a past life, experienced the guillotine, or perhaps suffered a major head injury. Headaches are also frequently the result of birth experiences; or, it might be more correct to say that the birth experience serves as a trigger to a particular past life wherein the client died from the decapitation, a blow to the head, or similar trauma. An inability to enjoy sex may suggest a possible rape, or sexual torture, or abuse in past lives.

As we will see, past-life regression can help us to allow ourselves to release these old repressed pains, to detach from the pattern, to reconcile relationships or separate from them completely, forgive others, and most importantly forgive ourselves.

At some point during the regression experience, it is important to work through the death experience. One's death is an intensely focused time in the life of a human being. Those last thoughts, or the way the death occurs, can be crucial in determining what unresolved situations we carry with us today. Most often at death we leave behind a great deal of unfinished business—not always, of course, but certainly in those pivotal cause lifetimes that come up during a regression session. At death, as a person leaves the body, that person takes those unresolved issues with him or her—locked into the cellular memory. Only a remembered, relived trauma can be released. For instance, a person can walk around through an entire lifetime with a fear of snakes, but remembering and reliving that cause lifetime will, more than likely, release that fear.

At the point of transition, if the conscious mind can let go of anger, resentment, pain, fear, and in essence finish it there, then there is no need to repeat the pattern. But, it seems that's not often the case. I still find it so interesting and intriguing that the moments of death in a past life can be carried over into the present, and that our present existence can be ruled by our dying thoughts from back then. Thoughts such as, "I'm a failure," "I don't deserve any better," "I can't do anything right"—these old patterns, these bits of residue from the past are the actual thoughts we live by now, as if they ruled our present lives. And the sad thing is that often they do.

Wise Ones

My work is as a certified clinical transpersonal hypnotherapist, specializing in past-life regression. This work literally grew out of my own fascination with reincarnation and my work in astrology, which I have done professionally since December 31, 1972, to be exact, when I read my first chart for one dollar. My client was my best friend, my sister of Spirit, Barbara. She gave me the dollar bill, framed and inscribed. I still have it. It meant a great deal to me. I had actually found my calling, my service. I could *feel* Spirit prompting me.

Working with a teacher can be of tremendous value on one's path of liberation. My first and dearest teacher, Evelyn Rhae, my mentor, but more importantly the grandmother I had never had, forced me out of the nest. I didn't feel worthy to read an astrological chart for compensation, for money! I couldn't possibly be ready. But she insisted I was. She said it was time to try my wings and fly, so she pushed. My wings worked. Already in her seventies when I met her, she died eleven years later right after my first child was born. I knew she was dying. I could feel it. Even though we then lived a continent apart, she was always in my heart, actually on my right shoulder, especially after her transition.

After she died, a part of me was saddened that I didn't have a memento, something of hers to have close. But, I now know I have much more than that. I have memories—memories of her greeting me at the door of her apartment for my private lessons, for which she absolutely refused any payment, her brown eyes sparkling, dressed in her turquoise kimono, her white hair embellished with Japanese chopsticks. I have memories of her, so excitedly, taking me to the Metropolitan Opera to see *Aida,* then coming back to her place on Central Park South and our sitting together chatting metaphysics like two little chipmunks, while we munched on honey sesame cookies and drank Chinese tea.

What I have are memories of sitting across from her at her desk discussing astrology, and of experiencing a tingling sensation, little rushes of electricity, running up and down my spine and up into my head, making me feel sure my hair was standing on end blazing. She was always trying to fill me up and I was unquench-able. We were a great match, she the Virgo and I the Sagittarian. She holds a reverent place in my heart—she was my Teacher. There is no one more profound in a person's unfoldment.

There was another Teacher, another Virgo, my dear, dear mentor and friend, Sanford Meisner. He forced me to sharpen my instrument so that I could recognize truth within myself, and he taught me to honor it by leaving it alone—to let it *Be.* That is probably the soundest piece of advice I've ever been given. There are memories there, too, like the day I got so exasperated with *him* that he threw me out of the Neighborhood Playhouse School of the Theatre. I refused to leave. He closed his office door. I knocked and knocked again. He opened it, saw me, and closed the door in my face. I knocked again. This time when the door opened I grabbed it so that he couldn't close it again. We talked. I stayed. I think it was a test. It was a "classic" exercise. Always there was common ground with Sandy, and it was sacred. Now some thirty years later, I know Meisner's method of acting as a highly spiritual art form, no different really than the art, or act, of living. It's simply *being* the truth of who you are moment to moment.

Sacred Work

Over the years I found my own path to astrology. It was inevi-table really. After my lessons, I remember leaving Evelyn's as if entranced, intoxicated by the way the symbols danced with my mind. I spent days and nights studying on my daybed, or sitting with my feet in the oven, after the heat in my fifth-floor walk-up was cut off at ten o'clock at night. Gazing out the window of my 99th street Spanish Harlem apartment, as an absolute product of the sixties' revolution I could feel, even hear, the doors of memory slowly opening. For me learning astrology was a process of remembering. I had done this before. While in Egypt I discovered where, very specifically where, one of those places had been. Standing there on the roof of the Temple of Denderah, looking out over the land, I knew. I knew that I knew this place intimately. There, in New York City, then, too, I knew.

To me, astrology is sacred. It is the study of spiritual law. It has taught me much about my path this time around and has helped me to see more clearly the depths of my being, putting me more gracefully in touch with my soul. Astrology is a grand metaphysical tool that we are blessed to have. Truly it is a sacred art, as well as a sacred science, of symbols that go beyond the physical, earthly life to put us in touch with Universal Truth. The more our inner understanding deepens, the greater the meaning we will discover in the astrological symbols. Our service as astrologers, as metaphysicians, is to help our clients become more aware of themselves and of who they really are, so that they can ultimately be their own healer and their own counselor.

My approach to astrology has always been from a karmic point of view, looking through the doors of the past to see how the past is affecting the present. In doing so, sometimes I receive pictures, images of my client. In the beginning I would not speak of these impressions because I couldn't always point to one specific aspect and say yes, it comes from here. With the admonishment of Evelyn emblazoned on my brain—"Never read psychically, just read the chart"—it took me a while to realize that I had to listen to my whole being, and that my impression *was* coming from the chart. Once I felt free to impart my feeling to my client, it was always greeted with deep emotion and revelation and connectedness. From the chart, I could also tell when an individual needed to release the karmic residue of the past. Not knowing at the time anyone personally that I could recommend, I came to know I was to help them do that.

The Birthing Place

Reincarnation had always seemed for me a constant, a natural way to evolve. How fitting that *we*, not the devil, in whom I didn't even believe, should be responsible for our thoughts, our words, and our actions. How freeing a concept.

As a young girl growing up in the mountains of Kentucky, I always had memories, familiar feelings, when I was alone in the hills, when I drank with my cupped hands from the creek that ran down from the mountains, when I ran lithely across the river rocks barefoot, swiftly, never slipping, never stopping to think, just doing, in such rhythm and harmony with myself and the land. The land was my savior, my comrade in arms, my witness. I knew I had lived before, that the Southern Baptist Church was deeply wrong, when it ranted and raved about a god of wrath and hell fire and damnation. A part of me knew we created our own hell. But my old spirit in my young body was weighted down with the negative energy of the culture around me. The land, however, kept me sane. It cradled my young body while it rekindled the embers of my spirit.

As I floated down the river on an inner tube, one lazy, sunny, summer afternoon, I knew this beautiful land was my salvation. I felt like a prisoner in my own home, in my own body, and like a true alien when I ventured out among people. My thoughts and ideas were so far removed from the ideas of those around me that I knew not to give them voice. Occasionally, however, they would burst forth in anger and frustration and despair. How could they not burst forth, with Uranus in my first house opposing my seventh house Mars? Impulse let loose! My revolutionary ideas could inflame others and did.

I now believe that I incarnated into this birthing place of limited consciousness because I had abused power in past lifetimes. This time, in order to be here now, at this amazing vibrational opportunity, this point in humanity's evolutionary history as we move into the new millennium, I had to truly *want,* strive, and long for what I had had available to me before and had misused. My destiny was to long for something that lay a million miles away—such a deserved learning experience. That's how I think of it now. I needed within my character the positives of the experience. I am a survivor. I have come back from the brink of what seemed like insanity. I have tasted many fruits and I have learned my lessons well . . . enough.

The Times We Are A Livin'

We are living in a time like no other. It is a time when multi-dimensional reality has stepped off the pages of science fiction and is now part of many of our experiences. We are being made ready. Time is metamorphosing, its parameters stretched, contracted, suspended. Learning to live in these new parameters becomes a serious lesson for us—a challenge that extends our boundaries. There is no time, it does not exist. It is simply manufactured—a product of human consciousness. But there are cycles, cycles that rise and fall. Most evident on Earth is the cycle of the moon, from new to full and back again, the day to night, the coming of the seasons, one following the other. But something is afoot. The seasons are unruly, unpredictable, late, early—*unseasonable.*

Mother Nature is upset and reclaiming herself from the unbelievable abuse she has endured, especially since the coming of the industrial age. As a natural consequence, Earth changes are upon us. The prophecies of olden days speak of now, these days—as do the seers of more recent times, such as Edgar Cayce—and that frightens many. Are these the last days? I hope so! I, for one, am ready and willing to step beyond this dimension. No, I do not mean I want mass destruction of the planet, nor am I certain that a spaceship will lift me and mine, including the dogs, on out of here.

What I *do* mean is that greed, hate and fear have taken us as far as they can, as far as we can allow. A massive shift in consciousness has to happen, is happening, and will continue to happen. Yes indeed, these are the times, the times of Revelations, the times of sorrow, the times of Light, of illumination—the times we all came here to participate in, to experience. Each has his/her place to fill. Where do we each fit into the hologram of this unfoldment, this life, this magnificent journey?

It seems to be each to his own. For some people, these coming years may well be Armageddon. There are many who will not make the transition to the necessary evolution in consciousness. It is told that such people will exit in large numbers. For others this time will be a spiritual manifestation of Light—a coming into our *true selves*, living as One in an enlightened state of being. This is our choice. For many, the choices have already been made, their lines having been drawn in the sands of time eons ago. For others, there is a quickening. Spring is happening in the lives of many who have until now lived a dormant existence—an existence cloaked in fear, apathy, and self-pity. The Light is bursting forth in the consciousness of humanity and a reawakening of the spiritual life is blossoming. Yes, it is the dawning of the Age of Aquarius. We are the dawn. Our purpose is to serve, to serve humanity, to serve the human spirit in its journey home.

In Unconditional Love

To get to do the work I do, I am blessed, honored, and humbled. We are One Humanity, each connected to the other by gossamer threads of light that create a web of interrelatedness. The key to our success is Love—*unconditional love*. We must love ourselves, *learn* to love ourselves, and only then can we truly love others. There is no separation by gender, race, or wealth. We are all equal. Some of us are further along our evolutionary spiritual paths back to the Source, but there is no differentiation, no one person less valued than another. We each open as *I AM*. The Rose unfolds upon the cross of life and God is Love.

The greatest gift I can give my clients is to help them to love themselves, forgive themselves, and know their true worth, their

Divinity. I help them to realize they are co-creators of their destiny. Within each of them lies the Power to Be who they are and to manifest, to create their life as they would have it be, living life to its fullest potential. The *empowerment of the self* is an idea that has burst forth from the cocoon of darkness that had kept it shrouded for thousands of years.

We are more than the sum of our parts. We came here with the Light within us. But always we have a choice. For some people, material riches and power are the great levelers. Such persons succumb to the desires of the lower self and their light is dimmed by the desires of the Ego—the great separator. Over time their true purpose is forgotten, because lust for power breeds a parasitic need to feed off others rather than draw from their own light.

Why do you think almost all references to reincarnation were taken from the Bible? I'll tell you. I'd love to tell you. It's because the *powerful* leaders of the church were no longer filled with their own God Light. Therefore, they needed the light of their followers. So, those who had been entrusted to hold the Light, and profess the Light, became the ones who hid the truth, who used fear to control their followers, losing the Light within themselves, in order to have more power.

The Council of Churches has met at various times throughout history to serve its own agenda. These meetings included the Council of Nicea in the fourth century A.D. as well as the Council of Constantinople in the mid-sixth century. These councils were comprised of historians and scholars whose purpose was at times to remove sections from texts, especially the abstract and the mystical, to condense, and to arrange what is now the Holy Bible.

The mere basis of reincarnation and thus the Law of Karma—the law that says we are responsible for every thought, word, and deed—gave absolutely too much power to the people. Yet, power belonged to the people. This reality became a frightening thought for those who felt the need to hold the power, to have the power, to wield the power—the Almighty Church. But people themselves had created their own downfall by letting others do for them, control them, letting the Church be all-powerful, instead of retaining power themselves.

Thus the Church became where people had to go to worship—inside a building! That works if there's inclement weather. But to give thanks, to meditate, to be at one with the Creator, to be Cosmically Attuned comes from within, not without, and can be done anywhere, no place being more powerful than outside in nature.

We are not less than, we are one with the Father-Mother-God. We are each individual lights seeking the Greater Light—the Source of our Beingness. All we ever have to do, all that is ever expected of us, is to be who we are. Truly, we are not in competition one with the other—only with ourselves. We are here to be the very best that we can be, to live our lives in unconditional Love, and to be a part of the great Cosmic Quilt—each in his or her own sacred space.

III

Time Destiny

All babies are yogis.
— Baba Hari Dass

The little ballerina danced barefoot in the grass in her ice blue tutu, to music that only she could hear. Her body remembered dancing in other cultures, dressed in clothing of other times. If she had her druthers she would have immersed herself in dance, a high art to express her soul with no words, just the language of movement. There were no teachers ever, in her youth, just longings, and the rhythm of the dance reminiscent in her blood—a part of my karma I know now. I always knew that I had lived many lifetimes before and that I had danced throughout time. When I look back on my childhood I see myself dancing, a melancholic dancing, a soulful exercise of release.

That time was a time of destiny, growing up with the memories of having danced in the temples of Greece, of having communed with the land as an American Indian, of having lived in the desert of Egypt with the hot sand under my sandaled feet. Perhaps these memories were just flights of fancy, a young girl's imagination lifting her up and away from a lonely and less appealing childhood. Lying in the tall, dead grasses of autumn as Running Cloud, willing my breathing to be silent lest it be heard by the marauding white men who stood close at hand, puzzled by my sudden disappearance—my mind remembered the stealth required to stay alive. Yet in my physical reality, I was only playing make-believe cowboy and Indian games with my friends, never ever lowering myself to be the white man.

One summer, as the late afternoon rays of the sun sliced low through the thick leaves of the trees, I felt drawn to make my sword, as if beckoned to yet another time. I observed myself outside of myself, as I purposely and meticulously went about drawing and designing and cutting and sanding, so enjoying the familiarity of what I was doing. Sure my sword was wood and not metal, but I felt as if I were lifted out of time while my soul sang.

I spent many hours sitting on the back porch steps, listening to the sound of the river, and letting it transport me back to the banks of the Nile. I *daydreamed* of time spent afar, perhaps I engaged in spontaneous regression—a remembering. There was never a time when I didn't know that I had lived before.

Of course, this belief in having lived before wasn't taught in the church. But it made more sense to me to know that my spirit is eternal, never dying, simply changing form, as I move through my lives, learning through my experiences to be more Godlike, to be Love. Reincarnation was so much simpler a concept, more real, and all-encompassing.

Unnerved by the vilifying sermons that I had to sit through in church, I kept myself steady, driven by the desire to be free of this narrow place called *home* in the mountains of Appalachia, where I had landed this time around. The minds were narrow, much like the land. Most people worked in dark small places deep in the mines. The mountains reached high and closed in, leaving room enough for the river, the road, the railroad tracks, and what houses could fit in the spaces left. Then there were the small fingers of the hollers (which the outside world knew as hollows), threading up between the sides of the mountains, creating small cavities of isolated community. It was hard to breathe. Sometimes I just had to run to be able to stay in my body without losing my mind.

My dad understood. He taught me to drive a car when I was eleven years old. As I grew old enough, he always made sure I had wheels, so my restless self could tear along the mountain roads in the dark night air and I could breathe . . . barely. Only after my dad had been dead a few years did I understand our full relationship to each other, why we had chosen to be there together, trapped in such a narrow mindset. In Egypt, in an earlier, darker time, he and I had played with power and this was our reward, our just desert. His fear, his reticence now to play those larger games of power, would never let him leave, but he made sure I had my chance. Here, for him, the territory was known and could be controlled. He chose to stay, I got to fly free. That was my dad's greatest gift to me. He knew. But, he also made the best of his choice. He was a good man who did good deeds daily in his community. He lived a life of service, a life of atonement.

In our present life, I felt closest to my dad when we worked in the garden, just the two of us, as we feverishly staved off the darkness to get the tomato plants set out after dinner, and after he had worked all day. I savored the unbroken silence of sacred time spent with the land and my dad, working as one, with a focused energy that was familiar and extremely comfortable.

Two Fiery Spirits on Common Ground

When the corn was high, I liked to sit in the garden with my best friend, Candice. She would slip into her grandma's kitchen and steal some warm cornbread and we would sit hidden amongst the corn and beans and eat scallions and tomatoes, and cornbread, as our dirty bare feet dug down into the soft, cool, rich earth while we sat on our haunches. I don't remember how many times this happened. It could have been only once, but the warmth both of the day and of our companionship is a rare memory, a fine memory.

Candice and I were two wild things figuratively thrown to the lions, though we knew we were both survivors. We enjoyed adventure and derring-do, perhaps I a bit more than Candice. At least she now adamantly says so. Once we found an inverted car top tied to some branches at the river's edge. We hesitated only momentarily about taking it since it obviously belonged to someone else. But then again, we weren't stealing, we were simply borrowing it, taking advantage of opportunity.

It was really thrilling going down the river in a car top, using a long tree branch as a paddle. Only after we reached the deeper, other side of the river and discovered a huge bed of water moccasins, under a large overhanging rock below the surface of the water, did Candice suddenly realize why an old tin can lay in the bottom of our rusty boat. We had a leak and hadn't really noticed the water rising around our feet, we had been so fascinated and intimidated by the bed of snakes.

Candice proceeded to freak out and did a little crazed dance in the middle of the car top. We were then truly in danger of capsizing, with all the shenanigans going on in the boat. We *had* to become still. This part I don't remember too clearly, but it had to be a moment of eye contact, of grabbing her arms and creating focus. Knowing me I probably screamed to gather her attention, whereupon she bailed water and I steadied the boat with the tree branch, as we moved away from that side of the river. This adventure was really different from that of turning over rocks in the shallow water to search for baby snakes when we felt bored. On the water we were vulnerable, but once ashore we became giddy and exhilarated.

The thing I remember most about Candice's house is listening to Elvis's "Jailhouse Rock" and dancing until we dropped. We were jitterbugging fools, as was her mom. So, we'd push the furniture back and dance until we couldn't. Candice and her family moved away when I was in the seventh grade and she in sixth. The day that they left for Gary, Indiana, as her family's car slowly pulled away, our eyes locked in the moment, saying goodbye in silence. I knew that this moment marked an ending of a part of my life that I could never get back. Two like spirits treading common ground had now moved apart. Two fire signs, an Aries and a Sagittarian, had taken separate paths and begun to go it alone. That separation proved not to be the end of our friendship though. Many years later we both found ourselves living in Southern California and simply picked up where we had left off in *Spirit*. Interestingly, in later years, we both moved back east within a year or so of each other and continue to keep in touch.

Snakes—Unraveling the Mystery

Yet, let's not forget the snakes. Weaving throughout my youth were several incidents that had to do with snakes. One Sunday afternoon, I was with my dad when he killed a large black snake. My dad was curious to see what it had swallowed that was making such a huge bulge. It turned out to be a whole frog. Of course, Dad also didn't want the snake killing our baby chicks.

Then there was the day that I arrived home from school and headed underneath the back porch to check on Mr. Macaroni, a stray cat I had brought home much to my mother's disapproval. Before my parents could get rid of it, Mr. Macaroni had produced three baby kittens and turned out to be a she. One afternoon when I went under the back porch to visit, I noticed that Mr. Macaroni had a huge piece of her neck flesh hanging open, but her three babies were fine. Off to the side was a large, very dead black snake. I was so taken aback that I sat back off my haunches and right onto a rusty nail, which required a visit to the doctor's office for a tetanus shot.

Then there was the time I was charmed by a blue racer snake in the high hedge in front of our house. I had been playing on the riverbank with Wilma, another childhood friend—barefoot of course. Who wore shoes in the summertime? But she had cut her foot pretty badly on a piece of glass. I tried to carry her, but she was too heavy. So I left her there while I ran for help.

When I got to the front of my house, I was stopped dead in my tracks by a large blue racer. It came up out of the hedge slowly, undulating, as if it were doing a dance. I found myself mesmerized by this snake. I didn't even realize that I was screaming. I must have cut loose when its tongue started darting out of its mouth. My mother ran to the front door to find me blue in the face and unable to move or stop screaming. Our neighbor, who was giving his son a haircut on his front porch, grabbed a hoe and killed the snake with one blow. Only then could I start blabbering about Wilma. I believe that our neighbor went to save the day again.

I remember several other instances involving snakes while I was growing up. The details aren't important. What is important is my feeling toward them. I was utterly fascinated by snakes— afraid and yet not afraid. Looking at them seemed to take me back to parts unknown. A part of me wanted to stare them down, but that part wasn't the young girl in the physical body; that was a more knowledgeable person, one who held secrets. Somehow the snakes held wisdom, knowledge, but at the same time they seemed swathed in an aura of fear and negativity. Maybe the fear stemmed from those mythical stories told about Adam and Eve in the Garden of Eden. Whatever the origins, snakes tell a story of power.

Over the years my mother would swear that it didn't look as if I had slept in my bed, because I slept flat on my back with my arms crossed over my upper chest, much like a mummy in an Egyptian sarcophagus. I never moved. I never turned over. Making my bed, my "coffin," was a snap. There isn't much room in a sarcophagus.

One night as I lay there in the dark I found myself mesmerized by a lively technicolor scene that unfolded before my eyes. I stood above a pit of snakes. It was obvious what was to happen. As part of an initiation I had to move through the pit without being bitten. So many snakes writhed, hissed, waited . . . for me. I needed to overcome my fear and be in control of my being. As I looked down into that pit, I felt totally, fully aware that the key would be to show *no fear*. If I showed no fear, the snakes could not and would not bite me. I spent many nights and many hours lying in my bed, remembering the feeling of becoming still enough and centered enough to take this most important step.

All that training seeped back into my consciousness, all those lessons in stilling the mind, quieting the emotions, teaching the body to move as one through its surroundings. Here was the test. I would pass the initiation by now using my training, or I would die in a pit of snakes. Not a pleasant thought. Yet, exactly that kind of thought must never enter the consciousness. It's a matter of lifting oneself out of oneself, and yet being totally present and seminally aware. Then it's easy, a piece of cake, if you maintain total control of the mind—that slippery eel that is out and about before you know it. But how to control that blaze of fear that jerks and darts and bursts through, blindsiding you, just when you think you have it all together? It's about being in the moment, being in the Here and Now as Ram Dass first brought to my attention with his book, *Be Here Now,* many moons ago. It's about being free, totally free and at One with All. That's it. That is the secret. That is what we all must do in our own way, whatever way that is.

There are many paths up the mountain. None is more right necessarily than another. But each of us must travel the one that resonates with our electromagnetic field, with who we are. What is right for your best friend may not be what you need to experience. Maybe snakes represent knowledge and wisdom in your life, and maybe you adore them. Or maybe they represent fear and the dark side to you, causing you to loathe them. Maybe your journey home is as a Buddhist, a Christian, a Native American. None of that matters in the end. That is just the way you took to get where you are going. Just don't let the way narrow the journey. Often with the establishment of beliefs comes separation. We are all going to the same place . . . Home. No matter the path—every avenue, every trail—leads to the top of the mountain, where we sprout our wings and fly.

All souls are equal. We are all a part of God. We are One. Some souls may have more life experiences, more awareness, more soul-growth, may have progressed further on the evolutionary path, but all are still equal in value. Some are just further along the path back to the One.

Years later on a plane coming back from Sweden, where I had lectured and conducted workshops and private sessions on past-life regression and astrology for two weeks, I was reading a book that I had picked up in a second-hand bookstore. The book, by

Joan Grant and Denys Kelsey, was called *Many Lifetimes*. In the book Joan Grant recalls her memories of living the life of an initiate in ancient Egypt. When I read about the test in her initiation that had to do with a pit of snakes, I almost jumped out of my seat in the sheer energy of recognition. All those earlier incidents with snakes in my childhood now took on a deeper meaning. Once again I knew that while in bed that night all those years ago I had experienced a spontaneous regression to a moment in my own past. All those previous experiences with snakes had merely been preparation for a step into power—my own.

Ptah Winks

Eleven years prior to this airplane ride, I had stood in a huge line for a long time with two of my dearest friends to see the King Tut exhibit at the Los Angeles County Art Museum. The exhibit was truly grand, but of course they tried to rush everyone through much too quickly. I don't remember many of the artifacts that I saw, with the exception of the one that winked at me. I know, I know, but it happened. I know it happened, and that's all that matters. I found myself entranced by a small statue of the God Ptah, the god of artisans—known to the Egyptians as the Supreme Architect of the Universe.

As I stood there, still as stone, I knew why a few years earlier at The Roscrucian Museum in San Jose, I had stared for so long at the artwork of Egyptian jewelry, especially the neck pieces. I knew then that I had, indeed, done this before, had crafted those pieces. I remembered the feeling of doing it, the rhythm, the precise movement of my hands. I had doodled all my life in the shapes of those beads, one after the other, having experienced one especially profound memory in the first grade of elementary school.

More memories came flooding back as I gazed at Ptah, not wanting to leave. And after I did move away, I had to go back, even as the guard motioned for everyone to exit. It was as if I had recognized a part of myself. Compelled by my impressions, I found myself once more standing in front of the small statue, staring into another time, pleading to Ptah for affirmation. I only had a small compressed moment to find out—was this real?—and then he moved his eye, not both, just one—his left. He winked—at me—for me, as if he were saying yes, my dear, yes. It was enough, more than enough. I would never be the same. Visions are like that. They put us in touch with our true Self.

IV

The Big "I"

There is no present,
only the past repeating.
Don't tell this to people,
they will say you're crazy,
but try to understand it.
— Baba Hari Dass

Understanding that we have all lived many lifetimes brings each of us to a deeper sense of responsibility for our actions. We have a greater glimpse of the larger picture. We become aware that it *all* matters. Once each of us comes to realize that we cannot avoid absolute responsibility for any and all of our actions, regardless of our intention, reasoning, or motive, then, and only then, can humanity evolve into its true destiny.

No one, or no organization, can do this for us. Some church doctrine says that Jesus died on the cross in atonement for all our sins, and that this act therefore absolves all of us. Perhaps this doctrine is a misinterpretation of the truth. Consider that Jesus the Christ came to teach us, by His example, unconditional Love, and not that He needed to carry the sins of the world on His shoulders. We each must carry our own. Each individual must bear responsibility for her, or his, actions, as evidenced by the Law of Karma—the spiritual law of moral cause and effect. If each of us lives our life in unconditional Love, as Jesus did, we can break the karmic cycle of rebirth. Remember Jesus said, "All I do, ye can do, and more."

When an individual "repents," resolves to make better choices, meditates or prays for Divine guidance and help through attuning with the Christ Consciousness, she, or he, begins a cycle of new birth, in a mystical sense.

The power of past-life regression is self-evident when a person is able to see the connections, the threads of attachment that link one incarnation to another. Once a person recognizes these patterns, she is able to make better choices. This change occurs when an individual realizes her own value and can then love and honor the self by releasing old patterns, forgiving the self, seeing how these choices of the past have affected the present, and moving forward from that moment with a greater awareness.

By connecting with our Higher Self—that part of us that is God—we begin to live in harmony with the cosmic laws. This act on our part destroys intolerance, as we realize our universal oneness with all of humanity.

Intolerance is one of the great separators. If we take a walk down memory lane, we can't help but see all the cruel inhumanity that has continued through the eons of time, all because of one group's intolerance toward another. Yet we are all One. There really is no separation. All races are the same humanity. All ethnic cultures are groups of people. If we are ever to evolve in a group consciousness, we have to recognize our Oneness. Through our commonality we can overcome the ignorance that is bred by intolerance, and can move as one into a higher vibration. This concept is quite an idealistic one, but through visualization we can create the reality.

Intolerance permeates our society. Certainly anyone who works in any metaphysical field has dealt with more than his or her share of ignorance and intolerance. Living in California is no exception. However, California does tend to offer a more progressive, more forward-thinking, spiritually-oriented environment that spoils one. Such an environment does not prepare one, transplanted to the

Bible Belt as I was, for a rather startling leap back in time. Having grown up here in Kentucky, I knew what to expect, but I was surprised to find that so little progress in tolerance had been made in over twenty-five years.

Behind ignorance and intolerance lies fear—the true crippler of humanity's potential. If a major portion of humanity were asked what they feared, the reply might very well be, "Everything!" Christianity has taken us into a very small creative space, a separate space. Very few are open to new possibilities, expanded avenues of thought, larger or more potent realms of experience. And yet most of humanity's limiting beliefs are not self-determined but based on doctrine. "This is what *we* believe." Any true mystic knows that truth must resonate within a person. It is not something that one accepts, but something that one experiences.

Much of humanity's mystical journey is hindered, blocked by fear. If an experience starts to unfold and so-called reality begins to lose its edge, immediately fear raises its head and says, "Get a grip." This fearful response needs to stop. Humanity needs to be willing to broaden its horizons. Most people see the unknown not as exciting, but as something to be feared. We, as a humanity, need to be able to stand in our own sacred space, to be truly present. Then life becomes an evolving unfoldment. We are aware. We sense the energy that emanates from all things. We feel, we are truly alive, we vibrate. Our spiritual lessons and insights arrive through our feelings. Our insights are our sacred Truths, derived from our own experiences. It is important for us to be still and allow our spiritual self to come out and dance the energy.

We all must learn the lessons of patience and—oh please—tolerance, so that we can be ready to pursue, or grow into, our true function on the planet—that of service. We must be careful not to shorten our vision when we think of service. A woman may be of great service to the planet in the way she nurtures her children, or the way she tends to her lovely garden, as she offers a colorful array of beauty to the world.

Often we worry too much about the material things of life, apparently unaware of a law that says when we become sufficiently

alive to the inner workings of our being—our true inner power—
the material things of life will not only follow in a natural and
healthy order, but they will assume their right proportions. They
will take their rightful places in the scheme of our lives.

We each have our talents to give. We each have our way to
serve. We each walk our path seemingly alone, yet buoyed up by
thousands of Beings of Light, held in the arms of the Cosmic, as
we find peace within ourselves. A form of spiritual oneness with
God is Grace.

Laws of the Dance

All life on Earth is linked to the dance of the cyclic rhythms
of the solar system. There are actually five dance steps, or laws,
that govern humanity's evolution. The Law of Correspondence is
the first. It's quite simple—as God, so man. Its idiom "as above, so
below" recounts throughout time and is the law on which astrology is based. In astrology, the planets in the heavens serve as a
mirror image of life on Earth. The second step in the dance is the
Law of Reincarnation, which draws the soul to incarnate into an
earthly body in order to learn the lessons of the Earth school.
Next, comes the incessant beat of the law that doesn't let you get
away with anything, the Law of Cause and Effect—the Law of
Karma—the law that says we must take responsibility for our
thoughts, as well as for our words and deeds. It's time we realize
our power to create our reality, come up to the table, and make a
difference in our world.

Once this cycle of life, this Earth dance, has been completed
and the transition made, a soul reviews its completed life to see
what choices it made well and what choices it made poorly. Then
at a particular point in time, based on the Law of Opportunity,
the soul is insured a birth at exactly the appropriate time, and into
the environment best suited to offer the greatest opportunity for
the experiences of earthly learning. Those experiences will most
further his/her spiritual evolvement. This spiritual evolvement is
further insured by the fifth movement of the dance, the Law of

Balance—the law that says all life develops according to its own rhythm. And so it goes.

Wouldn't it be fascinating to walk through a graveyard, or a library, or even a movie of all of your lives and see what was inscribed on all the tombstones, what was written in your book of life, or what characters played across the silver screen? All of those crossed, intertwined memories will eventually set the soul aright when all is settled and accounted for. We've all been a little bit of a lot of things. It's the human condition operating through the law of cause and effect. What will it be? We travel through the "Land of Trye." For the most part, we keep trying to go out when we should be going in. Try, try again, until it is gotten right and the path is one of Light.

The Threads of Time

When we are little we always think that anything can be fixed, rectified, made all right again. But with age we come face to face with the sad conclusion that not all rifts can be sewn together again, not all fences mended. Yet we are, for the most part, a reasonable lot. Why then are we often unable to sit down *like adults* and hash things out, especially when we are supposed metaphysical beings, spiritually inclined, and tremendously motivated to work through our karma as much as possible this time around? Perhaps the threads of time weave old designs into the cloth of now. For example, perhaps long ago an argument ensued between two pirates who happened to be twins. One's ship went down at sea, leaving many issues unresolved to push their way into the now, when relationships are different, yet emotions remain bound by twists of the past.

Actually, a matter often comes down to the ties that bind us together over lifetimes. Threads of emotional imprints are soul threads that we carry with us in our emotional experiences and in our cellular memory. Perhaps we cannot for the life of us come to an agreement with another person about something that is unresolved from the past and that resides in both of our individual

memories. Each of us sees the situation now from our own pecu-
liar sense of reality, and each can be seeing it from a very different
perspective.

An emotionally explosive event can occur in the present between two people who are close. This event can be triggered by
something seemingly unimportant. What needs to be understood
is that a major "something" still exists from a past-life association
between the energies of these two people. This "something" is both
painful and as yet unresolved. Both people may remain totally in
the dark as to what may have happened in the past, or one person
may have uncovered more emotional fodder on his or her particular path than has the other.

The point is that unless the cause lifetime of the present leak-
age is reexperienced and resolved, the two friends may never regain
the harmony that they had once experienced in the relationship.
By going back to the original cause and exploring that event, seeing what attachments each person carried from that lifetime, they
can let go of the past and heal the present. Sometimes one person
needs to forgive, or simply to understand. Whatever each person
needs will be available through the reexperiencing of that cause
lifetime.

Then, of course, if these persons have been together in other
lifetimes—which is often the case—where the pattern has again
been played out, reexperiencing those other lifetimes can be beneficial also. The goal is to clear as much as possible, so that both
persons are ultimately free of the threads that have held them in
the old pattern. Then, they are able truly to let go and be fully in
the present moment.

Two in One

During the 1980s my work took me to Sweden, where I experienced a rather rare occurrence in past-life regression work. Two
women who didn't know each other in the present uncovered
memories of the same past life, but they did so in private sessions
with me that occurred three days apart. These women had pre-

sented similar physical symptoms. Neither knew that the other was having a session, nor would it have mattered to either of them since they had no connection to each other in the present life.

Interestingly, the two women lived in different parts of the country and had not met until just weeks before their sessions when both had taken the same metaphysical trip to Peru. From traveling in the same tour group they recognized each other by sight, but they had not gotten to know each other. However, a visit to a sacred site, such as the Mayan ruins in Peru, can unleash memories, heighten awareness, open doorways, and loosen the threads of time.

The first session was with Anna. She had requested a private session with me after having attended my weekend past-life seminar, only to have been told that all the openings for private sessions had been filled. Nevertheless, after leaving Stockholm she had felt compelled to return to the city to speak with me. She felt strongly that she *had* to have this experience. I could see the urgency of the woman's need and so I agreed to do a session with her later that evening.

Anna wanted to regress back to the cause lifetime of the pain she suffered in her right ankle, knee, and thigh. She also complained of an everyday buzzing in her head. Twelve years earlier she had been involved in a bad car accident that had damaged her head and the right side of her body. During her trip to Peru, these painful sensations had intensified. She desperately wanted to free herself of the pain.

As I directed Anna's subconscious to move into a tunnel of time that would take her back to the cause lifetime, Anna remarked that a figure of an angel stood before the tunnel. Stepping into the cause lifetime, Anna became aware of a window, a window of yellow glass. It appeared to be night. She stood outside the window and became aware of shadows, people moving. The building, made of red stones, was a house of nuns. The ceilings were high and the house felt cold and empty of feeling. Anna felt cramped here, numb, without a voice. As she entered the gate, someone grabbed her from behind by the throat. This man forced her inside the building and into the room behind the window of yellow glass. He became one of the monks responsible for her death. In the present life, Anna saw this monk as her husband. Of course there was more, but Anna's story would prove similar to that of a younger woman whom I would soon meet.

Three days later I facilitated a session with a woman named Sophie. Five or six years earlier, when she had felt burnt out, Sophie first experienced a buzzing on the right side of her face, neck, and back. She attributed this sensation to being over-stressed. Both Anna and Sophie referred to a nervous or stressed stomach and discomfort in the solar plexus, navel point area, and lower abdomen. Sophie also expressed a desire to know if there would be a stop to her living alone, if she could have a relationship with a man.

Coming out of the tunnel, Sophie described a light coming from a house to her left, a house with a wall. The light came from openings in the wall—windows. She immediately felt weak, as if her blood had drained down to her feet. She recognized the cause as something inside the house, inside the house of nuns.

"They do some kind of operation. I am one of them, one of the nuns. I see inside. There is a bench. They are taking women and hurting them in their bottom where sex is. They are doing sex with them, the nuns, against their will. Many people around— men, another religion. The men are raping them. It is a struggle between religions."

Both women described being on a bench in a room where they were both raped and sexually tortured by men. They referred to several men who regarded these actions as fun. The men laughed. Anna referred to the men as monks. Sophie recounted being cut with a knife, a big knife cutting her female parts. She described the men as cruel. Sophie spoke of her liver being cut with small knives, and of the men making fun of her religion. She said the men had no religion, to do what they were doing. They wanted to destroy the nuns. In their shared past life, both women had expressed feeling pressure in their stomach and abdomen, areas that bothered both of them in the present.

Extremely interesting was that both women spoke of being tortured on the head, neck, back, legs, feet, hands, and arms with some kind of electrical instrument. Sophie saw a woman dressed in white, holding the instrument. She perceived this woman as the head of the convent. She did not understand why the woman acted in this way, but she knew that the woman did so of her own free will.

Sophie knew that this woman, "who does not deserve to be a Mother Superior," was the reason she had been locked up in another lifetime, as yet another nun, a novice, who had met a young man in the garden of the nunnery. They had only talked, but they knew they had known each other before. Sophie had fallen in love. However, this "Mother Superior" had her locked up for four weeks for speaking to the young man. After that Sophie never left the convent, although she had planned to leave to join the young man when she had completed her training, when she had fulfilled her duty. This experience obviously related to Sophie's lack of a relationship in her present life.

Sophie appeared to be more fortunate than Anna in that while the men tortured her, she felt the same weakness that she had felt at the beginning of our regression. She felt faint, aware of what they were doing, but she felt herself fading away. She said that they didn't know what they were doing and that she felt sorry for them. Sophie made her transition very quickly. Once out of the body looking down from above, she also referred to the red bricks, or red stones of the building.

Feeling the hair on my arms stand up, I now had no doubt in my mind that the two women had relived lifetimes from the same shared past experience. No wonder they had not related to each other in the present. Who would want to attract this particular memory to themselves? No one, I assure you.

Unlike Sophie, Anna had been very present during her excruciating past-life ordeal, but she also spoke of an electrical instrument, like a cattle prod, used to inflict pain. In fact, the pain became so intense during Anna's regression that I decided to try physically to move the pain out of her body so we could proceed.

It felt important to me that Anna reexperience exactly what had happened to her, especially since she continued to carry the pain during her present life. However, in her regression the ferocity of that pain was consuming her. The pain seemed worse in her left arm and the left side of her head and forehead. Her body shook, shivered, convulsed involuntarily, as if she might vibrate right off the massage table on which she lay.

My intuition had tried to tell me to take my bag of crystals with me that morning, but since I was not doing a crystal workshop that day I had decided to leave them where I was staying, thinking it would be one less thing to carry. Wrong. Another intriguing thing that had been happening all day was that my arms and hands from the elbows down felt a slight numbing sensation, similar to the way hitting the "crazy bone" would feel. I kept thinking that I must not be clearing myself well enough between sessions, and I kept trying to clear the energy out of my arms. But, it would not budge. Now I was to understand why.

It would have been perfect if I'd had a large crystal to work with, something I could use to pull the "electricity" out of Anna—at least that's what was going through my mind. But I had only the small crystal point that I hold when I do regression work. I hadn't listened to that little intuitive voice, and now I had to come up with a working solution. Something had to be done quickly and this crystal, approximately one inch in diameter sitting on a two-inch horizontal base, was all I had at hand.

It occurred to me that the crystal might break, since I would be asking it to do more than its size would normally allow it to do. Seeing no other choice, I simply asked the Cosmic for help and gently blessed the crystal. When I placed the crystal above the most intense point of pain on Anna's upper arm in order to draw out the pain, it was as if the electrical energy immediately jumped into the crystal. It became so hot that I couldn't hold it. The only other thing I had with me was a silk scarf in which I wrapped the crystal when I wasn't using it. In order to continue, I decided to wrap the scarf around the bottom of the crystal, so I could bear to hold it. As I drew the electrical energy out of Anna's body, her breathing, which had become a labored panting, slowly calmed. Gradually the pain subsided.

I knew instinctively that I was using a lot of energy and had stepped into unknown waters. Yet I had no doubt about this process that felt entirely natural and old . . . even ancient. I gazed at a drop of water on the massage table next to my client, as if I were transported out of known time. I wondered where that drop of water had come from. Anna wasn't leaking from her arm—I had checked. The tears that flowed softly from her eyes fell too far away. Then, came a slow realization . . . it was a tear from my own eye.

Whether from the intensity of the work, or the pain in my own arms, this lone teardrop appeared foreign to me, as if it belonged to something outside of myself. When the force of the electrical energy coming out of Anna's body became so great that I could no longer bear the pain myself, I switched the crystal into my other hand. Both arms then experienced an intensification of the numbing sensation that I had carried in my arms all day.

The crystal proved to be too small to handle the amount of electrical energy that flowed through it, so this energy seemingly backed up my arms. The arm and hand that held the crystal were numb. It felt like an electrical shock. I now knew what I had been feeling throughout the day. It was as if my body had been sending me messages of what was to come. Earlier that day my arms and hands must have been precognitive of what they would experience later that evening. Perhaps it was the Cosmic's way of reaffirming to me that yes, this is right. Some would consider my actions a little radical, but these actions felt very right, and in the moment they offered the most direct course of action.

Shortly after this point a man, who had agreed to work as a translator, since Anna's English was not really all that good, had to leave the room to let someone into the office upstairs. I knew something had needed to happen to remove him from this very private, intimate experience, of which he was not really a part. Grateful for the interruption, I thanked him for his assistance and told him that he did not need to come back, since under hypnosis Anna's

English appeared to be fine and his reentry might disturb what was going on. It was indeed interesting to note that Anna's English was far superior under hypnosis than in a normal state of consciousness. I had thought this would be the case and had given suggestions to further enforce it. We were then able to move through her rape and to complete her past-life experience. Anna found this process much easier to do once the male energy had left the room. This session certainly helped Anna, but I knew that she would need further work.

It was unfortunate that I did not meet these two women until my last few days in Sweden. I suggested to each of them that they continue past-life therapy with someone locally. Of all the people I came in contact with while sojourning in this Aquarian country, these are the two who wrote to me later. They continued to do so for several years, always at Christmas time and sometimes at points in between. Perhaps it would have been helpful for them to have shared their stories with each other, but that option did not occur to me at the time, partly because I am always conscious of client confidentiality. Also, Anna had already left the city, I was booked solid with other clients, and the two of them lived in different parts of the country. Plus, they had had opportunities to meet while traveling in the same group, but they had chosen not to get to know each other.

The traumatic stories of these two women provide horrific examples of the intolerance and cruelty that humanity has inflicted upon itself, infliction that is often done in the name of religion. The fact that these two women seemingly reexperienced the same past life and in the present dealt with similar physical aftermaths speaks volumes as to the credibility of past lives and the concept of reincarnation.

Sweden proved to be a place of absolute freedom for me to work, a place wherein I could be of service. From the first moments that I stood on the foreign soil of that country I felt keenly aware of my distinct lack of karmic connection to this land. Having Aquarian energy quite evident in my own astrological blueprint, I felt very much attuned to the vibrations I found there, yet found myself feeling totally free and unencumbered by any kind of ties that bind. The people of this land were so open and receptive to my work and so loving, kind, and thankful, that I felt very blessed indeed.

V

Mayday

You must save yourself—
it is your duty.
— Baba Hari Dass

We are living in the present, yet the past trails behind us as our legend. Fragments of our power are held hostage by past choices. One of the strongest benefits of past-life regression therapy is that it frees us to take back our power, to own it, and to trust ourselves, to take counsel from our inner guidance in major life decisions that affect our health and well-being. As we become less disempowered by the past, we become freer to live more fully in the now. Past-life recall serves us well in helping to achieve this freedom because it makes clear our need to find our answers within ourselves rather than from some outside authority. Are we willing? What needs to manifest in our society before we give ourselves permission to take on our own mantle of power? Something worse than AIDS? Something worse is hardly conceivable, but possible.

The power lies within us. This truth is a major realization, but a difficult one for many sectors of society to reach. Why is that? Why are we so afraid to be who we were meant to be? Sure, the almighty Church has managed to control its followers for thousands of years, causing many of us to believe that we need an intermediary to speak to God for us because we are not worthy. Aha!

There it is again, the true affliction of humanity. We aren't good enough to have our own conversation with God. Well that, my friends, is a huge pile of malarkey, as I'm sure many of you know.

It is well past time for all of us to take hold of our lives and embrace the dear souls that we are. How better to do this than to allow ourselves the personal integrity of healing ourselves, of playing an active role in that process, of knowing that we have the power to bring ourselves back into a state of balance.

Yet, have you ever noticed how powerless most of us are in the presence of a doctor? Immediately we hand over the reins of power as if to an omnipotent being, sometimes to an idiot, often to a person not trained in nutrition, relaxation techniques, stress management, not as well-read as we are, but who knows how to write prescriptions for drugs that he often knows little about, and to treat only symptoms, not the ailment itself. Seldom does a physician take the time to ponder the symptoms to see what they are related to, or to ask what is going on in the patient's life that would trigger such a reaction. But, you see, most of them can't. They don't know how. They didn't learn that technique in any of their textbooks. And besides, they have a room full of patients who are waiting to see them. Plus, they may now be getting paid by the HMOs and insurance companies not to treat you. In many instances doctors have become the mouthpieces of pharmaceutical companies. So, do you really think you are getting the best health care around? Doubt it. A simple reality check will take care of that.

Did you know that the wealthiest country in the world is populated by the unhealthiest people in the world? Why is that, you might ask? Well, look at the diet. Look at the mindset. Many people behave as sheep walking around, pushed in one direction then the other by a fear prod. Look at those people, sedentary in lifestyle, who spend hours in front of a TV set, and who live on white flour and sugar, caffeine and carbonated soda, alcohol and cigarettes. Need I say more?

Let me ask you this. How many times have you, especially you women, gone to the doctor and tried to explain what was going on with you, only to have the doctor talk down to you, act as if you were some child who had no common sense, or else dismiss your symptoms as purely psychosomatic and then proceed to prescribe an antidepressant? This is a scenario I have heard repeated time and time again by female clients, many of whom have given up on doctors. Perhaps it's time to realize with whom we are dealing.

Those in the Know . . .

Some time ago when I went to a doctor for a routine pap smear and mammogram, she sent me to see a gynecologist for abnormal bleeding. I told her that at my age I didn't think two periods a month was "abnormal," but simply my particular version of menopause. She didn't agree, and she thought it important to find out why. I knew the why—I was having a period! But out of curiosity, I went to see this gynecologist, figuring that the more I knew about my hormonal balance, the clearer I would be about how to help myself.

Both doctors were anxious to get me started on hormone therapy right away. Since they hardly knew me, I thought it appropriate to ask why. Condescendingly, the gynecologist answered with a question, "Do you want to die of a heart attack?"

A bit taken aback, but at this point in my life not surprised, I replied, "No, nor do I want to increase the possibility of breast cancer or ovarian cancer due to synthetic hormones."

"Hogwash," the doctor responded, "that's never been proven."

Perplexed, I simply said, "Really . . . ?"

When I told him that if I needed hormones, which the test results confirmed I didn't, I did not want to take synthetic hormones, but wanted to do it naturally, he really got out there. After a short diatribe he blustered, "This natural thing has gone too far!" I had just told him about a progesterone cream made of wild Mexican yams, which when used transdermally allowed the body to absorb more of the progesterone because it bypassed the liver. "All this natural stuff is dangerous. Nothing tells you how much to use, and I'll tell you the result of all this wild Mexican yam business—cancer!"

Good God, I thought, this man's an idiot, but calmly I replied, "How can you say that?" My incredulous response prompted his quick regrouping to a more mild-mannered approach.

He had no idea he was talking to someone who had been drinking Kombucha tea for over three years, who had seen cancer totally disappear in a friend who had been given less than a year to live, and who knew that doctors were not healers. I was disappointed . . . again. I had hoped to find a doctor with whom I could actually talk. I'll keep looking.

A few do exist and the number is growing slowly, although the insensitivity factor among doctors still runs high. Most recently my current gynecologist answered his cell phone in the middle of my pelvic exam. That's right. You heard me. I looked at the nurse who smiled sheepishly as I heard the doctor between my spread legs say to the person on the other end of the phone that he was with a patient. The doctor was actually taking a personal call. He didn't even apologize for the intrusion, and he certainly didn't apologize for his rudeness.

I suppose I fared better than a client of mine who had to suffer the indignity of having her doctor actually leave an instrument hanging, uncomfortably I might add, off the lips of her vagina while he stepped out of the room to take a phone call.

Earlier, when I had been escorted past my doctor's office to an examining room, he was on the phone then, too. Upon my arrival the reception area had been empty. It had seemed that I was the only patient there. Yet, I had had to wait undressed, except for the "little paper gown," in a freezing room for almost thirty minutes, which was an improvement over the last time when the wait had been well over an hour. When the doctor did arrive in his three layers of dress, the first thing he commented on was how cold the room was, but he did nothing about it. That was before the phone call. Suffice it to say I will continue to look for a compassionate, caring human being who is also a gynecologist without a cell phone.

Some doctors indeed use their medicine to heal, and seek alternative ways to help people, and live spiritual lives themselves. However, they are few and far between. I had the pleasure of meeting one such rare woman doctor on a metaphysical journey that took us to England, Ireland, and Wales in search of the Holy Grail. We shared some sacred moments, knew it was not the first such time, and bonded as women in common, each recognizing the other. Regrettably, we do not even live in the same part of the country.

My primary care physician, chosen because she was a woman and therefore, I had hoped, more understanding, met with me to discuss the results of blood tests she had ordered. My biopsy showed a normal level of estrogen and so did my blood work. But this doctor still insisted that I needed to start hormone replacement therapy. I had trouble comprehending her diagnosis, but she seemed in a hurry to finish up and get on with her day. When I questioned her reasoning, she abruptly barked that she was treating the patient, not the blood work! My mouth dropped open, but no words came out. I was too stunned. I let her write her prescriptions, as I studied this piece of art and wondered how she could be so insensitive and still be a woman.

After our initial appointment I had started having hot flashes, which I now mentioned. She took this symptom as added proof that I needed hormones. She had made up her mind before I had even entered her office. She needed no additional fuel, such as my own personal history, to reach her conclusion. I felt that if I were an entirely different person I would have received the same diagnosis. The only route in her mind was hormones. This attitude is not uncommon, as many of my clients attest.

When I mentioned wanting to deal with my menopausal symptoms naturally, she scoffed at me as if I were a child, and dismissed my statement without even bothering to ask me why. When she insinuated that my being a vegetarian was a potent reason to take hormones, I knew I had sunk deep into the quagmire. Sadly, this mindset is due to her training, or lack of it. She is no longer my doctor. However, she and all the other doctors who daily play out these demeaning scenarios are the standard, not the exception. This is not just my singular experience. A disproportionate number of my clients and friends have gone through very similar, or worse, experiences with their doctors.

Doctors are seemingly taught in medical school that any treatment not sanctioned by the American Medical Association is quackery. What are officially sanctioned are drugs and surgery. I think it is important to remember that doctors are not always right; they do not have all the answers. In fact, they deal from a narrow point of view and are wrong more often than the public realizes.

The Alternative Path

In the February 1997 issue of *Psychology Today,* an article on mainstream physicians who are blending traditional and alternative medicine stated that . . . "at last count, 34 out of the country's 125 medical schools were offering courses in alternative medicine." Times are changing, but not rapidly enough. Our entire system of health care needs to change its focus so that it addresses the needs of the patient rather than the needs of insurance companies.

How do we educate those doctors who, as the ones described above, have their heads in the sand and refuse even to open their minds to what might be out there? Perhaps they don't want to know. Yet they continue to make major decisions about our health and well-being with only a cursory knowledge of our situation and medical history.

Daily they prescribe drugs such as the one that has repeatedly been recommended to me to combat osteoporosis. Yet, one of the side effects of this drug is that it burns a hole in the esophagus, hence the instruction not to lie down for at least a half hour after ingesting it. No wonder I was not surprised recently when a person who works in the medical field told me that about 89% of women who take this drug suffer from gastrointestinal problems, and that in many cases the drug had not even helped in increasing their bone density. Somehow this information did not stop a doctor from prescribing it for my mother while she was flat on her back in a hospital bed, unable to sit up, and already on medication for acid reflux. Thankfully, being her advocate, I discovered the problem after only two doses and immediately had it stopped. I left that doctor's office, as I have many times in the past, shuddering at the thought that such doctors wield power daily over women's lives.

For my own treatment of menopause, instead of making a trip to the pharmacy I set off to the health food store. There I told a self-educated and well-informed vitamin specialist that I had been taking herbs, but perhaps not enough to turn the tide. She suggested I try Remifemin, which is standardized so that each tablet is consistent in its contents. This product has been on the market in Germany for over forty years and is popular in both Europe and Australia. It is advertised as the natural choice for women who experience normal mid-life changes. The downside was a statement that most women notice a difference only after four weeks of use. I did not look forward to another four weeks of hot flashes, especially since night sweats had begun to wake me up several times each night. Amazingly, after the second day of use I noticed a difference, and within a week all my symptoms were gone.

It is my belief that we are an over-medicated society. Obviously, for a severe infection and/or pneumonia, antibiotics make sense. Although, how many children would have benefited, if only their parents had been aware of all the alternative remedies available for childhood illnesses, such as St. John's Wort for an ear infection? Then, all of those antibiotics and their downside could perhaps have been avoided. The over-prescribing of antibiotics is a demon with whom we are just starting to deal.

What these doctors and, sad to say, others before them have done is to confirm my own feeling that anyone who goes to a physician must be seated in her own power, be fearless in questioning, and expect to be treated with compassion and respect. Of course, sometimes surgery is needed. However, those situations may be rarer than once thought. Surgery, we now know, is often performed to line pocketbooks rather than to serve patients. Nevertheless, if bones are broken, they should be set by a professional—I would hope by a doctor unlike the one who refused to set my mother's broken wrist. He claimed that setting it would only cause her more unnecessary pain since she was "too old" for it to heal properly anyway. I'm sure that the medical profession includes many fine doctors. I've personally met three or four myself, one being my current primary care physician, whom I consider a rare find. *He listens.* He reminds me of my childhood doctor.

When I was sick as a young child and the country doctor came to my bedside at three in the morning, I found that his reassuring, caring bedside manner did much to make me feel better. Most doctors seem to have lost this bedside manner over the years. Compassion is not something that can be taught. It comes from the heart. Doctors need to take time to listen to their patients and to treat them as human beings. That's not too much to ask. Medical schools have actually started to address this issue. It could be called "Sensitivity Management 101." It's certainly time to realize that healing often has more to do with *caring* for someone than dispensing medicines. It is the intention with which we go forth that makes all the difference. It would help tremendously if more doctors could rediscover this truth and realize that their energy has a marked effect on every patient they treat.

Provisions of Gaia

Planet Earth is an amazing cornucopia of pharmacological hardware, if we can stop destroying it all before it's ever discovered. Why is it that jewelweed, a natural antidote for poison ivy, is often seen growing very close to it? Once many years ago in the middle of summer, I visited a friend's farm. He and I set out for a walk. We found ourselves out in the very middle of a sea of green, where upon closer inspection I realized that most of it was poison ivy, to which I was highly allergic. I stood smack dab in the middle of it! I told my friend to wait because I *really* had to make peace with this before I could move on. And, I did. Then, he pointed out the jewelweed and told me that it usually can be found in the vicinity of the poison ivy. We took some jewelweed down to the creek that ran close by, and rubbed it on my body before we continued our walk. I never broke out at all anywhere on my body. I knew I wouldn't. How much of this outcome came from making peace with my surroundings and how much was due to the jewelweed, I have no idea. Either could have worked by itself.

What we need is provided naturally, often without severe side effects. When studying herbology many years ago with Dr. Sidney Yudin in Los Angeles, I found it mind-blowing to realize that pharmaceutical companies use only the active ingredient in an herb when they create a synthetic prescription drug. Did it never occur to these well-trained people that the inactive ingredients in the herb serve the function of allowing us to ingest the active ingredient without any harmful side effects? I guess not.

The Empowerment of Self

The point is that we need to maintain our health. The best way to do that is to take control of our well-being. We aren't currently blessed with the healing temples of long ago that I'm sure some of you remember—temples that healed with light, love, color, sound, touch, crystals, herbs, the mind. Now doctors try to cure things. The way they do that is to make the symptoms go away. They know little, if anything, about the emotional toxins that often lie at the root of a problem. They seldom go to the heart of the matter. Most don't know how. What is really needed is a healing of the problem that caused the symptoms to manifest in the first place. Symptoms are the body's signal that something is out of balance.

Most people don't realize that disease is simply a *dis-ease* in the body. If you are able to have a truthful conversation with yourself you can figure it out. For instance, when a woman develops cysts in her breasts, instead of abruptly having them removed she should simply try doing for herself for awhile, nurturing "me," instead of everybody else. Then the cysts, having done their job, can leave. Sometimes many of us need help in reaching these realizations.

Our bodies are remarkable instruments, and yes, there is a connection between the body, the mind, and the emotions, as well as the soul. Thankfully, this connection is no longer being ignored out in the community. Many dedicated people are writing books, talking about it in the media, and teaching by example, so more and more of the community is hearing about the mind-body connection. Now, we have to reach the hundredth monkey syndrome regarding this fact, as well as the fact that all of humanity is connected. We are all one, all part of the same handiwork, the same fabric, and we can no longer continue to be blind-sided by the work of separatist and elitist thinking and beliefs.

No, we are not all equal. Yes, we started out that way. Now we are each a compilation of all that has gone before. We are the culmination at any given moment of every thought, action, and word said or done throughout all of our "being" time on this earth, or elsewhere. Some of us have had purer thoughts than others, performed better deeds, spoken more compassionate words. All of our thoughts and actions are tallied in that great big book in the sky, the Akashic Record. So no, we are not equal, because we each have free will to do and say and think what we will, and all of those decisions have put us where we are today. There is no one else to blame. Blame is a sickness in itself.

The Choices Are Ours

Karmically speaking, you are where you are because your actions put you there. If you don't like where you are, it's up to you to change it. The way to do that is through your own creative energy. Some people will read this and say, "How was I, at seven years old, supposed to be able to take control of my life and stop my father from molesting me?" Obviously, a seven-year-old child does not make a conscious choice to be molested. I would reply that the child's choice of that parent did encompass the possibility of that situation coming to pass. It was something that the soul chose to endure, however horrible, based on something that had happened in a past-life situation. Ultimately, the soul's decision to have that hideous experience served a greater learning experience.

It helps if we think of Mother Earth as a great big school. We are all students. Some of us are still in nursery school, while others are in advanced studies, with the majority of us at various stages in between. All of us are learning our own individual lessons, each paying our karma, based on the law of cause and effect—the law that says whatever you sow, that shall ye reap, the law that says we must take responsibility for every thought, word, and deed. Interesting, isn't it, when you realize that you have to be conscious of your thoughts, that they are extremely powerful. It is time for humanity to reach some basic realizations, if we are ever going to be able to make this imminent jump in consciousness that many people are aware of, as it approaches closer and closer to our relative reality.

This is a truly amazing time to be alive. We are living at a time of conclusion, a time of beginnings and endings, a time of stepping out into a new frontier. The only criterion for going to the party is to leave your fear at the door. If you look back over the history of humanity, either in a conglomerate sweep of nations and peoples, or as individuals, you will see a pattern of fear as the motivating force for many actions.

The results of those kinds of actions and decisions are not of the highest caliber. They can't be, because such actions thrive on the lowest common denominator. Think what the world might be like if we were willing to live our lives beyond fear. Most of us have heard over the last thirty years or so that "love is letting go of fear," and so on—all kinds of little axioms for living. These axioms are easy to voice, but not so easy to live—certainly not in a society that employs fear as a weapon of control.

A great debt is owed to the love generation of the sixties, simply because we recognized the old form to be an albatross that wasn't working. We knew from deep within ourselves that a change had to happen. We were, of course, raised in the fifties and much more used to conformity than individuality. That was the beauty of flower power, the simple act of being who we were. A large group of a whole generation stepped out. Naturally, young people being very naive, it got rather convoluted. There were, as always, special interest groups who had their own agenda. But the message got through.

It always was revealing to me in the *forward-moving* eighties, to hear people ask, "Where have all the hippies gone? Into corporate America, that's where. That was some movement." What really happened to those who had been involved in the sixties as a spiritual journey was our realization that in order to change the system we had to start within ourselves. So many of us turned inward.

As the spiritual journey has continued over the years, it has become even clearer that the best, most productive way to induce change is by going within and using the power of the mind. Through meditation and creative visualization, we are able to manifest in the world what we create on the inner planes of our being.

Just think for a moment about those people in the world, whose numbers are growing daily, who have experienced spontaneous remission in their diseases. That is what the medical establishment calls it. Others might call it cosmic attunement, a miracle, or simply the process of having learned to honor the body as the temple of the soul, and choosing to treat it that way. It's as basic as honoring the self. Remember what Socrates said, "Know Thyself." Precise and totally to the point. That is the journey—to know the self. In so doing you are able to recognize any obstacle in your path, whether it manifests as a health crisis, a financial slump, or an emotional bloodbath.

What is needed is a good long look at the self. What do you really feel about everything—your partner, your children, your job, your position in society? Whatever the area of your life that is being affected, you can change it only by becoming aware of it. That's often where past-life regression becomes a wonder tool. It is an amazingly simple, yet profound process. When I facilitate the release of deep emotional wounds and witness the freedom that this release brings to my clients, repeatedly I am humbled.

Key to Healing

Past-life regression is a process whose time has come. It is no longer out in left field somewhere being used only by people like myself, who are not medically trained psychiatrists or psychotherapists. I do tend to be grateful for that fact, because my mind has been free of dogma to simply take in what is, without judging or trying to have it fit certain parameters or labels. It just is.

During the nineties, due to the work of the prior two decades, past-life regression rapidly became a cutting-edge tool in psychotherapy. Because of its success rate, this therapeutic tool can no longer be denied its place in the scheme of things. We all know success determines a winner. Traditional talk therapy, which often takes years, if ever, to get to the bottom of a problem, is having to take a back seat, because past-life regression bypasses the conscious, intellectual, logical mind and deals with the subconscious directly. In a relaxed state of being, we simply ask the client to go to the cause lifetime of whatever problem we are addressing. The key to healing lies in reexperiencing the cause lifetime.

For example, several years ago a young woman came to see me. She was a singer with a beautiful voice, yet she complained that her throat felt tight, restricted, and not at all free to sing. She wanted to be able to let go of whatever was blocking her, and thus release the throat tension. She said she always experienced insomnia before she sang and she felt as if there were pressure in her throat, much like a volcano. It felt as if she were choking herself.

We discovered the cause lifetime to have occurred in Kansas during the mid-1800s. Soldiers had found her and her brother hiding in the back of their wagon. Indians had killed their parents. While she and her brother hid from the Indians, her brother had covered her mouth and told her that if she made any noise she would be killed. At the time she was four years old, and after the shock of this experience she never spoke again.

She and her brother were separated and she was taken to live on a farm with an aunt and uncle. They were cold people who had no idea how to deal with her. They left her alone, and lonely, to

wander in her own little world. She had no one to play with, or to
love or help her.

One day many years later, when she went into town with her
uncle, she saw a young man whom she believed was her brother.
She became emotional, feeling a deep love for him that she found
impossible to express. He, too, looked deeply at her, but she sensed
that he wasn't sure. Too much time had passed. She was now sixteen years old. Almost choking in her effort to speak to him, and
feeling intensely emotional, she began to gag. Her uncle, embarrassed by this overt spectacle, dragged her away.

At this time in her regression, my client commented that her
lips felt tight, as if her mouth were closing up. The young girl,
feeling so alone, never saw the young man again. She had no way
to communicate, to express herself, not being able to speak or
write. The people who took care of her couldn't write either, and
did nothing to bond with her or try to reach her. In abject frustration my client exclaimed, "I'm not a dummy!" Sadly, she simply
never received any care, any stimulation. She just seemed to exist
in a quiet, lonely, dark, solitary place.

Her death came one night in a house fire started accidentally
by her uncle, who was drunk. She died in her sleep of suffocation,
hence her inability to fall asleep the night before she sang. Subconsciously she believed that if she did sleep, she would not wake
up. She also realized that the tension in her neck came from her
inability to express herself in the past, a problem that stemmed
from the incident in the wagon, where if she had made a sound,
she and her brother would have been discovered and probably
killed. Of course, too, when she later did try to speak out to the
young man, she couldn't express herself and thus was dragged away.

At this point my client started to breathe deeply, realizing the
air was friendly. It became a freeing and healing moment for her.
She now knew that she would not be killed if she breathed, and that
if she sang out the air wasn't poisoned. Her situation had been
reinforced in the prenatal period when her mother often partied
and smoked while pregnant. Thus, my client found her time in the
womb to be uncomfortable due to the smoke, and she found herself

unable to rest because her mother remained perpetually on the go. Now, she realized that she was no longer in either situation. She needed to trust breathing deeply. This regression helped her to resolve this problem, freeing her to share the beauty of her music.

Past-life regression is a metaphysical tool of self-awareness, transformation, growth, and insight. Working with this process allows one to let go of deep-seated fears, anxieties, and phobias, release emotional blocks, and karmic residue, alleviate stress, deal with eating disorders and addictions, and connect with one's Higher Self and the soul's purpose.

Through self-knowledge comes the realization that we are all a part of God. There is no real separation. I know that Love is the most powerful force on the planet. Yet, in all my years of work in the metaphysical field, it continues to be my experience that the most frequent *dis-ease* of humankind is a deep-seated feeling of unworthiness, a real lack of self-love. It's truly time to change that, to heal ourselves, to let go of fear, to accept ourselves as who we are, and to bring ourselves to a state of wholeness. We have incredible opportunities for soul-growth available to us now. It's time to take responsibility for creating our reality.

There are many self-help paths available. Past-life regression is not necessarily right for everyone. Some people may feel that another way is a more correct path for them to take. That's fine. Just do something. Don't continue in a state of stagnation or fear for one more moment. The time is now. Don't lose another opportunity because you were wrapped in your web of denial.

Through the Eyes of a Child

Denial is rampant in today's world. For many of us, it's hard just to keep up with the day. Time seems to be moving so swiftly for everyone. People go through their daily lives feeling overwhelmed, just holding on, trying to maintain, to make it through this day, so they can hurriedly get to bed in order to get up, to then get through the next day, repeating the vicious cycle that keeps them farther and farther from themselves.

I first became aware of this speeding-up process around 1983, certainly 1984. It seemed fairly subtle then, but happening. At that time I had two toddlers, four and two years of age, and was consuming Marilyn Ferguson's book *The Aquarian Conspiracy* every weekday afternoon while they watched "Mr. Rogers" and "Sesame Street." I thoroughly enjoyed viewing these two television shows with my children. Actually, my own joy came from observing them react to what they were seeing. I missed getting to do that. But, I knew an important shift was taking place. I could feel it. And from my view out my kitchen window, as I sat at the table contemplating, I knew that I was not alone.

It's hard for a woman not to feel isolated from mental stimulation while she is raising her children, especially when they are really young, but there is no greater gift than to see the world anew through the innocent, incredibly honest, trusting eyes of a child. It is without doubt one of my life's greatest blessings. Being a parent teaches you to get the attention off yourself. You have to. Often there is no time for you. And that's when the going can get a little rough. But the lessons your children teach you can be the most profound lessons of your life.

Experiencing life through the eyes of your children can certainly broaden your doors of perception. I'll never forget the tone of the young voice of my son, Ethan, as I drove him home one afternoon from preschool, which he insisted on attending. He sat glued to the window in the back seat. It was a typical, beautiful, sunny California day. The back road I had taken to the school wasn't well-maintained. Some tall bulrush-type plants grew beside the road. When Ethan saw them, he exclaimed gleefully, "I remember those! That was in my other life."

Nor will I forget the first time Ethan was given a fork. My husband and I sat there in amazement watching him hold it as if he were of royalty and had already been taught the proper etiquette. Too bad that memory didn't stick with him. Watching him gulp his food as a teenager is quite a different experience. This incident with the fork also coincided with a morning drive, when he was sitting in the front seat across from me. I glanced over to find him sitting much the way you would think a young prince might sit, poised on his royal cushion. When I conveyed this observation to Ethan he responded indignantly, "King, not prince!" "Oh," was all I said, chuckling to myself. His kingly Leo ascendant made itself vibrantly known, as he sat there with his long, blonde, curly locks creating his own crown.

Until a child is seven or so, the veil has not totally dropped. Children still retain memories of "before" in their consciousness. Often children are pooh-pooed, laughed at, or reprimanded when unconventional statements issue forth from their young unsuspecting minds. How dare we not respect the mind of a child! But, sadly that is much the way our society operates, so that slowly, as children, we shut down what may later take us years to reopen.

When once I asked my children what past lives they thought they had had, their answers did not astound me, although these answers certainly seemed correct and in keeping with the persons I had observed them to be in the present. At the time, I think Ethan and Mikaal were in the fifth and seventh grades, respectively.

Immediately, Ethan said he had been a soldier—a soldier in a World War killed by a tank, someone exploded in a million pieces, a soldier during Abraham Lincoln's time, a king, a cowboy. Meanwhile Mikaal responded with lives as a black person, an American Indian, a person in the Orient, a soldier, and someone stabbed in the back.

If you have children, you might know what I mean when I say I used to watch them grow and change overnight. I could never figure it out. They would go to bed looking one way and get up the next morning with their feet looking bigger, or their bodies taller, or with something else different, and you say that's impossible. One thing I always noticed about Ethan was his hands. They were always so strong-looking, a worker's hands, capable hands, even when they were the small hands of a little boy.

As our sons grew up, we did not allow them to have toy guns or G.I. Joes. During those early years we made sure that I stayed home with them. Consequently, I was present the first time Ethan was exposed to another child's toy gun. I'll never forget how his hands looked on it. The gun could have been an extension of himself. It seemed familiar to him and he appeared glad to have it with him again. He handled it easily. His hands behaved as if they had handled many a gun, as if they could take them apart and put them back together. He looked so natural with it in his hands. Needless to say, I was genuinely intrigued.

It made me realize that no matter what we may want to do as parents in our child's best interests, some patterns of the past override all of our good intentions. That kid was going to be fascinated with guns, probably for his entire life. There wasn't a whole lot I could do about that except continue not to buy them, and yet, give in enough to keep his interest from becoming fanatical. For instance, he and his brother got squirt guns to play with in the pool, which helped somewhat to satiate his fascination.

Most of us have no spiritual nurturing when we are young. I'm not referring to religion. I'm talking about honoring the psychic, intuitive beings that we are. We are all psychic, some simply more developed than others. When a young person says, "There is a pretty woman in my room and she makes me feel good," we must listen and give credence. Perhaps you are just too closed-off to be able to see what your young son or daughter can take for granted, because he or she is still open to Spirit.

Cosmic consciousness is what we all seek—an attunement with God, a peace that surpasseth all understanding. If children were honored more, as beings one step away from the Divine, perhaps so much could be avoided. The hardest thing for parents to bear witness to is the integration of their child into society. It is a grave travesty to watch them hurt with non-understanding as another child who has had a less spiritually inspired childhood abuses them in one of countless ways. And you witness the sacrifice . . . the change.

Today many children in our world know more about violence than about love. Violence is more familiar to them, and to some children it seems a better, safer way to go themselves. Or you hear a child exclaim, "I had to cheat! Everybody else was." Or, "Why should I go to school? They're not teaching anything useful. I'd make a better living selling drugs on the street."

A turnabout needs to take place and soon. A regeneration of our sense of community is sorely needed. Perhaps something large and major will have to happen in our world to bring society to its knees, so that a gentler, more loving path can rise out of the ashes of destruction. I do know that we are responsible for our actions. I do know that we have to see all children as ours. I do know that change is vital. I do know that the responsibility for that change lies with each of us. *We must save ourselves.*

VI

Innocence – Done Unto

Religion of your upbringing is like a cloak—
you must know how it is made
in order to take it off.
— Baba Hari Dass

When I was a little girl I sang to my Father, but my earthly father made fun of me and I never sang again, not if I could help it. How could I have known at such a young age that my father's innocent comment had triggered a past-life trauma that I carried as a painful embedded memory of a time gone by—a time when my worth had been called into question and I had failed by not being good enough.

In this past life, I was a young opera singer in Europe. I was very much in love with a male opera star who had a huge ego. During the run of the opera we were performing, the soprano developed laryngitis and I was forced to move into that role, even though I was a mezzo-soprano without the vocal range to sing the soprano's part. In rehearsal, I had managed to hit the high note, but that was just a fluke. The pressure of being put on stage—in a situation where I was expected to sing in a range that was beyond me, just so the show could go on—proved too much. In the actual performance I failed miserably. The crushing embarrassment of standing before that unforgiving audience was bad enough. Yet, as soon as the curtain hit the floor, my lover rushed to me, not to put his arm around me and offer comfort as I had thought, but to lambaste me for my failure. He saw it as a personal affront to him that I had let him down. He humiliated me in front of everyone backstage and ended our relationship on the spot. He left me shocked and utterly devastated. I never sang again.

In the present life, I found myself once again very much in love with this same soul. His ego was still large, but was used to cover his own pain and insecurity. I believe we chose to meet up in this life. He genuinely cared about me, but this time around I didn't need comfort. What I did need was a place to hone my craft as an artist, an actor, and I have him to thank for directing me to The Neighborhood Playhouse. Karmically, I would say he repaid his debt in spades. My years at the playhouse were two of the most formative years of my life. However, at the playhouse I found myself in a voice class and once again having to sing on stage. Sheer will got me through it. My fellow students respected my acting talent, along with my guts, and did not make fun of me but supported my effort. One of my voice teachers, who later became a good friend, continued to give me voice lessons after I graduated from the playhouse. I never improved. He was encouraging, upbeat, and patient, but I'm certain his ears were in distress by the end of our lesson.

Throughout my life I have always loved music but have considered myself tone deaf. It was only years later when as a parent nightly singing at bedtime to and with my children did my husband comment, "Sam, do you know you are carrying a tune?" I consider this another gift from my children.

Of course, in my younger years in the present life, I was put in situations where people expected me to sing, but fear had replaced the joy and I felt lost and lonely . . . an alien in a foreign land. But I had felt lost and lonely earlier still—when I was born. I remember the doctor holding me upside down of all things! I was a mixture of severe emotions. Number one, I had no penis! I could tell *that* from my precarious position. The overriding thought I had, overriding my anger and disgust at this brutal way of entry with no Light Beings in charge, was that someone had made a major mistake here!! I could not be here in this God-forsaken, red-necked, double standard hell-hole and be a GIRL—a female! I knew then that I would have to fight for every breath I would ever take until I was out of there. I knew, too, that there was very little Light . . . *there was very little Light*—and I was so little and help-less, and so very far from Home.

We arrive here on the Earth plane carrying our embedded memories of times past. As our recollection fades, the belief sys-tems that are in place here override our deeper wisdom and distort things that a part of us continues to remember. When this distor-tion happens we often find ourselves reacting to a stimulus in the present that has literally set off a response that stems from a life experience in another time. Obviously, one example of this distor-tion was my reaction to my father's comment when I was between three and five years of age. A second example would be the dogma of the church of my youth that served to trigger a failure in yet another past life as we will see.

My childhood was often one of deep melancholy, alternating with volatile outbursts of rage and frustration. My parents dearly loved me, but most of the time they had no idea what to do with me, or for me. How could they? How could they have answered the unasked question that burned inside me, "Is this all there is?" I grew up in the Appalachian Mountains of Kentucky, in a coal mining area where drinking men had shoot-outs in the street, most often on Saturday, one of their two days off. Some of them spent the next day in church repenting for their sins, provided they weren't dead or in jail, while others really didn't seem to give a damn that their souls were on the "fiery road to hell." This, too, I never understood. If they knew something was wrong and they continued to do it, why didn't they just stop doing it instead of showing up in church dressed in their Sunday best, to do penance time and time again with no apparent change?

I found going to church to be a bit like going to hell. My parents made me go, and once there I was pushed into the choir. Still traumatized by the words of my wonderful father, who had no earthly idea that his earlier light-hearted kidding had seared my soul, I either mouthed the words of the hymns, or I sang under everyone else. Only later did I understand that I had sung harmony and could probably be heard more clearly than if I had tried to sing along. I loved the hymns in the Southern Baptist church. Actually that was the only thing I did like about church. The hymns connected me to Spirit, but they were often sung in such a high key that most of the time the congregation sounded like a bunch of cackling wild things.

Token Heathen

Church was a hard place to be. I mean, by the time I was sixteen, up there in the pulpit was a preacher dedicating one of his sermons specifically to the evils of dancing. Then he singled me out as a prime example of youth gone awry. It was all I could do to stay in my seat on the back pew of the church. That's where most of the young people tried to sit—as far in the back as possible. I wanted to jump up and run down the aisle screaming, "You bloody hypocrite!" and claw his eyes out. But, that would never do.

Why hadn't my father jumped up and defended me? Surely he knew. He liked to dance, too. So did Mom. Dancing is natural, an innate response to the rhythms of the music, a creative expression—a release. I had done nothing wrong. I was innocent.

Yet, I knew Dad would have killed me, metaphorically speaking, if I had been presumptuous enough to challenge the emissary of God. So, I had to sit in the midst of the entire congregation, writhing in the pain and humiliation, however unjust, of condemnation. My churning stomach had twisted itself into knots, while my insides silently burned white hot, threatening to avalanche at any moment and spew a truly "righteous" fire upon all their heads. On the outside, though, I kept my back straight and my head high. I refused to let them see my pain.

All the while, dancing a wild cacophonous beat through my head were rumors that this *man of god* was having an affair with the song leader's wife. She played the piano for the services and always sat up front, dressed to the nines. She even got to wear red lipstick. There was no sermon about that.

Oh yes, the preaching was always about a god of wrath and the hell fire and damnation that we could expect after death, if we had not accepted Jesus Christ as our own personal Saviour. I could never understand that. How did we get to be such blithering idiots? I often thought if there really was a God like this, then He had really messed up in creating Man; or else, He surely had every reason in the book to be angry and intimidate us with all that brimstone.

Sunday School became a torturous proposition, too, in that I remained the only one in my class who hadn't accepted Jesus; therefore, I was the proverbial thorn in the side, since my class never got to have a hundred percent on those little white envelopes we had to fill out, because I wasn't a Christian. Thing is, I didn't want to be a hypocrite like the rest of them. If this was Christianity, then I would pass. I didn't have to stay for church those days since my dad hadn't joined yet. That came a little later and that's another story. So, staying for church accounted for something like twenty percent, but so did belonging to the church and thus being a Christian—so a hundred percent was out of the question for me, and thus for our class as a whole. My peers would glare at me, as the Sunday School teacher would ask me if I believed in Jesus Christ. I would say yes and then it would begin—the interrogation. I learned just to keep my head down, make no eye contact, my hands clasped tightly in my lap, and just retreat inside myself until the inquisitor had given up for that week. She always went straight for the jugular. The other teachers were more polite—condescending, but polite. I was the token heathen.

Yet, I so longed for a sacred place where I could go to be with God and to be with the feelings I had inside. I yearned for a place where I could sing the songs of my soul. The mountains were my only solace. Thank God for the mountains. There, out in nature, I found some peace as I clung to the Earth, my best friend. I spent lots of time there, up and away from the madness below. In summer I loved the way the green leaves of the tall trees whispered in their canopy above me. I loved the sunlight making its way in intricate messages, encoded through the clusters of leaves. Although autumn was always my favorite time of year, with the thick rustling of its multi-colored spectacle splashed in wild abandonment up and down the hillsides. Running in the autumn wind with the sound of the leaves chanting their evolution under my feet, I could almost, not quite but almost, propel myself out of there.

Often I would lie on my favorite rock, a big one, large and flat on top, with little crevasses made by the rain. Or I would lie on the dark, black, rich earth dressed by a layer of whatever the season. As I lay there I could feel the Earth's heartbeat, and its sadness, and I knew that somehow we were in the same fix. I've always felt a deeper emotional connection to the Earth than to any person, especially then. I loved my family deeply and so wanted us to be the ideal I had in my mind. Of course we weren't, and it took me years to reconcile that one.

Bearing the Weight

When I was young I harbored so much fear that if I didn't do enough penance or show enough humility, God would kill my family and it would be all my fault. The church had done an excellent snow job. I obviously perceived myself as a sinner and unworthy to boot. My imagination would often take on some grim demise and I would genuflect on the floor in contrition sometimes for well over an hour, on the cold hard floor by the side of my bed, until I believed it okay finally for me to go to sleep. No wonder I had to be pried out of bed in the mornings, almost always waking depressed. Sometimes the cloud took hours to lift. Sometimes it never did.

In retrospect, I can see clearly that my early, church-induced belief system initiated my obsessive compulsions that escalated in eighth and ninth grade and continued throughout high school, often leaving me in tears of dread and frustration. The *real* reason for these compulsions lay in a past life and would not be revealed until years later. My classic compulsion involved doing the dinner dishes. Similar compulsions tried to move into other areas of my life, but something told me that if I let that happen I would be in deep trouble. Yet my compulsive reading and rhythmic repetition of every road sign while traveling did present a real challenge.

My dad didn't work in the mines, but managed the commissary, so we had dinner later than my friends whose dads got off work at the three o'clock whistle. When Dad left managing the commissary and began to work in the insurance business, he came home even later. I would beg my mother to let me do the dishes later, so I could go outside and play first, when everyone else was out. No way would my mother allow the dinner (we called it supper then) dishes to remain on the table.

So there I was in a fever pitch to get the dishes done as quickly as possible. I was fast. But then I had to dry them and put them away. This was where I started to run into trouble. The main problem was with the silverware. I felt compelled to place them in the drawer evenly, each one representing a member of my family. If I didn't pat each one just right—equally that is—then I believed that something terrible would happen to my family. Their fate lay in my hands and I had to do it *perfectly*. Ahh, there's that word that would continue to drive me through the rest of my childhood. The pats quickly developed into a much more complicated pattern of four times four times four times four, all having to be exact and equal, until I was literally driving myself crazy trying to get out the door to play.

There were four members in my family including my younger brother, who was the teaspoon, and who, interestingly enough, never had to help with the dishes—a small example of the double standard. But then again, why didn't I just sneak out the back door and be gone? Well, I was much too responsible to do that. Besides, the punishment would have been much more than fit the crime—and somebody might just die. So, here I was still in the kitchen with twilight fast approaching, and the plates and glasses to contend with. Thankfully, these were not as complicated but were time consuming. Then, lastly, it came down to the four chairs at the table—if only there had been five. The kitchen chairs soon became the straw that broke the camel's back. I couldn't pat them evenly for the life of me. Totally exasperated, I would find myself in my umpteenth round.

Occasionally my mother would hear me crying and would take time from her reading, working puzzles, quilting, or whatever, to come into the kitchen to see what was the matter. When I explained as best I could what was the matter, she didn't set me down to talk to me, or even think to hug me, but said to stop acting "crazy." After she had walked out, I would assemble the splintered forces of myself to continue until I got it right. Then there would be the doorway. I had to pat the sides of the doorway out of the kitchen in just the perfect well-balanced rhythm needed finally to make my way outside to play, often only to find the fun was over and I was alone with my crazy self.

Salvation Is Mine

Once in my freshman year of college, I must say I was much relieved to hear my psychology professor refer to this phenomenon that I had lived with for years as "obsessive compulsions." Strange how just having a name for it somehow validated my sanity. Transfixed to the paragraph that explained in psychological terms what I had been going through for years, I felt a subtle lifting of weight from my soul. That year I started to be brave enough to let them go. Of course, it helped that I didn't have the dinner dishes to contend with at school, but I had taken the doorway compulsion with me to the dormitory. However, I found it a bit difficult to engage in this remaining compulsion without appearing a complete idiot. I was very subtle.

It took a great deal of courage, and faith in my psychology professor's statement that nothing horrible had happened to him when he finally was able to go to bed without rolling his socks up a particular way, putting them in his shoes, and then placing his shoes in a certain position by his bed. I figured if he could do it, I could, too. And, I did! And, nobody died!! But old habits die hard, especially compulsive ones. When home visiting, I would find myself starting to fall back into my old pattern. It was a wonderful feeling to be able to say no and walk through the door, knowing that my doing so would not rain down death and destruction on my family. The first time I slammed the silverware drawer shut was a real coup. Liberation was mine!

Unbeknown to me at the time, my compulsions had all been due to fear—a fear steeped in a memory of another time when, after being unable to keep my baby safe, my mind had broken down, had given way to the pressure, to the guilt, to the loss. And of course, there was my fear of God—the God that organized religion had presented to me. Oh, how I missed the memories of another religion in another time, with rituals outside in nature, initiations of passage, and wise and compassionate teachers! Where was that God?

This other God of fear and retribution had been forced down my throat by a group of frightened people—people who in later years would listen to another Southern Baptist preacher, also a hypocrite, preach about astrology as the work of the devil. This was after he had picked me up at the airport when my dad was having emergency surgery for a blocked colon, which doctors had found to be cancerous.

In the years that had passed—I mean we had lived through the sixties, seventies, and most of the eighties—I had thought that maybe some things had changed. Maybe this church had taken some steps into the Light. So when this younger and, wrongly I thought, hipper preacher asked me about what I did, I had told him. I had said I was an astrologer and did past-life regression work. To my astonishment that wasn't the end of the conversation as usual. He continued to ask a lot of questions and I responded as openly as I would to anyone. I should have remembered I was in *devil's land*, but at this point in my life I truly didn't care what he thought of me. Turns out he thought I was the devil's handmaiden.

At least he found himself able to put something new into one of his sermons. I suppose it wouldn't have helped to tell him that the Three Wise Men, the Magi, who followed the "Star" in the East to find the Christ child had been astrologers. Nor would it have helped to tell him that the Council of Churches in meetings some fifteen hundred years ago had removed almost all references to reincarnation from the Bible so as not to empower the people. Heaven forbid that people be empowered! Let's excommunicate them instead. No . . . it wouldn't have helped. I felt as if I had been had because I had viewed our conversation as an indication of the growing tolerance in the world—that two fellow human beings with divergent views could have a nice, warm, friendly discussion. That was simply not the case.

Herein lies my main problem with organized religion. It is a separatist movement—us against them. Often its members are judgmental, hypocritical, and condemning of others and of things that they literally know nothing about. In my own personal journey outside the church, I have found God to be Love.

VII

Pieces of My Quilt

I have always been and still am a seeker,
but I no longer do my seeking among the stars
or in books. I am beginning to hear the lessons
which whisper in my blood. Mine is not a pleasant story,
it does not possess the gentle harmony of invented tales;
like the lives of all men who have given up
trying to deceive themselves, it is a mixture
of nonsense and chaos, madness and dreams.
— Herman Hesse

Our entire lives are full of patterns, remembrances, knowings. Life is a gift of unfoldment. Some might call it a puzzle. All of us remember something of our past lives. Fragments of memory surface while we are children, but by adulthood we often carry only unexplained feelings.

To be or not to be is not the question. It's not even an option. The truth is we are. We have been and we will continue to be, always. The question is how far into actual *being* are we? What have we gained from the journey? How well do we know ourselves? How realized is our path?

Past lives bear many gifts. The most obvious gift is a letting go of the pain. We all carry pain, whether we admit it or not. Whether it's clothed in guilt, shame, rejection, loss, it's there. Certainly we have the choice as to what we are going to do about it. We can keep our heads in the sand or we can go for a revelation that leads us toward transformation. I opt for the latter.

Every moment holds the potential for Cosmic understanding of who we truly are, and of our trip this time around. All of those past-life experiences can enrich our knowing and free us of the pain that keeps us trapped in fear. Every moment is a point of Being.

Out of the Mouth of Babes

Sometimes such moments come unasked in the guise of spontaneity. They are just there, rising unannounced out of the past, bubbling up from the subconscious. This happens quite often with young children. One of the most amazing and well known examples of a spontaneous regression took place in India, in the heart of regression territory. Unlike the United States, which lags behind most of the rest of the world in its acceptance of reincarnation, India embraces the concept of multiple lifetimes. Shifts in the winds of consciousness that are now upon us may eventually change that statistic. The following is a recounting of the famous regression of Shanti Devi that has since been widely reported.

When a little girl named Shanti was three years old, she spoke incessantly of her family. She did not speak of her present family, mind you, but of her husband and their three children. Her parents chalked it up to an overactive imagination, thinking that in time her incessant talk would pass. It didn't.

Four years later, when she was seven years old, she continued to speak of her "imaginary" family. Now she even referred to her husband and children by name, and she described them. She said they lived in a town called Muttra, not very far from her present home in Delhi.

The most disturbing detail of Shanti's story was that she reported having died giving birth to a fourth child in 1925. Shanti had been born in 1929. Shanti gave her past-life name as Ludgi. This death she described in alarming detail. How could she possibly have known these things? Her parents took her to a doctor thinking that she was mentally ill. The doctor found her to be in good health, both physically and mentally, but said that she knew an incredible amount of very specific information about dying in childbirth, information that would have been impossible for a child of her age to know.

At this point, an amazing "coincidence" occurred. Her father had a business acquaintance come over one evening. The mother asked Shanti to answer the door. Shanti immediately recognized the visitor as a cousin of her past-life husband. Enthusiastically, she asked about everyone and pretty much forced a quick expansion of this man's reality. The man did indeed live in the town where she said she had once lived and he did have a cousin by the name that she mentioned, and that cousin's wife had died while giving birth to their fourth child, and the dead woman's name had been Ludgi!

Shanti's parents now decided to ask her supposed past-life husband to come to their house one evening without Shanti's prior knowledge. He agreed to do this, and upon his arrival Shanti very excitedly ran up to him and hugged his leg and immediately asked him how their children were.

All of these events took place in a land where reincarnation is a given. But the story generated so much talk about Shanti and her amazing recall that the government set up an investigative committee to determine the truth of her claims.

Shanti was taken to Muttra by train and was blindfolded. Still, she knew her way around the town. Once the blindfold was removed she took them directly to her former home and instantly recognized her mother and father-in-law as well as her husband's brother. Then with a great deal of emotion she recognized her children, except for the fourth child, who had been born at the time of her own death.

She then took the researchers to her mother's home. Once there, she correctly spoke of structural changes made to the house since she had died and decorative ones, too. The mother appeared uncomfortable with this, but went along with it until Shanti declared that as Ludgi she had buried some of her rings in the back yard. With the mother's permission she dug up a small bag of rings that the mother conceded as belonging to her daughter. Now, overwhelmed by these events, the mother asked them to leave.

Obviously Shanti had been Ludgi in a past life. Nothing has ever been established to prove otherwise. The scientific committee formed by the government eventually filed a report stating that they had found nothing to disprove Shanti's assertion. This is one of the more famous cases of reincarnation, because Shanti remembered so many details of her past life and knew so much about dying in childbirth, a subject that she had never been exposed to in her present life.

Children, as we know, live in the moment, in the truth of the moment. As with many children before the age of seven, Shanti was not bound solely by the present. She had carried these memories with her. They had become a part of her present-day reality. Perhaps part of Shanti's reasons for coming back into a body so soon was that she had a difficult time letting go of her family when she died, and she wanted to be as close as possible in physical form as soon as possible. Perhaps part of the reason, too, was to help prove the truth of reincarnation. There is no doubt that such spontaneous regression happens. It happens more often than we realize.

When the Time Is Ripe

Once several years ago, when my husband and I had returned from a Dick Sutphen Past-Life Seminar, I felt fit to be tied. I thought I was upset with myself because I had been unable to stay focused enough to participate fully in the exercises we had done, as we foraged into past-life experiences. This was my field of interest. Why would I have trouble staying awake or connected to the moment? In the final session of the day, we were to see and talk with our Master. I had really looked forward to that experience. But I had spaced out! I couldn't rid myself of an anger that had begun during the previous group regression. My anger had continued to build until I had become absolutely furious with myself. Why is it, I thought, that when I have this opportunity to do something that I really want to do, I refuse to allow myself to experience it?

The real reason lay in that previous group regression earlier that afternoon. The facilitator had asked us to go back to an event in the past that carried relevance in the present. I now believe that the past event had been so emotionally charged that my conscious mind knew better than to allow memories of it to flow in that setting. Yet subconsciously, triggers were going off, seething to the surface, manifesting as incredible anger.

After the final session, not having gotten even close to contacting my Master, I felt that I had to get out of there as quickly as I could. I was ready to spit at Dick and strangle my husband for having such a good time. I bolted from the room out a side exit. I was so livid I couldn't even speak. Finally, in the car coming home, it hit me—*self-defeat!* Yet what was it that I had done that had created such guilt, such strong feelings, such intense anger? This was not the first time I had self-destructed, but I found myself ready for it to be the last.

By that evening both of us agreed that something had to be done. I felt truly primed and ready to burst. After a tearful discussion, my husband agreed to hypnotize me and try to take me back to the cause of these intense feelings. I must say that having to guide him through the proper process, while simultaneously experiencing a past life myself, proved distracting. Not ever having done this before, my husband missed moments that needed to be pursued. I continued to point these moments out to him, and he proved to be a very sensitive facilitator. Most alarming to him was my extreme emotional reaction to this past life, but I assuaged his fears and assured him I was all right. This is what we learned.

Sitting on a stool in a nice wallpapered room, I saw myself as a young girl about eight years old, wearing a green dress and brushing my hair in front of the mirrored dresser. (Due to my husband's inexperience as a facilitator, I had asked him to move us forward every five years until we reached whatever "*it*" was.) At thirteen years of age I played with my cousin, an older boy. His hair was the color of carrots. We ran across a field. Then I followed him into the barn. It started out as "I'll show you if you'll show me." I felt hesitant, but I did as he said. This evolved into playing "nasty." I didn't like what was happening and did not want to ever do it again. However, after that he forced me to have sex with him for years, threatening to tell if I resisted.

In the present life, when I was about five years old my mom and I went to visit a neighbor. While my mother visited inside the house, I went under the house to play with the children there. The house stood on legs, actually concrete pillars, with sides open to the light. Underneath the house, two little neighbor girls and one little boy played "doctor," using popsicle sticks. A large incomprehensible feeling swept over me and told me that this game was very wrong, so I left. As we walked home together, I told my mother what had happened. Later, as I sat alone on the front porch swing, I pondered feelings that I had no way of understanding at the time.

When I was about nineteen years old in that past life there was a dance. That evening, sitting at my mirror getting ready to go, the eyes that stared back at me were solemn, as if prematurely saddened by something deeply hidden. Of course, there was. I kept it hidden, this extortion of my soul that had occurred for years. As I stood at the top of the stairs, in a long dark dress with a floral design and my hair swept up on my head, the price of long silence weighed so heavily upon my heart that I could do nothing to remove it.

At the dance I was accompanied by an older man named Frank, whom I was courting. Our engagement to be married was to be announced that evening. Instead, my cousin showed up raucous and drunk and made a mess of things. He insisted on my dancing with him, and tried to cut in while I danced with my fiancé. My fiancé resisted because my cousin was so intoxicated. At that, in front of everyone, my cousin began to say deplorable things about me, about us, and about what we had been doing. He spilled the beans about our "trysts" in the barn, and gloated that he had had me for years. I stood there stunned, horrified, my worst fear realized. Turning to my fiancé for support, I could not believe the look on his face! He shunned me. Devastated by his intolerance and his lack of trust, I ran outside sobbing. Blindly I wandered back through the parked buckboards and wagons and collapsed on the ground in a heap behind one of them.

A little later my drunken cousin and some of his cronies stumbled out, found me, and decided to have some fun. I tried to fight them off and obviously couldn't. They dragged me into the stable and forcibly had their way with me. Worse, is that my fiancé heard the commotion and proceeded to get into his buckboard. Then he drove away without investigating or even trying to help me. My life now destroyed, I didn't know where I could go. I couldn't go home. I could never face anyone. I felt too ashamed. My father would disown me anyway, so there was no point in subjecting myself to that.

Of course, time found me pregnant with nowhere to live. I survived as best I could. I lived pretty much on the streets, in a hand-to-mouth existence, in a neighboring town far enough away. I managed to have the baby. Shortly thereafter, it died, and with it a part of me died, too. Then came the guilt. Up to this time I hadn't blamed myself. But my little baby, my little boy, died in my arms, sick and hungry, because I couldn't take care of him.

This unfathomable loss brought on a rage and horrible anger that consumed my being. By the time I made it to my parents' home, I was truly crazed. I stormed in, headed straight to the mantel, brushed my father aside, and took down the rifle from the wall. Consumed by grief, I blew his face off. At first it was hard to determine just whom I had murdered—my cousin, one of the men who had raped me, or *my fiancé*—my fiancé, who supposedly loved me yet did not offer any support, who had not even tried to listen to my side of things, who had not even bothered to come to my aid, when he had to have known what they were doing to me. Only his pride, his ego, mattered. Yes, I blew the son of a bitch away. I was not sorry.

After the killing I appeared to be totally bonkers, having completely lost my grip on reality. Its accomplishment—to make him pay—had been my only thought. Subsequently I was placed in an insane asylum where I lived out my life, alone a lot, and sometimes with others. Totally denigrated, with no humanness left, I clawed at my vagina mindlessly. I squatted against the wall for hours, utterly self-defeated. I couldn't deal with what had happened to my baby, and so I punished myself unmercifully. There seemed no end in sight. I remained there for a very long time before I finally died, after years and years and years of self-imposed torment, lost to myself.

Through the days that followed this regression I gained more insight and certainly a great deal of relief and release. I felt a deep sense of kindness and compassion for who I had been in that past time. I realized that my child from that lifetime was my firstborn now, which explains why I would become so emotionally distraught when he would have a cold, a slight fever, or a simple stomach virus. I would be so afraid of losing him that I behaved as if he were in serious physical distress. I was petrified to leave his bedside. Although a part of me knew I was overreacting, another part of me remained locked into another time when these fears had been realized. This unresolved trauma of losing my baby had been restimulated every time my present child became ill. This pattern had continued to the time that I attended Sutphen's past-life seminar.

Of course, I had never let my baby know my fears when I was with him, but I'm sure that, babies being what they are, he picked up on it, at least somewhat. When in another room away from the baby, I would break down and refuse to leave the house for anything, including once my husband's planned birthday celebration for me. But after I had resolved this past-life trauma when my son was almost four, I found myself able to keep things in perspective. What a relief!

This past life also showed me a place in time when I had been truly crazy. I always knew I had been. From a very young age, I felt that I had known what it was like to cross that thin line between sanity and madness. It bled through sometimes, that feeling of such interminable darkness and utter despair I had carried for so long that it seemed as if my soul were permanently marked.

The lesson here is that memories of this past lifetime needed to resurface so I could come to some major understandings and do some major healing of myself. Obviously the seminar had kindled the healing process, but such a traumatic memory needed a more appropriate time to come forward. When one has lived such a traumatic life, and suffered for so many years, and died in such a living hell, much resolution and transformation are needed before one is able to leave those experiences in the past and move forward without carrying the weight of them in the present. That dark shadow that had always come unannounced throughout this life and had threatened my very being had a beginning, a place of origin of which I was now conscious. Its discovery proved to be not only freeing and comforting to me, but also very healing.

It's extremely important, of course, to realize that was then, and this is now. "Then" doesn't have to overshadow "now." Once a prior event has been reexperienced it can be released to the past, separated from the present and defused. It no longer has the power to wreak havoc in the present. It has in essence been laid to rest. The memory of that event is present, but the emotional intensity is not. Much needs to be realized, and connections to the present need to be made. These connections often happen spontaneously during the regression itself.

For me, I immediately recognized that cousin in my present life. I also became aware of why my feelings toward him in the present are as they are. He has always seemed a bit slimy to me, dirty, unclean, someone certainly not to be trusted. After this regression I was able to see him in a different light. I even tried to help him in the present, but he has proven himself not to be very trustworthy in this life either.

It was some time after this regression, however, that I recognized this past lifetime as the real root of the obsessive compulsions that had driven me during my younger years, when my mother had told me to stop acting *crazy*. I had feared that once again I would lose a beloved family member and it would somehow be my fault. That fear became enough to keep me rhythmically patting those kitchen utensils and chairs! After the processing of a past-life regression, and all of its accompanying realizations, one is truly *free* to move on.

The Path of Preparation

Even though doctors had told me in my present life that I would never bear children, I proved them wrong, partly because I needed to take back my power and heal myself, and partly because I unconsciously needed to have the soul of my former child with me again. My healing took about a year. I hadn't had a period for over five years through my late twenties. When I asked my doctor about the side effects of a lack of period, he responded by saying, "Enjoy yourself." I must admit, at the time, I did enjoy the lack thereof, but I knew I had to bring myself into balance. Only later in life did I find out the high cost of such an imbalance. It seems that when the menses are interrupted, especially at an early age, there can be a tremendous loss of bone density. It is as if a vacuum cleaner were suctioning calcium right out of the bones, the result for me being a significant percentage of bone loss by age forty-seven. However, I haven't chosen to accept that as my reality either.

The diagnosis from the medical establishment back then was a malfunctioning pituitary gland. I was informed that this condition was serious; however, they knew of nothing they could do for me. They wanted only that I please come back in six months. Oh joy! I wasn't about to become their guinea pig. When the hospital started misbilling me after I had already paid for their tests, after phone calls and letters failed to clear up the matter, I returned the next bill unopened, writing across the envelope, "She died!" That's one thing they do understand. I never heard from them again.

Now that I knew the problem, I had to figure out the solution. First I discovered a book called *GLANDS—Our Invisible Guardians* by M.W. Kapp, M.D., published by AMORC, the Ancient Mystical Order of the Rosy Cross, better known as The Rosicrucian Order, which I had joined in May of 1973. I must say my path as a Rosicrucian has been the single most important factor in the evolution of my spiritual journey. It has served as a beacon of light, a sacred sanctum, an avenue to my Self. Over the years, no matter my life situation, my studies have provided a never-ending stream of solace and peace most profound that has served as an unfailing source of strength for me and a constant lifeline to the Cosmic.

During the time of reading this book, I felt compelled to drive up the coast of California, literally crying all the way to San Jose, to Rosicrucian Park, where I sat in the rose garden. You see, this time period coincided with my "dark night of the soul," so sobbing offered a good release, and where better to do it than in a garden of roses. I spent the next day or two there figuring out what I was to do. I knew I needed to fast on the new moon, which I did for a little over a year, the fasts usually extending at least seven days. Once I fasted for thirteen days, another time for only three or four days. I also knew I needed to be celibate, to retain my energy within my own vessel.

Since the pituitary gland is associated with the sixth chakra, purple felt important for my healing. I dyed my sheets purple. They turned out lavender. That would do. My wardrobe was already rich in lavenders and purples, I simply added more. I wanted to paint the inside of my car lavender, so that every time I stepped inside it, I would be in a healing bubble. I realized that such a step would be a little too impractical, so I used my imagination instead. Living in California, naturally, I spent a lot of time in my healing bubble, my little yellow Toyota, Mary Sun. Something else I knew I needed was a purple stone to wear as close to my third eye as possible without drawing too much attention. It was not long in coming.

Monday morning rehearsal of a play called *The Long Christmas Dinner* found one of my fellow actors, whom I didn't even know very well, coming up to me and saying, "I don't know why, but this is for you." She had been to Mexico over the weekend and had brought back an amethyst cluster. I'll never forget the look of it lying in her open hand. I was blown away. It was exactly what I had needed. Then in a matter of days I struck up a conversation with a man who *just happened* to be a silversmith. He set the stone in a silver band that I could wear underneath my hair at my hairline. I tied it around my head with a purple cord. It was subtle. It was perfect. The only time anyone noticed was when it flashed in certain light. It was too private to explain. So, I didn't. The month I met my future husband I had my first period. I had completed preparing the way for the return of this soul—my son.

There is such a deep, deep soul connection with this child, a connection that stems from this as well as from other past lives. In this life, I felt his presence about five years before I became pregnant. But I had thought that the soul who hovered was a Native American boy child, whom I felt I would one day adopt when I grew older. I knew his name as soon as I saw a set of books from Glastonbury, England, about the Lord Mikaal, the Archangel. That name leaped off the cover of the book and I knew it would become the name of my son.

Astrologically, I also knew I had a barren sign on the cusp of my fifth house of children. There was perhaps one child. I pushed the envelope and had two. But complications then that, unknown to me, had begun with the first birth would have made it too dangerous to have a third child. I was just so thankful that my second child made it through some harrowing moments. He came out looking perfect, the epitome of a beautiful baby.

My firstborn, on the other hand, had come out looking as if he had just been in a boxing match. He had. I had endured back labor and he had already rotated when his head emerged—not a lot of fun for either of us. But, I'll never forget the moment when I knew after almost twenty-one hours of labor that I couldn't continue much longer. I buried my head in my pillow. Ignoring my husband's tired pleas that I breathe, I connected with Mikaal's soul and told him telepathically that we had to do this together—now. The doctors had just determined that it would be at least three or four more hours before I would be dilated enough to give birth. How dare they tell me that! I could feel our minds and hearts and souls merge, as movement, almost infinitesimal at first, started to happen.

Funny. All of a sudden my husband exclaimed, "Uh, the baby's head is crowning!" The doctor jumped to attention and had the audacity to tell me to hold it. I felt ready to kill him, but I was jubilant because Mikaal had responded and we were as One. I had no doubt of the truth of this oneness when I looked into those steel grey/blue eyes of my newborn and saw his soul, his essence staring back at me, totally present, with the most gorgeous heart-shaped lips ever imagined.

This child has shown himself time and again to be the kindest person I have ever known and one of the most spiritually profound. As I watch him grow in his wisdom, I know I am in the presence of a true Spiritual Warrior, and a very dear old soul, a friend, who is my teacher, as I am his.

Claustrophobia—Rooted in the Past

Birth, it is often said by my clients, is much like dying. The same sensations are often present and the same thoughts as those at death. Over the years, I've often pondered the death of one of my high school beaus, Taylor Sanders, and wondered if he felt the same sense of smothering, making his way down the birth canal toward the light, as he felt under the layers of dark, black coal that took his breath with that light.

Smothering is a sensation I've had to deal with in this life, too—not obviously with the same results as Taylor this time around, but before. Where we grew up was bad enough. The mountains closed in and the mines were dark and forbidding holes in the ground. Just standing at an open mine shaft with the cool air coming up always gave me the willies. That was one place I did not want to go.

I've often tried to determine when I first started having those claustrophobic feelings. I believe it was when I was born, or actually before, with the realization that I knew I was choosing to come in to a place where it would be hard to get a breath of freedom, a place where there would be no room to spread oneself out, let alone fly. It would all be too close. My childhood felt like a race against time. If I didn't break free, I knew that I faced strangulation. The restlessness kept me moving, yet it smothered my breath at the same time.

As a young person growing up, I knew I had known darkness. It was a fearsome thing, and it was always there sort of off to the side in the shadows. I could never see it, didn't really want to, although I didn't want it to know that I knew it was there. If it knew, it would smell my fear and I would be had. Something like that. I didn't know much more than that. It was just a feeling, a feeling of not being alone. But I knew that there were other energies out there that kept the balance. These energies kept their distance. I mean, it wasn't a real close personal relationship, but I knew they were there.

These feelings were most prevalent sometimes when I was up in the mountains alone, where I often had to go just to breathe, before I was old enough to drive. Up there, though, was different. The energies up in the mountains were often just nature sprites, the spirits of trees, things like that—powerful, different—but I knew they wouldn't hurt me.

It was those that came when I was alone in the house at night that I didn't like and I sure as hell didn't trust. Madness reigned, or else I was being watched by eyes that pierced the walls as if those walls were paper-thin tufts of gossamer that let the rays of uninvited beams dissect my fear. But, that's another tale that might not be told.

Then there was the wind and the speed of the car to assuage those smothering feelings, as I ripped along the winding mountain roads at breakneck speed, with just the wind, the night, and the trees whispering to themselves, "There she goes—again." There was an artistry to it. I could drive all the way home without using my brakes, maintaining my speed, without being what I would call reckless. I knew those roads like the back of my hand. As I've gotten older—after years of meditation—gazing at a beautiful tree out the window is all I need to still myself.

One night, as I drove home in the pitch-black darkness, an owl slammed face first into my windshield. For a few terrifying moments we found ourselves eyeball to eyeball, creating a truly freaky moment of immense proportion from my point of view, before the owl's body slid off the windshield. Momentarily it snagged on the wiper as if the wiper were my heart, before it disappeared off the side of the car. Unsettled by my experience and wondering what the hell it meant, I stomped my foot through the floor and I became the wind.

Living in New York City in the late sixties and early seventies, I felt discomfort sometimes on an overcrowded bus, subway, or elevator, wherein hordes of humanity were packed much like sardines in a can. Most of the time I could control my discomfort. When the feeling grew a little too intense, especially exacerbated by layers of winter clothing, and the sweat started running down my back, or my breath started acting funny, as if at any moment I would be gasping in search of it, I would get off the means of transportation, no matter the destination.

After I moved to California, I was no longer in tight groups of masses of humanity and so didn't have a problem. Once, however, at Disneyland on Tom Sawyer's Island, my two young boys went running into a manmade labyrinth that looked like a mountain. As soon as I followed them and people started crowding in behind me, I knew I was in trouble. Immediately I began to hyperventilate. *I'd never done that before.* Hurriedly I told the kids I was going back out and would meet them at the top, and I proceeded to excuse myself out of there, which wasn't easy. I found this incident rather alarming, and it made me seriously consider what I would have done if that had been a situation where my children's safety was at stake. Would this overwhelming feeling have crippled me so that I would have been unable to assist them? I found such a thought horribly frightening.

A few years later, during my transpersonal hypnotherapy training, I chose claustrophobia as what I wanted to work on, when it was my turn to be the subject in a practical training session. Well, the fellow student facilitator could not move me beyond a tight, pressing, close feeling. A heavy slab of stone lay on top of me, making for a very uncomfortable situation for quite a long time. I could have helped her along and made it easier for me, but I thought it was her turn to be the facilitator and I shouldn't interfere, even though it certainly wasn't a pleasant place that she kept me in. In retrospect, I can see my lack of response as a fault of mine, not taking the initiative when I know, but waiting for the other person to take the action. I'm much better at that now.

Some time later, with the director of the Transpersonal Hypnotherapy Institute, James Maynard, who had become a dear friend and colleague of mine, serving as my facilitator, we approached this subject a few weeks before I was to travel to Egypt, a land of many memories for me and the culmination of a lifelong dream. I did not want to be hampered in any way from being in the Great Pyramid, or any of the tombs, or close quarters where I might find myself. I needed to clear this smothering, closed-in feeling once and for all.

What is always interesting with past-life regression is that you may think you know where you might end up in working on a particular issue, but you find yourself somewhere else, or in circumstances that you never would have imagined. I knew I had never cared to know anything about the Aztecs, and now I was going to find out why.

In asking to go to the origin of my claustrophobia I found myself in a state of intense pain, crying out that it was too tight and I felt afraid. There was not enough space around me. I was in a gold, shiny metal box-like structure that pressed in on all sides, slowly and painfully crushing me. My arms were being pushed into my body, my legs were being pushed up, my chest hurt, and eventually my spine would be driven into my brain. Then came the realization that someone was doing this to me. "He's killing me," I managed to say through clenched teeth. I seemed to be choking, gurgling in my throat.

"Someone, like a shaman, with a headdress on, wearing a skirt to above his knees, is doing some kind of voodoo. It is not good. It is evil. This is being done to me because I don't like what they do and I won't do what is expected of me. I feel very hot and I'm having trouble breathing. They put a curse on me. A steady flow of saliva is coming out of my mouth. The main guy is saying a five-sound incantation. He forces a bitter potion down my throat.

"This whole culture is evil. He has dark skin. The drug makes me sweat. It's dark, it's at night. The priest . . . he's a priest, is shaking a rattle-like thing with feathers on the end, that he has in his hand . . . What I wouldn't do has to do with blood. I feel I'll be damned forever if I do this. It's the blood of sacrifice. I'm a young boy, maybe fourteen, fifteen years old, being trained to do these things that I know are very bad. I'm expected to drink blood and perform ritual sacrifices. It's what they all do. I can't do it. I try to tell them there is a better way. My dreams tell me this. They think I've been touched by evil because I don't do what they do.

"My culture is fear-based. The fear is so thick, everything is wrapped in fear. From gazing at the night sky I know there is more. There, up there with the lights, I know there is not fear. I can feel it, a part of me knows it is different. It is the only solace I have, but it is too far away.

"They then place a heavy, old, stone slab on top of me. It is large and very heavy and has writing, or symbols on top. I can't breathe. I go through a lot of heavy emotion. Then, this gurgling, choking thing happens, and I have all of this stuff in my mouth. (I'm literally choking on the couch and keep spitting this overflow into tissues as we continue.) It got so hot, I couldn't breathe. Then it's all swirling darkness, and finally I am free.

"There is a god waiting there for me, a big winged multi-feathered god. In our religion he is the one who takes us through the underworld. Then I go up to where it's not dark. Now my soul separates from this life of twisted belief and my soul is very light. This is better than the night sky. It's really soft, way beyond all that ugliness. Here I realize that fear is an illusion, death too. My culture's beliefs were not true. I am seeing that they did what they did with fear clouds. My primary purpose in being born into that situation was to stand up and choose a better way. I am free."

Later I did research on the Aztecs and their need to sacrifice humans. According to modern references, the reasoning was literally to keep the Fifth Sun in the heavens. A deep sense of fatalism surrounded the Aztec legend of creation. The Fifth Sun, the last of the five worlds, was destined to end. The ultimate and most holy Aztec offering to keep the Sun in the sky was the blood and heart of human sacrifice.

Huitxilopochtli, the sun and war god of the Aztecs, received daily offerings of human blood and hearts torn from the chests of living beings. Religion was in the hands of priests who came from the ruling families. These families considered it an honor to give a child to the priesthood. Such children were dedicated young and were trained so as to progress up through the ranks of the priesthood. What I did by refusing to participate must have been blasphemy of the worst sort. I had reached the point in my training where I was expected to take a more active part. I couldn't do it. I could not cut out a living heart and drink human blood. I did not seem to be in the same state as those around me.

One intriguing detail that I later discovered was that the priests usually dyed their bodies black with soot. This is perhaps why I had commented on how dark the priest's skin was, although my own skin appeared to be a rich brownish red, not white. The priest also had white and red paint on his face, or so I thought. In my research I discovered that at certain times the priests would paint those to be sacrificed, using red and black stripes, and would make their mouths red with black circles then drawn around them. Perhaps my own face had been painted when they tortured me to death, or else I saw the face of the victim I refused to sacrifice.

What I do remember succinctly are the priest's eyes, dark pools of crazed intensity. He looked as if he were possessed. In the healing and transformative work we did at the end of the session, I traveled into the darkness of those eyes to the Light within, deterrorizing and defusing the negative energy as I went. It proved difficult in the beginning, to build up the courage to enter into those horrible pools of madness.

The Aztecs spent their entire lives awaiting doomsday, the arrival of the fatal day that would end the reign of the Fifth Sun. Their belief dictated that they must feed the sun daily with the sacrificial blood of the human heart, which was a symbol of life, so that the sun would remain vital and in the heavens. In their tension-filled world, their society revolved around these rites of human sacrifice. In their minds the continued existence of the cosmos depended on it.

Following this regression I traveled to Egypt and had no problem being where I wanted to be when the quarters were close. However, in two instances heat became a factor that I had to overcome. One was in the Great Pyramid, in the Queen's chamber, which seemed to me to be only an anteroom. The air flow system had been off throughout the night and we visited the Great Pyramid from six to nine in the morning, before it opened to the general public. Thus, the air felt really stale and it grew warm and very stuffy in the Queen's chamber. Sweat began to run down my spine as I could feel the familiar sensation start to happen. Several others in the group had trouble breathing. My dear friend noticed what was going on with me and merely said, "You are supposed to be here." I pushed my body up against the coolness of the stone wall, took a deep breath, and connected to the freedom of the nighttime sky of my Aztec past, as I willed these feelings to recede.

The other time of discomfort occurred at the Temple of Denderah where, I discovered on this trip, I had once worked with astrology. We were to move through a small opening at the foot of some stairs that led to an underground area where precious items had been stored. At the entrance, with people in front of and behind me, the heat rising from that small room hit me in the face with such smothering intensity that I declined to go in. I waited until everyone else had finished. Then, I was fine. The beauty of the artwork on the walls took my breath away, especially the splendid beauty of the workmanship on the god Horus. This beauty so overwhelmed me that all I could do was emit a sob of expressed ecstasy. And to think that I might have had to miss that beauty because of claustrophobia! On this trip I entered many tombs and tight spaces and remained perfectly fine, even in situations where other members of the group had difficulty.

The other lifetime that I needed to clear in relation to the issue of claustrophobia was one that I had lived in Egypt as a young initiate. I'll never forget the feeling when I first found my-self recalling that lifetime. All I could see was sand, my foot in a sandal, and a diaphanous blue, blue material I wore that hit my leg a few inches above the ankle. Off in the distance across the sand stood the temple where I would soon have my initiation. My feelings were those of deep comfort and familiarity, and quiet an-ticipation. I resonated with this ancient land and was soulfully connected to it.

My studies as a young, vibrant priestess had gone well. I was now being prepared for a very important initiation related to my own immortality. I had been taught that it would be best to have no emotional relationships with others during this time because one's focus and concentration are so crucial to one's success as well as one's survival on this plane of existence. I had been warned, but had merely laughed because I didn't feel it would be a problem . . . I was young.

I was in love with a young artisan who was not involved in the temple and did not truly understand the importance of not thinking of me when I was not with him, certainly not while I participated in an initiation. I had explained it to him, but I was too young and inexperienced to realize how much I was asking of him.

On the day of my initiation, I felt totally present in the mo-ment and very sure of myself and my abilities. I was destined for this role. This was who I was, and I had become very good at it. Once I lay inside the sarcophagus the priests closed the lid and then it would be up to me. Some people lose it when the sound of the lid ushers them into the darkness of the soul. They freak . . . and fail. Not me. I had fun doing my most favorite thing, being the ruler of my mind, body, and being. I began the construct and it was beautiful. I felt content simply to observe its emergence. It was pyramidal in shape, three dimensional, yellow and green in color mostly, with some red. It appeared transparent, as if it were made of light, but yet holding its own form. It existed outside of me and yet of me, created by me, with the power to raise the lid, *to open as I am.*

This realization came only in the writing of these words, and it felt so powerful that my equilibrium began to go. The feeling was one of shifting into a different state of consciousness, yet the physical body couldn't move that quickly, or adjust that readily. I thought I might have to lie down, to ease out of my chair at the computer and onto the floor, but soon the sensation passed. All my life those words, "*You open as I am*," words that first came through when I was in college, have had a profound bearing on my life. That, too, is another tale.

With the construct in front of me I found myself fascinated with it and totally concentrated on my task. To do this kind of work one must remain in a profoundly psychic state of awareness. At the same time my love began thinking of me as he painted. His thoughts constituted a lapse in his own promise to me, and I was so open, how could I not have received them, being as closely connected to each other as we were by our feelings? I can still remember his thought of me coming through like a line of energy that approached from my left side, level with my head just above my ear. In that one moment all was lost. I could do nothing, for as I realized what had happened my construct started to fall apart and dematerialize before my eyes.

My thought construct had already raised the lid of the sarcophagus about half an inch, and it now slammed shut, accelerating my instantaneous awareness that all was indeed lost. I had failed. I was doomed to have failed my initiation because I had thought I could handle more than one thing at a time, which is something I do now a great deal of the time, and enjoy immensely with my Gemini ascendant. But sometimes it proves to be too much still. I am often too scattered in the use of my energy and struggle to remain with one thing through to completion.

Here in the land that speaks to my soul most deeply even now, I had learned the cruel lesson of discipline, the discipline that is solely focused on the goal, the discipline that does not allow the emotions any involvement outside of the work, the discipline that leads to success. I had been warned, but did not heed the call. My superiors knew I was treading very dangerous ground.

In the beginning we were told to keep ourselves apart and virginal basically. Perhaps if I hadn't been so cocksure of myself and my abilities, I could have contemplated failing. Then I would have taken the need for abstinence much more seriously than I did. But, in the end, they wisely knew that the decision was mine to make.

This particular lifetime is an extremely important one for me on many levels. It speaks to several aspects of my personality. In this initiation, I did indeed smother to death. It wasn't a death of panic, but one of resignation and deep personal disappointment. I had come so close, the end was in sight, almost present, and I blew it. I held my failure as a sorrowful and extremely poignant and devastating loss. My death itself was immaterial. That I could do. But to deal with the actuality of what I had done, of what I had failed to do, would take lifetimes. I can still feel that moment of loss, of the realization, of the failure. It has resounded throughout the ages. Too many times even now in the present lifetime, I have gotten to a point of success and then walked away and not allowed myself to complete the picture. I have carried such deep disappointment in the self, such mixed emotions, such repetition—until now, until the time when the source of the pain, of the disappointment, is uncovered. Once it is uncovered we are free.

Interestingly, the man whom I loved during that time is someone I have known intimately in the present. Now there was an issue of trust—trust that he would do what he said he would do, trust that he would remain present and aware. This issue has proven to be hurtful to both of us because it has been so important, both then and now.

Visitors of Light

Once when I was young, maybe nine or so, I found myself awake in the dark in the middle of the night, knowing that I was not alone. It was in the back bedroom of our family home. My brother and I shared that room until my dad had the upstairs added. However, I don't remember my brother being there then, perhaps because he was asleep. What I do remember is a presence, a Light presence in my room. The energy spoke to me telepathically. I remember, lying there with my head against the headboard, thinking that they had made a mistake. I don't remember much of what they said. It was about big stuff. I do remember being overwhelmed, because I interrupted them to say that they must have the wrong room, for I couldn't possibly do all that. "I'm too little," I remember saying out loud. They assured me that I was here to help in the closing of the circle, but I believe I insisted that they had the wrong room. I now hope they didn't take me seriously!

A fear of the unknown, I suppose, unduly influenced me. No one had ever spoken to me about these kinds of experiences—experiences that go beyond the boundaries of what we term ordinary reality. I was a young girl, and just as in the rest of the world not a lot of credence was given to us in the mountains. Children were to be seen and not heard. No wonderful mystic, philosophical discussions had ever taken place in my life. Naturally, I had no one to talk to about this and I never did. I felt like an alien in this land, and there was no one.

Karmic Lessons of the Young

Throughout childhood, my best companions were my dogs. Yet they were constantly being taken from me, dying young, ripping my heart each time. I, too, was young, and I felt only the pain. I couldn't yet see these losses as karmic retribution for my past misdeeds. It would take years before I knew that.

As a young girl I played with the puppies of the pregnant strays I had a knack for bringing home. I would give them baths, sit with them for hours picking off their fleas and squishing the fleas' bulging backsides between my fingernails. Then I would dress the puppies in doll clothes and take them for walks in my doll carriage. I'm pretty sure I enjoyed this more than they did. Naturally we couldn't keep the whole litter, so my dad worked hard to find homes for them.

Over the years my parade of dead pets grew. Often they were poisoned. Seems there were some people who enjoyed riding around at night throwing out poisoned hot dogs as bait for the neighborhood dogs. One morning we found a piece on our front porch. It was one of those mornings when Whitey didn't come when I called. He never came again. I looked and looked for him, but could never find him. I wanted to think that he was up in the mountains hunting and had somehow not managed to find his way back yet. But I knew he wasn't coming back.

One day when I had long given up hope, as I was coming down from the mountains I went around the back of a big rock and found Whitey's remains. There wasn't much left of him, mostly maggots and a few tufts of his beautiful white hair. He had been totally white. I knew it was Whitey. I'd never seen a carcass so decomposed before, but I made myself stand there looking, and I gave myself time for a proper goodbye. I missed him for a long time. A part of me still does.

King was a different story. He did come down out of the mountains, wily and playful. But he was not mine. King was a big collie. He jumped upon me as if I were his long lost buddy. We romped and played in the crisp autumn air, rolling and wrestling in a pile of leaves the wind had whipped up to the side of the hill. But he didn't stay. I didn't blame him one bit. He left and I never saw him again until spring, when once again he came bounding down out of the mountains, out of nowhere.

This time he stayed—she stayed. She was pregnant. Guess she knew who to come to. I must have had a reputation with the dog population. "Go to her house. She would never turn you away." Even with her pups, King remained King. She was a great dog. She would run around with me as I rode my bike. She was my goodtime buddy.

A big problem did come up when King got her first taste of one of Daddy's chickens. There were dead chickens in the mornings, feathers all about. My dad threatened to shoot King. I told him it couldn't be her. Dad secured the fence and put a piece of board on top of the gate to make it impossible for her to get in, or so we thought. I tried to talk to her, but I could see the fire in her eyes. That very night the moon must have been close to full, and I stayed up to watch. Her eyes had told me that she was not to be trusted. I could see the chicken house and yard from my upstairs window. The gate lay directly in my line of vision. After keeping vigil, as it were, for quite awhile, I grew tired but felt relieved, when suddenly I saw her.

King made circles in front of the gate about fifteen feet back. Then before I could do anything, she was airborne, floating across the top of that high gate in the moonlight. I froze to the spot, and stared out the window, scared to death. Then I heard the chickens go crazy. It's funny, but I don't remember if Dad woke up and went racing outside with his shotgun that night, or if it was something he did the next day. I just remember begging him not to shoot her, and him telling me that he had to. The gun separated us as I continued to plead for my dog's life. Maybe Mom said something on my behalf because Daddy didn't kill King.

Instead, Daddy nailed another board on top of the gate and I breathed a huge sigh of relief. King was safe for the moment. It had worked. After that King couldn't get into the chicken yard. Boy, was I ever glad. After all that, you would think things would go well. But, they didn't.

One night after supper, I went out front to ride my bike. King always liked to lie underneath the back of Dad's 1954 pale green and white Chevrolet in the soft sand that the highway workers had put between the old sidewalk and the newly paved road. It was the first time the road had been paved. As I walked past King, headed for my bike, I stopped dead in my tracks. King's eyes were open, but they didn't follow me, and her tail didn't beat the ground as it always did when I was close by. Her eyes just stared, vacant. King wasn't there. I could see waves of movement in the sand where her paws had struggled with the pain of death. I stared at those waves for a long time. The pattern looked so pretty, so uniform, graceful and surreal.

When I finally could, I screamed for my daddy. Somebody had poisoned my dog . . . again! Thinking he was doing me a favor, Dad offered to haul her off. Hysterical, I screamed for him not to touch her. I would bury her. I did, down on the riverbank with the rest of my menagerie, all dead. I always held a service. I didn't invite anyone except my brother. He was there once, I remember. One time I arranged a memorial service, with Candice and her brother joining us one morning, but that was a different dog.

Lots of my dogs died. Two of them froze to death the night I brought them home. They were just little guys, way too young to be away from their mom, but the woman was going to get rid of them, as in drown them, so I had no choice but to take them. It was after dark as I walked home cuddling these two little fur balls in my arms, knowing my parents would not be happy. Mother did allow those two puppies in the house because they were too little to walk around and mess up anything. She helped me try to feed them with a baby bottle, but they were too weak to suck. I wrapped them in a towel and put them in a cardboard box, setting it next to the big furnace vent, which was the warmest place in the house. I wanted to take them to bed with me, but my mother wouldn't hear of it.

In bed that night, I prayed to God that they would be all right. When I got up the next morning and hurried downstairs, I found them dead and stiff. I was really pissed at my mom, and disappointed and saddened that God hadn't heard me. Of course, my mom didn't want me sleeping with sick animals, nor did she want me waking up to find them dead in my bed. But at my age, I didn't think along those lines. As for God, I already struggled with the God that the Church had presented to me. This God seemed real different from the One I remembered from before. I felt confused and alone, and I just knew something was wrong.

Once I brought a stray hound dog home. She had her babies that very night up under the house, nestled against the chimney. She was smart. My dad hated her. He called her "Gut." He didn't seem to understand that she had to eat for a family of eleven! That's right. We knew they were there, because we heard yelping and whining as we ate breakfast. I wanted to go right then, but I had to wait until after our meal. Then I went under the house with a flashlight and there they were. There were so many of them and just as cute as they could be!

Of course their eyes weren't open yet, but one little guy had already distinguished himself. He had crawled way over away from Mom, exploring and whining. I brought him back only to watch him blindly take off again. Yep, he was my favorite. I named him Big Daddy right then. Somebody later poisoned him, too.

His mom did a survival thing that totally freaked me out. One Sunday we went to my grandfather's house. My dad stayed home. When we got back a little before dark, I immediately ran outside to see the pups. I found only a few there. The others were missing. I asked my dad if he knew anything about it. He said he didn't. I started searching and found them all over the place. The mother must have carried them off and left them to die, because she knew she couldn't feed so many. Animals do that, eat their young or refuse to feed them. Some were cold when I found them. Others were still alive. Some I managed to get going again and I fed them myself. The whole incident was really traumatic and fraught with karma.

Then there was the puppy who almost drowned by falling into the sump pump down in the basement one morning. The very next morning there it was, pushing its fat little butt out through the fence, trying to follow Dad to his car in the garage across the road. He had put the pup back inside twice already, and he thought it was still inside the yard when he backed the car over it. Dad was really sorry. I was seriously wounded.

My dad felt really bad for me and replaced the pup he had run over with a purebred cocker spaniel pup, who died from hepatitis after I'd only had it a week or two. Sometime through all of this I began to wonder why me? What had I done to deserve this? My parents had reached the conclusion that all this loss was much too hard on a sensitive child such as myself, and decided it would be a good idea for me not to have any more pets, since I seemed to have such bad luck. Only years later, when I was a parent myself, did I finally learn the real reason that I had explored such heartache.

The Answer Comes

Once our own children were five and three years old we wanted them to experience having a dog. They brimmed with excitement as we drove to the pound to pick one out. Ethan went right over to Reggie and stuck his hand in the cage to pet him. Reggie trembled. Ethan, just as cute as he could be with his long curly locks and gregarious manner, announced that this was our dog. We all agreed. Only after our decision were we told that Reggie was scheduled to be put down that afternoon, a mere two hours later.

Reggie had obviously been mistreated since he cowered and peed as soon as anyone started to approach him. It took him a while to feel safe enough to stop that reaction. Throughout his life, he almost always raised his hind leg to urinate, but sometimes even years later still reverted to squatting. He was one year old when we got him and he lived to be fourteen. He had a good long life. Having never had the same dog for very long while growing up, I felt blessed.

Mikaal named the dog in the car coming home. Where the name came from I have no idea. I do know that Reggie was a beautiful dog inside and out. His markings were striking and he was filled with wisdom. Ethan, being a typical three-year-old, wanted to walk him as soon as we got him home. So, he and I did. Fairly immediately, Ethan got tangled up in the leash and fell on top of Reggie's back. At this time we hadn't had Reggie an hour. But instead of snapping at Ethan or reacting in the fearful way that one might expect, Reggie spread his legs and held Ethan up, until with my help, Ethan could regain his balance.

That showed me that Reggie was indeed meant to be our dog. He was extremely intelligent, and sometimes he talked to me as plain as day. One winter day as I walked past him, I heard him say in my mind, "It's too cold for me out here." There was no way I could not have heard that. Being twelve at the time, he suffered from a little arthritis, but he still loved to play ball, chasing it at a dead run. I guess he figured the limping around afterward was worth it.

When Reggie was around five years of age, he proved to be instrumental in my having another spontaneous insight into a past-life experience. The following day I planned to conduct a past-life regression workshop and I wanted to use one of my big crystals in the center of our meditation circle. It was a male crystal, Atlantean in its energy, that wouldn't let me not buy it. As soon as I had entered a crystal shop in Mount Ida, Arkansas, I had seen it. It made sure I saw it. I picked out several other pieces, but that one continued to draw me back to it. It seemed to insist that I take it, as if it were saying, "I'm the one." It's vibration made it become one of my favorites. On this particular day I had cleared the crystal with water and salt and had set it outside on the banister to bathe in the sunshine. As I walked away a thought went through my mind that leaving the crystal there might not be a good idea, but I was in a hurry and didn't listen.

A little later my son Mikaal, who must have been about nine at the time, threw a ball for Reggie to go fetch. Instead of leaving the porch through the doorway, Reggie was so ready to play that he jumped over the banister and knocked this beautiful crystal to the ground. Several facets broke off, all in the same area, but for the most part it was still intact. The damage was done to only about a quarter of the crystal. Both Reggie and Mikaal were very sorry, especially after they saw my reaction. I entered another zone altogether.

In truth, Atlantis had begun to rise—out of the depths of my memory. Above the broken crystal I found myself swaying with bent knees much as one might imagine a Greek chorus of women reacting to a grave tragedy. I heard a wailing sound emerge from deep within me. It was primal. I was outside of my present surroundings, caught up in a grieving of the masses. I continued to do this for some time.

Being a mother above all else, I did realize my young son was dismayed. He and the dog stood stark still and stared at the crystal . . . and at me! I forced myself to be in the present long enough to explain to Mikaal that it was okay. I assured him that I knew it was an accident and that he and Reggie didn't mean to break it. I explained that Mommy was just having some amazing moments here that were really important, some revelations, and I was fine.

I don't believe I could have stopped if I had wanted to. The momentum of the memory was sweeping over me. Out of the crystal that lay broken on the ground flowed the memory of *many, many* people dying. I felt as if I were crying for a land, for the loss of a people, for all of us.

All of my life I have carried with me the feeling that somewhere along the way I had misused power. Over time, I came to realize that this misuse had to do with taking away the free will of others. Over the years I had had inklings of insight about this period of time. I knew that it had to do with science. I knew that it had taken place in Atlantis, that I had been extremely cerebral as was the Atlantean society. I had been curious then, ohhh, sooooo curious. I had wanted to know what would happen if . . . if we crossed this with that. I sought knowledge at any price.

Now, through the coming together of three wise beings—my beloved son, our dog of ancient wisdom, and this crystal that had reached out and made itself known to me—I knew that the scientific experimentation that I had been involved with in Atlantis had to do with animal and human experimentation, the mixing of species without permission, without even asking, just doing, to see what would happen. This was what it had been! I now finally knew where those feelings of unworthiness had come from.

This experimentation was a perfect example of what had gone wrong in Atlantis. Anytime progress is made, we have to bring our whole self along for the ride. In Atlantis we left the heart behind. We led with our minds, with pure mental energy, devoid of feelings. The result of this approach was the technological nightmare that led us to destroy ourselves and our beautiful land and incredible achievements. The power wrought through our advanced use of crystals put us so out of balance that we found ourselves unable to stop until we self-destructed. We had simply run amuck. Naturally, this didn't occur overnight. Many generations came and went during the time that it took to reach the point when we literally blew ourselves up.

Obviously, my intense reaction to the crystal breaking did not in any way fit the event. My reaction was extreme. But when we are ready the universe provides the experience needed for further unfoldment. I was ready to receive the next piece of my life puzzle. I needed to receive that piece, and so the cosmic provided the components necessary to bring about my further realization.

As my weeping continued, I made my way with the crystal to a place where I could be alone to continue this experience without alarming my children. There I sat, holding the crystal, and I wept for a long time. Afterward, when all my grieving had subsided, I felt a deep openness, a peaceful place wherein nothing could touch me. From that space I could handle anything. I had let go. I gave Mikaal and Reggie each a big hug, and I thanked them and the crystal for their amazing gift.

Everything in life serves as a stepping stone to the next awareness, to the next shift in consciousness, if we go with the flow and allow our senses to register the experience on all levels. We each are multifaceted—crystals of light that are sometimes blue, sometimes green, going from color to color, from experience to experience, lesson to lesson, until we are all color as one—white light.

So you see, all those dead puppies, the premature demise of so many of my beloved pets provided a lesson of compassion, directly related karmically to my earlier time in Atlantis. My emotional pain in this life was merely an act of balancing the scales. In Atlantis I had no compunction about conducting genetic experiments. I was interested only in the results. In the present, through my beautiful menagerie of animals I was led to experience firsthand the true value of life, knowing at a young age the deep sorrow of loving and losing what I had loved.

One could say that I've actually gone to the other extreme. As a child I used to break down crying in the back seat of my parents' car when we would pass a poor old man with a potato sack on his back, who walked along the highway looking for lumps of coal, or shale, that he could use for fuel. It would break my heart to see people, or animals, in situations like that. I didn't see any difference between the stray, starving dog and a person. My mother told me repeatedly that I was too sensitive and that I would need a thicker skin to survive in this world.

Atlantis Still Rising

Another example of this lesson for me in the present life came about through the acquisition of our second dog, Aussie. The kids named her, sight unseen, while in the car on our way to look at a litter of pups that a woman had advertised in the newspaper. Mikaal asked me what kind of pups they were. I said Lab and English Springer Spaniel mix. He then asked, "And what kind of dog is Reggie?" I replied that he was an Australian Shepherd mix. I then heard Mikaal say, "We'll name it Aussie." So, go figure.

Anyway, we had the name and now we needed the pup. This litter was scheduled to be destroyed at the Humane Society, and the woman who had advertised them would take such litters and try to find them homes. When we arrived there, Aussie was obviously the most lively pup and Ethan, having just turned eight, again decided that this was the one! So we took her even though she had a pretty bad cut on her neck and her mother didn't look too well. The woman gave Aussie her shots and we stopped at a pet shop on the way home to get her some puppy food. She was thought to be about ten to twelve weeks old.

We then swung by the vet to have her checked out and he said she was fine. That was on Thursday. By Monday morning Aussie had become really sick. She was passing blood and yuck from both ends that didn't look like anything I had ever seen before. I gathered some samples to take with me and got her to the vet. Aussie was really, really sick. While we waited in the examining room for the doctor I had another cosmic moment around the Atlantean energy. I knew what this experience was about. When moments like that happen there is no doubt, there is only truth, and in that truth lies revelation. What I realized proved more real to me than the reality of my sitting in that examining room.

Aussie's sad brown eyes never left me, even though she had become so weak she couldn't even move. I felt overcome with the enormity of the concept of our lives and the incredible role my beautiful dogs were playing in my total realization. I felt so blessed and honored by their presence. It seemed that, lying there as sick and as little as she was, Aussie was cognizant of what was happening. It was her gift to me. Weeping in abject awareness, I petted her and prayed to God to please let her live. I did understand what was happening here.

After examining Aussie, the doctor suggested that we put her down, since we had only had her three full days. He said it was unlikely that as young as she was, she could pull through this, and besides the treatment would be expensive. One look at my face told him that his suggestion was not an option. Once he fully realized how I felt about the dog and that I could not under any circumstances let her die without trying, he started to discuss ways we could cut financial corners. He then put her in quarantine and tried to figure out what was wrong. He never knew for sure, but he suspected it was parvo. She remained in quarantine on medication and an IV for five days.

My husband and I took turns visiting with her. We would go twice a day and just sit and hold her and tell her how much we loved her. When we would come in to sit down on the floor in front of her cage, no matter how sick she was she would try to wobble over to our lap where she would remain until we had to leave.

The doctor really didn't think she had much of a chance. All of the staff were convinced that it was our caring and loving that had saved her. They commented as we left that they had never seen a sick dog receive so much heartfelt love and attention. Perhaps that explains why she is now so protective of us.

After I left her at the vet's that first day, I stumbled to my car, blinded by my tears, and sobbed uncontrollably all the way home. Once home, I still couldn't stop and I continued to weep so profusely for over two hours, even I thought I needed to get a grip. Yet through my tears I received many understandings and further insights into that life in Atlantis, and into the major release that was now possible and occurring spontaneously in this one. As a result, I am no longer so hard on myself. I've been able to let go of the guilt under which I've labored for so very long. I'm able to honor myself more and allow myself to accept *me* as I am, the sum total of *all* the parts.

If You're Known, You're Dead

Another time in Atlantis warrants being spoken of in relation to this one. It came into my consciousness only as a result of a statement that came through loud and clear during hypnotherapy training when James, the director, guided us through a visualization wherein we took note of what we saw, felt, or heard as he took us on a journey up the mountain. At one point he said to be aware of what was to our right, as it had to do with what stood in our way, or our greatest fear, or something to that effect.

There on the side of the hill I saw an opening, much like an old mining shaft. It appeared dark and dangerous. I distinctly heard the following words, "If you are known, you are dead." This statement carried an ominous ring to it and I knew it was vital that I truly understand its meaning. In my own astrological chart there is a definite reluctance to be known in the world, as well as there being obstacles to overcome. Throughout my life a pattern has emerged. Once I get to a certain point of success, once I know it is something I can do, I leave it, or never finish it, or opt to go in another direction, or have it taken from me. So I knew immediately that this statement held great import for me and my further unfoldment.

At a later date we chose to pursue this statement using hypnotherapy. We asked to go to the source of the statement, "If you are known, you're dead." The following is what took place.

"There's a light. . . ." I became aware of a light above me. "It's really bright, but it's not just a light. It's scary. It's invasive. I feel numb. It's this light. . . . It's . . . I don't know, I'm just getting numb. . . . My cheeks are numb." I realized that these parts of my body felt numb because they hurt, and they hurt because of the light. It's not so much that they felt numb. It felt more like a vibration, a frequency invading my own space, my own electromagnetic field. "Some power, like a vibration, that is getting stronger." My legs separated, pulled somehow. My face grew numb and I heard a noise.

My body started to shake uncontrollably in response to that vibration, that noise. I realized that I was crying. The vibration became stronger. It came from the light. It felt like a sound. It was whatever made me feel pressed to the table, as if paralyzed. All of a sudden I experienced intense pain in my upper right arm. It felt as if an instrument of some kind had taken a sample of me, of my bone marrow. I didn't know. I did know I felt extremely intense pain. When this happened I reacted to the force of the pain and practically bounced out of the recliner.

Screaming and in great pain I said, "Ohh, stop it you son of a bitch. Cut it out!" It felt so inhuman, what they were doing. I was no more than a lab specimen. "Oh God!" The light was still there. I lay on a table. These beings communicated. I didn't hear words, didn't see any mouths. I was in a round room. "Oh, God damn it, they are not through!! Oh, Jesus Christ!"

I felt such rage. . . . It was futile. I couldn't do anything about it. At this point, James asked me to express my feelings, to express the rage and anger that I felt. "You're a pile of shit! Go to fucking hell!! You can do whatever you damn well please, I know that, but you can never kill me. You can't kill me!! I am eternal! You can take this fucking body and shove it up your ass, you little shits!!! You little peons! You don't deserve information. You don't deserve anything. You have *no right* to do this. . . . No, nothing has the right to do *this*. (Just as I didn't have the right to treat people and animals the way I did in Atlantis.) I'm leaving. You won't be able to hurt me. Go ahead. Give it your best shot." What I meant was that I could go within myself and out of my body to where whatever they did couldn't touch me, my soul, my essence.

They did what they would do. They didn't touch the body. "Jesus Christ." When I was told to move to the outcome, I found myself in a desolate place. They took the best and the rest just wasn't enough to go on. I felt dead. I saw my body as if I were above it. It appeared to be the body of a young girl, wearing a dress. Whether this were just an image, a projection of how I felt, or the reality of the aftermath, I could not be sure.

Later, in another session, I went to when this event had supposedly happened. It appeared to be my present life when I was around thirteen, fourteen years old living in Kentucky. It seemed to have happened about the same time that the obsessive compulsions started to escalate. Perhaps those fearful neurotic feelings of being watched at night, feeling that something was out there on the other side of the windows, watching, observing, waiting, weren't so crazy after all. Growing up I often felt I was being watched. Perhaps that is a symptom of a neurological disorder, but for me it felt very real. It happened at night when I was home alone, or just with my brother. This feeling was always there. I didn't like to walk past the windows. The presence of an actual "peeping tom" a couple of years later increased my discomfort.

In that session, I seemed to be in the kitchen late at night. Everyone else must have been asleep. Maybe I was there to get a drink of water. The sink was right below the kitchen windows. I don't know. There was a bluish light at the window. I seemed to be floating. The next sensation was of being outside and off the ground, moving toward a bluish white light. That's all. This part was not easy to retrieve. I was so conscious of not wanting to make anything up or be influenced by anything I had read or seen, that it was very difficult to get the conscious mind out of the way.

I do know that I have always been interested in UFOs. But, when the book *Communion* came out and I saw that face on the cover I could never read that book. I didn't want to. Even though a friend loaned it to me, I still did not want to go near it and I returned the book unread. Whether this memory is accurate as to when, or even if this happened to me, two things I do know. Lying on that table under the light that emitted that vibration was certainly real, and remembering it goes a long way to explain and eradicate a lot of fear I had always carried. I don't anymore. Quite recently I had the opportunity to have an expert in this field read over my experience. He called it "classic."

During the regression session, as James asked me what I was aware of, all I wanted to know was why this had happened. James then suggested that I go to where it all began, go to where "*If you're known, you are dead*" comes from. I knew immediately that I was in Atlantis.

An incredible looking clear turquoise-blue crystal hovered above me like a seeing eye. If you're known, you are dead. I'm one of the ones who know what's wrong. "God, I'm known!" The feeling that accompanied this utterance felt old, familiar, and oh so heavy. An instrument above me looked sort of like what a doctor uses to look into someone's ear, only it was longer, and colored light came out the end of it.

"There are no secrets, you know." They used this instrument to penetrate the third eye. I grew very upset, extremely so. In a flooding torrent, I exclaimed, "I'm not doing this anymore. I am not. I am not being known anymore. I'm not doing it. Find somebody else to do your work. I'm not doing it. I'm not doing it anymore. . . . Oh, God. Oh God. . . . If we don't do it, who will? . . . Who will? . . . I'm not. I am not. I am not! I'm not putting myself in this place again. . . . Death is easy. To die is easy . . . but this."

This remembered experience dealt with trying to stop what was going on in Atlantis, knowing that it wasn't right to do the things that were being done. The result was that I and others of like mind were basically lobotomized. We were then reprogrammed to perform what they wanted us to do. In essence, we became their instruments of experimentation. One realization I had during all of this, which many of my clients describe in their own sessions, was that I had not of my own free will done all that I was now in this life unconsciously blaming myself for, and had for centuries. Yes, I had participated up to a point, as a scientist, but my own humanity *had* made me draw the line. I then tried to effect change, but it was too late. Things had gone too far.

The whole puzzle had now fallen into place. I now knew the cause of so many behaviors, feelings, and thoughts that had affected me negatively, even down to knowing why I had always abhorred science in school. In those classes, I had spent as much time looking out the window as I possibly could. I also now knew that I never had to have those feelings again, ever. This is the whole point of doing past-life regression therapy. One becomes able to understand, forgive, and free oneself from the hold the past has had, so one can move forward in the present unencumbered by the past, able to honor the self, make the best choices possible, and support oneself to live one's life to its highest potential.

Forgiveness remains an essential part of our journey. Forgiveness of self is crucial. It often takes work, much more than even we suspect as we begin to peel back the layers of our guilt, of our sense of failure, of our feelings of unworthiness. But forgive we must, forgive ourselves and others. Forgiveness brings liberation, pure and simple. Sometimes it happens in the twinkling of an eye. There is a moment when all is understood. Then comes the letting go as we feel the tremendous weight we have placed on ourselves being lifted by ourselves, by our hard work toward realization, by our attunement with the Cosmic, sometimes by gentle Grace.

Sometimes in this work we have a tendency to jump the gun, so to speak, by trying to forgive before we have understood, before we have worked through our anger, sadness, and pain. These efforts come first. Then we are ready to forgive. Sometimes forgiveness happens automatically and spontaneously, while at other times it is a slow and gradual process of steps. We each have to follow our own path of truth. The light of that path is Love. The more we are able to love ourselves, the more we are able to progress in all areas of our lives in the way that is most appropriate for who we are. The first step is the most important and most often the hardest. But once that step is taken there is no going back. There may be side roads and detours, yet there is forward momentum. Love is at our back pushing us onward. It is underneath our feet holding us up. As our journey continues we become Love; we remember that we are Love.

The Synchronicity of Life

Sometimes answers to life's myriad waltz of mysteries come in all kinds of unexpected and wonderful ways, in small packages of illumination. Suddenly, out of nowhere, a meditation takes on mythic proportions and we get to push back our boundaries a little further. We are such amazing beings, each experiencing our own unique stories of personal enlightenment and soul growth.

Just such an occurrence happened for me in our monthly group meditation. It was the Harvest Moon, September 11, 1992. In retrospect, I saw it as a vision of Truth that took me on a broader journey—back to my roots—forward to my destiny. I led the meditation group that night. After aligning our chakras we left our physical bodies through the tops of our heads and moved back to the time when we had been at one with the Earth, to a time when we had knowingly walked the Sacred Path.

A Native American time was my experience. In color I saw the deer/elk skin dress of an Indian woman, but I saw her only from the knees down. She wore long-legged moccasins, and she walked through a field of golden grass or grain.

Then the scene shifted to black and white and came from up in the upper left corner of my mind, seemingly a place from whose direction truth flows for me. There I saw a tall, lean, rather wizened old Indian man. The planes of his face were very accentuated— high cheek bones with a protruding brow. He had large hands, big, dark, and worn. He lifted a sheaf of some kind of dried herb and shook the seeds from it. They fell into a cupped, round, black, shiny stone, or rock that looked as if it had been broken open. I saw a similar stone to his right. There seemed to be other such stones there, too, all of them black. He pummeled the seeds with another stone or maybe a longer object, as if he were preparing the seeds for use, and as if he were doing it specifically for me to see.

He stood in front of a large, tall black rock. On the top of the rock I saw black evergreen trees. At his neck hung a silver thunderbird with a black stone in its center. When I asked him his name, I heard "Black Elk." Funny, a part of me wanted something more interesting and a female. Hah! "What tribe?" I then asked. His response seemed to be Shawnee or Shoshonee, but then I realized that he had said "Shaman." This was not a tribe, but a path. I knew then my path to my true self was further opening for me. The "you open as I am" of my earlier experience resounded softly through my being as I knew I stood on sacred ground.

The next day I followed an inward urge to go to the local metaphysical bookstore. I almost didn't go because I really didn't need anything at the time, but on the pretense of getting a greeting card for a friend, reluctantly I heeded my intuition's call.

Interestingly, everything shifted as soon as I entered the store. My Higher Self took over and I found myself in an altered state of being. Not even looking for cards, not even close to where they were located, I found myself being pulled toward a U-shaped section of books. One side held UFO-related books, and the middle section included magic, ceremony, and ritual. In too many bookstores this section is heavily laden with books on black magic. Such books give off an energy that I really don't like to be around, but this section carried enough ceremonial white magic and women's ritual type books to make the energy bearable. The third side held all Native American books.

I stood there staring, but not focusing, until I saw Sun Bear's books. I pulled down one that gave information on preserving foods, how to make a root cellar, and so on. Then I saw another book of his called *Medicine Wheel Earth Astrology*, a book that I had recently read about in the back of another book, *Black Dawn, Bright Day*. I settled on the bench in the center of these three sets of shelves and started to read a little about the Scorpio time period. But I knew that wasn't it. This wasn't about my kids. This was about me. So I turned to Sagittarius. In the first short paragraph I read, "People born under the Long Snows Moon, November 22 - December 21, have the obsidian as their totem in the mineral kingdom, the black spruce as their totem in the plant kingdom and the elk as their totem in the animal kingdom. Their color is black, and they are members of the Thunderbird elemental clan." There was my meditation, all of it—the obsidian, the black evergreen, the elk, the thunderbird.

The time had come for my path to take another turn. I had always felt a little leery of obsidian, having read somewhere that if a person were not ready for the power within this stone, it could pull them in. I am ready now, I thought. I felt no apprehension, no fear. In the bookstore that day I purchased an obsidian stone. Later, I realized that the stone I had chosen was in the shape of an arrowhead, connecting not only to the Indian use of obsidian for arrowheads, but also to the Sagittarian shooting her truth-seeking arrow.

Of course, as soon as I started reading the title page for this chapter and read the word "elk," I started to emote. That's just my modus operandi. Tears have always accompanied the truth for me. Sitting there and experiencing incredible insight, wrapped up in that beautifully metaphysical mantle of illumination, while browsers moved all about, I felt totally alone, as if I were in another dimension, as if I were invisible to the other people in the store.

Through my tears and feelings of deep appreciation of the Native Peoples and their ability to live in harmony with the Earth, I found my gaze fixed on a title of a white bound book with black cursive writing. At first, I couldn't focus enough through my tears to read the title, but when I could, I saw that the title was *Black Elk*! Naturally I bought that book, too. There on the cover was a black and white photo of an Indian Shaman, Wallace Black Elk, who wore a silver Thunderbird around his neck! I loved the synchronicity of this experience. I had missed having such a profound experience. It had been a while.

We must remember that each day brings profundity on many levels if we remain aware enough to recognize it. I do know it is incredibly gratifying to follow our intuition, trusting it to guide us on a journey of spiritual upliftment and unfoldment that feeds us for many days to come.

Sacred Time at Mount Shasta

Other experiences that have happened to me while I remained totally conscious have absolutely reinforced my knowing that we are not alone, that Spirit walks with us. Power exists out there beyond our ability to comprehend. One of the most amazing and sacred experiences of my life happened in 1978 at the base of Mount Shasta on a moonless, pitch black late-August night. My dearest friend and I had been traveling about the United States that summer, visiting people and places and states of being.

We drove cross-country, taking turns reading to each other *The Treatise On White Magic* by Alice Bailey. In the middle of summer, in a car with no air conditioning, we had to be creative to be heard over the combined noise of the car's engine and the wind. We devised a megaphone to point toward the driver so that our words could ride atop the competing sounds.

Our route was a huge, uneven rectangle from Los Angeles to Houston and The Alamo, to the voodoo energy of New Orleans, to an island in the Gulf off Mobile, and on to the beaches up and down the Florida coast. Then north we traveled, visiting in North Carolina, Georgia, Kentucky, Pennsylvania, Maryland, New York, and Vermont before we made our way across the vast expanse of this land to Boulder, and to the incredibly huge skies of Montana, where we rounded a bend to see a large tree totally ensconced in white flames of fire in the middle of the day. Afterward we wondered if we had been the only people who saw it. On we moved up into Washington and Oregon, eventually making our way down the California coast back to Los Angeles, sometimes sleeping in strange and often, in retrospect, unsafe places, but feeling totally protected.

Our journey took nine weeks, three times the triangle. We experienced many lessons along the way—eyes forced open, relationships tested, discipleship forged. We found the journey to be hard and sweet, dedicated, and ego-stripped and honed—a true spiritual journey of major consequence.

The ultimate and most defining experience of our journey took place at Mount Shasta in northern California. We knew that we did not want to stay in the designated campsites. That was not why we had come to Shasta. Our entire trip had led up to this moment in time. So we waited until dark and drove around, letting our intuition guide us. We really didn't know where we were going, and I doubt very seriously that it was our decision that we stop when we did. We found ourselves turning to the right sharply off the road, such as it was, and up into a small clearing surrounded by trees, as if the location were just waiting for us.

Parking the car, we settled in to figure out what in the world had been happening to us, because we both knew our friendship was being tested in ways that we had never expected. Our relationship had always been one of great love and respect for each other. We were sisters in spirit, sisters of Light, and we had taken this journey of soul growth together. Before this trip we had never had a disagreement. We had always been willing to go with the flow, to acquiesce to the other's desires, which were never far from our own. Yet, on this journey there had been friction, some understandable, some out of nowhere—ego rips, personality snares, images of past times. We were indeed on a spiritual journey of growth, stretching the parameters, moving beyond the comfort zone, but always and foremost remaining comrades in spirit, disciples on the path up the mountain of trial by fire.

This tear in our friendship we wanted to discuss, clarify, and heal. Why was this happening? What did we need to understand? What did we need to grow beyond? We felt ready and willing, knowing that our love for each other and our spiritual fires would be enough to transmute the problem. We just had to see it for what it was. As we talked, slowly, our experience started to happen. I don't know how much of this experience I can share, or even if I want to. I only know it happened and is one of the profound experiences of my life.

A spiritual experience is almost impossible to speak of, for one can never in words describe the depth of its feelings, or even its physical sensation, and do it justice. It is an experience beyond words, beyond reason, metaphysical in nature. It simply is, and one is never the same. One is touched by Holiness, by Grace, by the Father-Mother, the Cosmic. One has received a glimpse of Home.

That is what I have carried with me as a result of this encounter. Our experience started slowly with a subtle coming of vibration, a sound, an essence so large that it took a good while to be totally upon us. In the beginning, we found ourselves parked in a palpable web of silence. Our first awareness was of a hum, a vibration that increased as we sat in the car, in the still night with the stars and trees as our only witness. A moment came when we realized that Lily, the car, was vibrating as if it were off the ground, not on it. It was as if what constituted Lily was vibrating at such a rate that we could see the actual materialization, the coming together of those particular atoms that made Lily appear as a car. Soon after this slight phenomenon, we noted that we, too, were vibrating, that the sound, the Presence was growing louder, and more intense, as it drew closer. The very air around us seemed to increase in vibration, to thicken, to be a *felt* presence. The energy permeated our bodies, coursed through our heads, became so incredibly intense that we vibrated in response.

I don't remember this now, but in my journal I had written that there were flashes of white and red light. I knew that we were being touched by a holy Presence, a large Presence, an incredibly powerful Presence. Telepathically, this Force communicated with us and at various times it channeled certain things through our speech. At one point we grasped each other's hand and ascertained that we were hearing the same thing although no words were being spoken. I believe that it was necessary for us to remain in physical contact during the experience so that we, as one, could become more of a conduit. At the peak of this experience so much energy pressed in on my outer body and so much electricity raced through my being that I heard little sounds in my head, much like the sound that two electrical wires would make if put together. I felt that I couldn't handle any more energy, that I had come close to overload. During this time all I could do was press Barb's hand and repeat the words, "God" or "Lord" over and over as we became completely immersed in the experience. I have never before or since felt so much in the presence, in the actual physical manifestation, of Spirit.

Gradually, the thickness and the outer sound of the vibration faded until only the vibration around our heads remained. Eventually, more slowly, that vibration also subsided. It took what seemed like a long time for complete recession of the energy. We sat there in silence for some time. Each of us checked in to see that the other was okay, and then we realized that both of us had to pee badly. That was definitely a humbling experience, getting out of the car, after what had just happened, and dropping our drawers in the coal black night! My imagination definitely needed to be reined in.

We exchanged no words as we made our beds outside on the ground and slept, blanketed in an aura of Holiness. I must admit that I wondered as I drifted off, just *where* we might find ourselves upon awakening. It didn't really seem to matter.

There are places we have seen, places we have traveled in this life and others that open our eyes to the larger vista, that help us to walk our path in the Light of Love and know that All is One. Each of us makes the journey alone, yet we come to know for ourselves that there is no separation. We all share the garden. We each stand alone of our own free will, one among many, each giving off our own particular Light in the garden of Roses.

PART TWO

Soul Threads through Time

VIII

All in the Mind

I knew that this was one of those moments
where the history of all mankind would be changed.
The Christians seek to blot out all wisdom save their own;
and in that strife they are banishing from this world
all forms of mystery save that which will fit
into their religious faith. They have pronounced it
a heresy that men live more than one life—
which every peasant knows to be true.
— Merlin, *The Mists of Avalon*

Sometimes a rare opportunity comes along when you are blessed to work with a particular client over a long period of time. This was the case in my work with Michael Montgomery. In a little over a year we did twenty-six regression sessions, producing a body of profound work. His original reason for coming to see me was a lower back problem. Our work on this issue clearly illustrates the idea of cellular memory. This is the idea that within the cells of our body we carry a memory of everything that has ever happened to us.

When Michael first came to see me he was thirty-four years old. He was married, with two children, one dog, some fish, a station wagon, and he lived in suburbia. Interestingly, in addition to his back problem, he noted a difficult time dealing with the responsibility of being the proverbial breadwinner. He felt that he had lost his zest for life and that he no longer believed what he espoused. He doubted his ability to continue, and he was tired. Basically, Michael felt disillusioned with his life and where he found himself, and he saw no way out.

A key component to Michael's story was his emotion, or his lack thereof. He had grown up in a house where the parents never raised their voices in front of the children, but instead took their disagreements behind closed doors. Therefore, Michael witnessed little expressed emotion. Not surprisingly he now tried to suppress his emotions and live through his mind.

Through all of his life Michael had suffered from asthma and allergies. Metaphysically, thanks in great part to Louise Hay's wonderful book *Heal Your Body* that suggests mental causes for physical illness, and metaphysical ways to overcome those illnesses, we can look at asthma as the result of a smothering type of love. When we feel stifled we are unable to breathe for ourselves. It is suppressed crying. In babies and children the underlying emotion may be a fear of life and a sense of not wanting to be here. With allergies we are denying our own power and have to determine who it is that we fear. Allergies often result from emotional congestion, a fear of persecution, or a sense of guilt.

Michael's mother died six years before his first regression. She died of cancer of the lumbar. He had tried with his mind to keep her from leaving. He believed that he was being successful. Naturally, her death surprised him—he felt betrayed. Revealing here, too, is his lack of expressed emotion, and an absence of grieving, of tears. He was very stoic. But then one must ask where the unexpressed emotion, the pain of loss, is stowed.

Four weeks after his mother's death, he played a game of touch football against a group of teenage boys. The boys were winning, when Michael's *pride* kicked in. Thinking there was no way this could be happening, he tried to become a one-man team, pulled his back and thought nothing of it. His back became stiff and did not improve with time. About nine months later, as he picked up his baby daughter and put her on his hip, something happened.

He began to experience problems with his sciatic nerve, often with numbness running down both legs.

After a CAT scan, other tests, and a second opinion, doctors reached a consensus that he had suffered a ruptured disc, and guess where—the very same place as his mother's cancer. He quickly refused the recommended surgery and continued to live with the pain and stiffness. Now experiencing a great deal of trouble getting out of bed in the morning, his movements had become more and more like those of an old man. Hot showers and yoga helped him to function, but the migraines he had suffered for years began to occur more and more often.

His wife found it difficult to deal with all of his physical problems and grew short on patience. As the mother of two small children she had her hands full. She considered him a space cadet, who didn't stay in his body. In her view, whenever he was confronted or had to deal with something emotionally, he simply left. He would sleep. When she lost it, in her anger she called him a wimp. For a long time Michael's favorite pastime had been *napping*—sleeping.

Michael knew that he could not continue in the manner he had up to this point. As a deeply spiritual man he had knowingly pursued his spiritual journey for several years. He believed in reincarnation and preferred a holistic approach in all areas of his life. He knew that he could get better only after he understood why this had happened to him.

At our first session we had planned to work on the cause of his back problem. But when he arrived he was suffering from a horrible migraine headache, so it was pretty obvious what we needed to work on that evening. I did not take the time to do my normal induction, one that used visualization, soft music, and progressive relaxation. Instead I opted for a repetition technique learned in my studies with Dr. Morris Netherton, author of *Past Lives Therapy*. I asked Michael to tell me about his migraines. The key phrases he spoke were "It takes over my whole being. It makes me want to throw up. It makes me dizzy." I then had Michael repeat the first phrase several times, and I used it to take Michael into the appropriate past-life experience, and told him to go with his first impression.

He found himself in Japan, lying prostrate on huge steps that led up to the temple. He was a young Japanese woman who felt abused. It's interesting that at first he used the word "prostate" instead of "prostrate," then corrected himself.

The next scene found him highly emotional, saying "It makes me want to throw up." Here was one of the key phrases Michael had used to describe his migraines. In this instance, "it" was a penis in her mouth. Having been treated as property, she was sexually used at her owner's whim and she felt horribly abused. At another point in time, while she sat on her knees, her owner without warning cut off her head with a saber. In her anger she screamed, but she could not be heard. She had no voice box. It had been removed. Without being asked, Michael indicated that his present mother had been the man who had killed her, and that his present father had been one of the men present.

Next I asked Michael to move into the prenatal and birthing periods, to see what had triggered this particular past-life experience as one to be dealt with and hopefully resolved in the present. Having the client go into the prenatal and birthing periods of his present life can be an invaluable tool in this type of work. What we found was a feeling of abuse. While his mother carried him in her womb during the seventh month of her pregnancy, cysts had to be removed from her cervix. The problem proved to be quite serious and the fetus could have aborted. From his place in the womb Michael felt upset. Sadly he wondered why he was not enough. Why did his mother have to grow something else, too? This medical procedure jostled him about a lot and he grew angry, *and his head hurt*. This pregnancy was not an easy one and his mother did not feel well herself a lot of the time.

He also wanted to throw up because of all the cigarettes and coffee his mother used. They made him feel sick and dizzy. This sick, dizzy feeling would often take over his whole being. Here we had all of his current key phrases being expressed during the prenatal period.

When Michael was born, the doctor used forceps to pull him out. He responded to this memory by saying that his head hurt. He exclaimed that the doctor was trying to *pull his head off!* When he had finally moved through the birth canal and out into the hospital room, he experienced sudden cold. With so much noise, and the lights too bright, he felt lost. He said, "They don't know what they are doing." I had him repeat this statement several times until he no longer expressed any emotion. He continued, "They are stupid. They are choking me to death with a bottle of milk much like the penis in my mouth in Japan. The pressure . . . I am full of milk. I think I was allergic to it. It's all up in my sinuses, everywhere. I'm so sad."

Here again I had him repeat the phrase *I'm so sad* several times until he said it without any emotion. Naturally, this repetition is important as it clears the unconscious of the emotion attached to the words. It's also important to note here that Michael's allergies to milk in his present life are connected to the same choking feeling that he/she had experienced with the penis in her mouth as a young woman in Japan. Right after Michael's birth, a nurse unknowingly smothered the newborn with "love" (milk). Same thing. As a newborn he found himself as powerless to stop this smothering as he had been powerless to stop the abuse in his past life in Japan.

Michael gained much insight from our investigation of the prenatal and birth experiences, as evidenced both here and in our later work in this area.

Migraine headaches can be associated with sexual fears and a resistance to the direction in which life is going. We soon uncovered another lifetime associated with Michael's headaches. This other lifetime related his headaches to the down-deep feeling that he really didn't believe what he espoused. That feeling made him doubt, feel blocked emotionally, grow tired, and believe that he did not know what to do now. Michael experienced some resistance to getting into this other past life, and we soon understood why.

Michael: There are lots of black robes, inquisition, robes over
           faces. First impression . . . the henchmen—guy who
           swings the ax. Stairs . . . platform . . . colonial
           times . . . knickers . . . pointed hats. . . .
Sam: Who are the people in black robes?
Michael: Clergy, the church.
Sam: ʾ   Why are they gathered?
Michael: To pass judgment.
Sam: On whom?
Michael: Whoever is to be judged this day? No. Just what they
           do. Don't speak.
Sam: Why not?
Michael: Just nod. Totally covered. All you see is black robe.
           No hands. Just black. Their nod is the judgment.
Sam: How do you feel about these people?
Michael: I am one of them. In one of those robes . . . I can feel
           fear. . . . Fear from people being judged.
Sam: How do you feel about it?
Michael: Makes my heart push up through my throat to the
           top of my head, strangling me.
Sam: Do you like being one of them?
Michael: No!
Sam: How did you come to be one?
Michael: You sort of become one. You end up one . . . re-
           spected . . . an elder.
Sam: Did you want to have this position?
Michael: No.
Sam: You have this position because . . . ?
Michael: Was expected to do it.
Sam: What would happen if you refused?
Michael: I would be defrocked.
Sam: How does that make you feel?
Michael: Confused. . . . What would I do with my life . . .
           what would I be? . . . (Said with resignation.) So, all
           I do is nod and nod and nod "yes."
Sam: Then what happens to the person?

Michael: They are exterminated.

Sam: What would you like to have done?

Michael: Not be there. Spend most of my time just spaced out and nodding. . . . I separate. (Here in order to survive Michael has had to stifle his emotions.)

Sam: How does your inner self feel about where you are?

Michael: I've been a royal fuck-up somewhere. How did I get to this place? Illusions of grandeur, that's how. I make a vow never to join an established church or order again. That's why I have great difficulty sitting in certain churches now. What happened to seeing God as Light, Love? This isn't right.

Sam: Can you try to change it?

Michael: I do—I die . . . in my *sleep*. (This is the way Michael deals with emotion in the present, he sublimates it by going to sleep . . . taking a nap.)

Sam: How old are you?

Michael: Forty-five.

Sam: How long have you been in these black robes?

Michael: Not long. Two years maybe.

Sam: Do you have a family?

Michael: Oh, no . . . except the church. In solitude . . . work your way to that through fasting, prayer, monastic. Total solitude—prison.

Sam: Is there any light in these people?

Michael: No . . . praying to who we thought God is . . . too powerful, whole group. The people who come before us are witches, heretics.

Sam: Anyone you know now in your present life?

At this point Michael named his wife, son and daughter, and two family friends. In communication with his Higher Self, it became clear that he needed to come to terms with his drifting, to remember what this drifting really was, to understand why he continued to drift off. Michael recognized his drifting as a habit brought forward from his past life. When things grew emotionally difficult in his present life, when he couldn't see any way out, he just drifted off. He spent a lot of time that way when things became too emotional. Or else, he slept.

Michael: Self-esteem, carried helpless aspect with me, taken on physical demeanors of helplessness, physical problems. Very difficult to stand there all day. Had to. Part of ritual. Didn't speak up . . . part of order.

Sam: How did you communicate?

Michael: You don't.

Sam: How old were you when you entered the order?

Michael: Seventeen, maybe younger . . . fifteen.

Sam: What was your reason for joining?

Michael: It seemed like the best thing to do. What other choice was there? A farmer or nobody . . . wanted to be something. There were those with power and those with nothing. Poor serf farmer or part of church. If had spoken up, wouldn't have changed one thing—a mockery. Wouldn't have been happier as a farmer. I would have starved. I was from a poor family, ate lots of potatoes, life of day-to-day drudge. At least up until the last two years, I felt alive, had a sense of order and purpose. Dying that way, leaving with such low self-esteem, gives me a headache.

Sam: How did you die?

Michael: Of a cerebral hemorrhage in my sleep. I had developed headaches after I started at job. Self-esteem suffered . . . a sense of total futility. No use . . . a terrible feeling. Burst bubble.

It's easy enough to see where the doubt, tiredness, and lack of belief in self were leaking from. Now it became important to take what Michael had learned, the insight and resolution, and move on from there. After these two lifetimes he had reexperienced, Michael's headaches grew farther apart and appeared with less severity. Soon he no longer suffered from migraines. He would occasionally give in to a typical sinus headache, but such headaches didn't debilitate him and put him to bed.

Now we were ready to move on to the issue of his back. Michael found himself on horseback:

Sam: Where are you going?
Michael: Going to war.
Sam: What kind of war?
Michael: The Crusades.
Sam: How are you dressed?
Michael: Armor . . . silver.
Sam: How do you feel?
Michael: Proud.
Sam: Do you want to go to war?
Michael: I want to be of service.
Sam: To whom?
Michael: To my God.
Sam: Who is your God?
Michael: Jesus, the Christ.
Sam: Are you alone?
Michael: No.
Sam: Who's with you?
Michael: Hundreds . . . thousands.
Sam: Where are you going?
Michael: Going East.

Told to move forward to a significant time, Michael found himself in a new situation.

Sam: Where are you?
Michael: I don't know. . . . Many have already died . . . or
           scattered. (Laughs.)
Sam: What's funny?
Michael: The bravado of it all has long since gone. But, I'm
           very bullheaded.
Sam: What are you doing?

Michael: I'm proceeding on. Looking for whatever it is that I'm supposed to, the heathens, the infidels.

Sam: What makes them heathens?

Michael: Very different belief systems.

Sam: And that makes them wrong?

Michael: This is confusing to me.

Sam: What is?

Michael: The purpose of the quest. I'm *doubting*—not part of my discipline. It's very disturbing to me. Many have already left . . . illness, fear, no food, lack of water. I'm wondering what we are all doing here. Whereas before, I knew. Don't have peers to reinforce the brogue, the bonny brogue. . . . I saw a theater, like a balcony, but the balcony was like my helmet, and it's a theater of the mind. . . . Think I'm losing it . . . losing my mind. . . . I'm awfully disheveled in all of my bodies.

Sam: What are you doing?

Michael: I'm hallucinating. . . . Think I've just been mugged, so to speak, from the rear, small of back . . . broad sword . . . something. Knocked off my horse . . . but so disoriented anyway. I'm just lying in the mud, hallucinating, seeing monsters, things like that. My mind tells me they are trees, but they have monstrous faces. Trouble discerning between what's real and what isn't.

Sam: Go back in your mind's eye and see what it is that hits you.

Michael: Like a big log or something . . . big board. It's wood and . . . who does it?

Sam: Who hits you?

Michael: I don't know . . . my mother, now it seems to be Andrew. (Andrew is a friend in the present life.) There's a gang of them.

Sam: What do they look like?

Michael: Urchins. Ragamuffins.

Sam:	What does it feel like when they hit you?
Michael:	Feels like a piece of salt water taffy . . . like been separated . . . pulled apart, but not. Incredible headache as I hit the ground. (His head has hit a rock.)
Sam:	What are they doing after you hit the ground?
Michael:	Taking away everything. Stripping the horse . . .
Sam:	Then what do they do?
Michael:	They are taking off my armor.
Sam:	Does that hurt your back?
Michael:	No . . . I think I'm out of my body. See my legs dropping, but don't feel anything anymore, except a dull ache in my neck and head.
Sam:	So, do they leave you?
Michael:	Yes.
Sam:	What are you feeling?
Michael:	I feel warm . . . feel good . . . (long pause).
Sam:	So, is your body now dead?
Michael:	Somewhat still in my body. . . . Enjoying the last moments here, incredible feeling.
Sam:	What's causing this incredible feeling?
Michael:	It's like being one with the waves of the ocean . . . so comfortable and so warm. Sun is bright in my mind's eye. Actually lying in sort of mud, mucky mire, sort of gross, but my mind is seeing fields of daisies . . . getting off on it. . . . It's a release from the stupidity of it all.
Sam:	These people did you a favor?
Michael:	Oh, yeah. I set it up. I couldn't go back. I had to go on till the end.
Sam:	What can you learn from this?
Michael:	When one realizes one is going in the wrong direction to be able to release the ego and change course.
Sam:	So, what is the pain in your back trying to tell you now?
Michael:	To relax and go with the flow and not try to push, be

	patient, allow the situations to dictate the direction.
Sam:	And how is that different from what you do?
Michael:	We live the illusion of past and future and we have this image of the direction we are going. I have to let all that go and try to enjoy the moments . . . the present and not get so stressed out. When things come at me unanticipated I tense up too much . . . don't allow to pass through me . . . too rigid. . . . Be able to accept people and their differences without tensing muscles.
Sam:	Have you seen all you need to see in this life as a crusader?
Michael:	Yes.
Sam:	Who hit you with the piece of wood?
Michael:	I don't know.

At this point I asked Michael if there was anything else we needed to know about his problem with his back. He immediately segued into another lifetime.

Michael:	A train trestle.
Sam:	Where are you?
Michael:	I'm on top.
Sam:	What are you doing?
Michael:	I'm about to jump off.
Sam:	You're about to jump off because . . . ?
Michael:	I don't know.
Sam:	Do you want to die?
Michael:	Yes.
Sam:	Because . . . ?
Michael:	Because I want to be free.
Sam:	What keeps you from being free?
Michael:	Because I'm an Indian in a white man's world now.
Sam:	Do you jump?
Michael:	Yes.
Sam:	How does it feel?

Michael: Asthma comes in. I land on my chest . . . crush my
           chest. Also my back. I took it in face. I faced it . . .
           right on the sternum. (Michael had suffered from
           asthma since infancy. Whenever life got to be too
           much in the present, the asthma would kick in.)

Sam: At the moment of death how do you feel?

Michael: Better, proud . . . (After a moment's silence, Michael
           resignedly says . . .) . . . stupid.

Sam: How is it stupid?

Michael: Again the pride . . . "pride takes a leap." I couldn't go
           any further . . . didn't know any better . . . didn't
           realize. I'd reached the end of what I thought I could
           handle. I had a picture of what I saw as the future
           and I couldn't handle it . . . think had to do with
           leading the group of Indians to a reservation.

Sam: Were you afraid of heights? Of jumping? (He had
           told me earlier that he had a fear of heights.)

Michael: No, again I was proud . . . full headdress and every-
           thing. I think afterwards there was a fear. My realization
           again of having created a picture . . . blown it for
           pride . . . the illusion . . . one's own illusion of reality, of
           the future. . . . At death as crusader, disappointment, I
           felt like I wanted to throw up. I'm so disappointed.
           (Tears.) I'm so angry . . . waste whole Goddamned
           life . . . hoity-toity . . . pride, armor, garbage,
           bullshit . . . pride, pride, pride!!! I'm so angry! I'm so
           stupid! I'm so stupid! (Starts repeating . . . laughs, then
           exclaims.) God! I saw an image of someone bigger than
           me patting me on the back and saying it's all right boy,
           and me saying back to the drawing board. It's the same
           thing. Again, first the disappointment, then the anger,
           then deeper realization of the stupidity of it . . . getting
           caught up in that whole garbage. . . . I'm trying to
           figure out why this all happened.

Sam: Allow the emotion to tell you. Keep it out of your
           head.

Michael: I'm choking on my own blood. The mind won't stop . . . the mind won't stop! My emotions were blocked. So disciplined, mentally disciplined. (Remember that metaphysically, asthma represents emotional congestion, and asthma became an issue for Michael when he took his leap out of this life.)

Sam: Let's ask your Higher Self for any insight that would be helpful.

Michael: There's a door with a number . . . Roman numeral . . . a Christmas tree and a candle . . . number XII.

Sam: What does that mean to you?

Michael: Twelve lifetimes need to explore.

Sam: Now let's move into the womb. What are you experiencing?

Michael: A sore throat, constriction in my throat.

Sam: What's the reason for that?

Michael: Recognition of what was to come.

Sam: How is a sore throat recognition?

Michael: Constriction of vocalization, not being able to verbalize what I felt, continuation of same *caca*.

Sam: What is that?

Michael: Illusion of good and evil, control of emotions, constriction of things that are wrong, constriction of things others can't handle . . . just got pain in heart.

Sam: What's causing it?

Michael: My funny self said cupid's arrow, but really realization of going through one more time. (Michael drew himself up in pain, I told him to take a deep breath.)

Sam: Now know the reason for the pain and it can subside. What's the reason?

Michael: *Pride, selfish pride,* superiority . . . this hurts. . . .

Sam: Why is it hurting your heart?

Michael: Just the realization that I'm not following my heart.

Sam: How are you not?

Michael: Because I'm suppressing my emotions and feelings . . . living in my head, concepts, rationalities, limitations of perception, judgment.

Sam: Is this what your wife gets on to you about?

Michael: Yeah.

In continuing to explore the prenatal period Michael let off some steam:

Michael: I'm pissed that she's smoking because it hurts my lungs. (This also triggers the asthma.) I'm just not getting what I need. It's too small in here. I'm not able to grow correctly, not getting . . . being limited physically . . . so I'm leaving early. (Michael was born three weeks early.) I'm angry because it's not the way it's supposed to be. I'm supposed to go to term.

Sam: What limitations, Michael? What makes it too small?

Michael: She's growing other things on the uterus. It's like I wasn't enough . . . makes me angry, makes me disappointed. This isn't how it was supposed to happen. I wasn't supposed to have limitations, be asthmatic. I'm supposed to be perfect. Because the place is too small, I'm being forced out for my own survival. If I don't come out now, I won't live. The people are so stupid. They don't know what they are doing here. (Michael appeared extremely upset during this diatribe.) My mother is being gassed. She's going to sleep.

This pattern also played into Michael's need to go to sleep when things got tough. That's what Mom did. He found himself in the middle of a crisis and Mom drifted off to sleep.

Michael: I'm stuck. People are starting to yank at me, pulling on my head. This isn't what's supposed to happen. I'm not supposed to come out like a conehead. I feel like a piece of meat . . . with forceps . . . just yanked right out. Sooo stupid! So dumb! Put you in this stupid place, with stupid people looking at you with stupid smiles in total ignorance, and here I am in this little body, and nobody knows that I know. If I could only tell them how stupid they are . . . so ridiculous . . . wrapped up so can't even move . . . with a conehead.

Sam: How does this change things for you?

Michael: Well, I don't think I forgave my mother. I was very pissed off because this was not the plan, not what I signed up for.

Sam: What did you sign up for?

Michael: I anticipated more awareness, that I could enjoy the transition, more painful than it should have been.

Here I suggested that perhaps his birth was perfect, to which Michael vehemently replied, "Perhaps it wasn't!"

Michael: It wasn't perfect because of the stupidity.

Sam: And how did you express that emotionally?

Michael: I was colic . . . *I told her.* . . . I was a bitch of a baby. I cried a lot. Of course, I wasn't breast-fed, that was disappointing.

Once again from the prenatal and birthing experiences we are able to see correlations between the prenatal and birthing experiences and the past lives.

In our next session we dealt with two lifetimes. Our purpose was to get to the bottom of his feeling of fear around the lower back pain. Michael found himself in the snow as a soldier in Napoleon's army. He was a sixteen-year-old foot soldier, nobody.

"Being a soldier gave me a place, a purpose, and a *pride* in myself," he said. "I'm very afraid, very cold . . . know death is near . . . *stiffening up.* Everyone seems to be in same stupor . . . little toy soldier. . . . Finally, give up, lie down in snow. Afraid of battle . . . so afraid of being killed and killing. Napoleon went by, while I'm lying in the snowdrift, his gaze straight ahead. I'm so tired, cold, afraid . . . think shot in wrist . . . pain. . . . Death . . . wagons are going over me. People are marching over me."

Michael displayed a lot of resistance to his lifetime in Napoleon's army. Here we had his back, which metaphysically is the support of life, stiffening, and again we had that tired feeling, with the way out being to lie down, close his eyes, and drift off.

In Roman times, Michael found himself dealing with the same issue. He saw himself as a man falling on his face in the dirt.

"I'm a slave. I've been captured. A man in a Roman chariot is beating me because I fell while pushing something. People are stepping all over me. I'm being crushed by peers, out of fear of being beaten themselves."

Here he experienced death with excruciating pain in his head and lower back. When he fell on his face he gave up, took the easy way out. He felt very tired and described his situation as a death march.

"We're building a road, people are sickly, dropping like flies. When he starts to flog me, I feel tension in my back, then in last moment like a board, then swoosh. . . . I'm afraid of what happens next, attached to body, mentally don't want this life, but *back* is saying, '*Fool*, don't you realize how precious life is?' . . . Too late. Being captured was so hard for me to take. I was there only about forty days. In Corinth, I was a soldier and a philosopher. I was captured because I was in the back of the retreat. I liked the danger of having them close, but not capturing me. . . . I lost a wheel. Now, I'm giving up, I'm sickly, *throwing* up. . . . *The lesson is that you don't give up, doubt, lack faith, and decide I'll stop here.* You go until you can't.

"In the present, I need to relax my back. When my mother died due to her back, I realize now she didn't feel supported in her own life, and yet ironically, I felt she was the support in my life. (Another lifetime bears this out.) Her dying triggered my own deaths. It's important not to *back out*, but to face life head on . . . don't lead with back."

These three lifetimes seemed to have triggered Michael's asthma and allergies. He hadn't had them this badly since he was a child. Obviously, we had hit a major nerve. Michael became aware at this point that when something was brought up from the past that he wasn't dealing with in the present, he would start choking with asthma and allergy symptoms. "I'm not dealing with my emotions in the present as well as the past."

We both realized that more work had to be done. Michael proved to be a very good subject, and he needed less and less input from me in order to see the patterns as they unfolded.

Japan became the setting for the next past life associated with Michael's back. The quality of Michael's own words tells his story. His voice was calm, and behind the voice was a man deeply centered and connected to his participation in this life.

On an Oriental rug sat Michael, a Samurai, praying to the Buddha. "I'm doing breathing exercises to replenish body, mind and spirit . . . to empower oneself with sense of invincibility . . . sense of real power. . . . Protect the right, God's right—Buddha's. *Being Samurai makes me feel at one.* No questions to answer. *No mind.* I've been a Samurai eighteen years, am now forty-two years of age. I live in a place near Kyoto. It is early morning. It has just stopped raining. The air is heavy. I feel a sense of my death today. I am drinking the essence of the moment of life. So pleased to have lived this life, opportunity to be with One. It is 1781, March the 16th. My name is Chiojo. I am called Jo."

At this point I asked him to move forward in time to a significant moment.

"Today, in battle, I just had right ear cut off. I am in battle with several dozen people in white and gold. I am in black and pink and purple and red. *Fighting for honor.* Power struggle . . . one group versus the other. *I'm having a marvelous time!* To be put on edge, to be totally in tune. Lots of blows are being struck. It doesn't matter. I just keep going . . . like a dance, total bliss . . . no pain . . . *no sense of separation.* I can somewhat feel the blows, but it's magical . . . the dance."

This is a very different attitude than any we had seen thus far when Michael had been confronted with death, fighting and dying.

"It's the end. I'm dimly aware, lying on back . . . pleased. I've done my best, fought the fight. I'm waiting for my friends from the spirit plane so we can continue the dance. Death, *some real tightening,* real jolt . . . electrical. Being ripped out of my body, feel tightness in midsection. I'm leaving through my navel . . . volcanic eruption . . . being thrown. . . . Floppy old straw hat person looking over my shoulder as I was making my transition . . . startled me . . . my next incarnation in America."

I now asked Michael to be aware of any connection between his back and his experience as the Samurai. He replied, "In many battles . . . was somewhat an invalid toward the end. But, in battle could lift up the body, in this state body would respond, from power of mind . . . work through it . . . stop thinking so much of day-to-day pain. My left side injured as Samurai . . . left side, middle of back to top of ankle. Incredible, very painful. Didn't heal right . . . tightness, drawing up. Present life mother was samurai who inflicted the wound. She was in present as karmic payback . . . she felt she owed me. It came back after she died because I now have to deal with it. Some invalid lives that followed . . . very hard on me . . . because of proud soul. Not a warrior type, but a frump, also a gay. I think I was supposed to be female but couldn't let go of male energy."

Still dealing with the issue of Michael's back, we found ourselves in jolly ole England in the late 1800s. Michael was gay, had a limp (his left leg, naturally), and emphysema. He lived with a male lover who became his present wife. This lover was a boisterous, loud, argumentative, in-your-face type. There was mental and verbal violence.

As Michael described, "We get along pretty well. I'd laugh at him, then he'd get back at me with lungs and limp, with my physical pride. That was hard to deal with . . . real conflict for me being who I was in that life . . . gay and invalid. We got along fabulously, sex was good, lots of laughs . . . most when fighting. We enjoyed the combat, mind games. We died in each other's arms . . . got real rip-roaring drunk and fell out of window onto cobblestones. Been together twenty years. Fops. We played, went with the moment, liked to get dressed up, especially me. I liked eye make-up. He'd get real impatient. So, I'd take longer . . . then another fight. I was always late. He couldn't stand it. He was so straight, serious, punctual, a cause. He would feel so guilty when he would have an occasional fling, such strong sense of right and wrong, would torment him . . . so, we'd have a little argument . . . make him laugh.

"We went to the theatre, talked with philosophers, actors, disbarred theologians. Dante Moore and Stephen Douglass. I was forty-six years old when I died. He was brash. We rapped and argued points. He gave me a pink stone, gold band, pinky ring . . . wore on right hand. I died Monday night, February 16, 1891, cold and damp, and independently wealthy.

"Two current-life friends were there then. Jane, a good friend of my present wife, was a buxom madam, and Anthony, who is a gay friend in the present, was a 'box boy,' who moved stage stuff. He was blonde, small in stature, about eighteen to twenty-one years of age, and Dante had an affair with him.

"Dante and I fell out a third story window and I landed on *my back*. I died quickly. Dante died soon after. He had landed on top of me. How fitting!"

This regression gave Michael the insight that his back problem was also tied to the *pride* of who he had been when a Samurai, and his inability to let go of that pride. He saw the inflexibility of pride manifesting as the inflexibility of his back.

Michael and I continued to work as he reexperienced several more lifetimes that gave him even greater insight and awareness around his issues. Our work took place in the mid-eighties. Michael never required back surgery, his migraines became a thing of the past, his asthma occurred rarely and was mild, he stopped being bothered so frequently with allergies, and he learned to express his emotions more easily.

IX

Pressure Cooker

The untrue never is;
The true never isn't.
The knowers of truth know this.
— The Bhagavad Gita

Mickey had been diagnosed with an anxiety disorder with some panic symptoms. Her heart beat rapidly. She couldn't think straight. She became nervous. She couldn't stand noise. Words often over-lapped because she spoke so fast. The symptoms seemed to come in spells. For days she could channel this energy into her work, until it got the best of her. Her problem became worse during her pre-menstrual days.

She had been given tranquilizers to calm her down, but they failed to stop the rapid heartbeat. Sometimes, she felt as though her heart were going to fly right out of her chest. Mickey could not drink anything with a stimulant in it.

A very real problem involved driving anywhere she had never been before. She would grow extremely nervous, irritable, and unable to think. She would lose her sense of direction and feel lost, terrified that she would be unable to find her way back. She had experienced this feeling of panic for as long as she could remember, but it had gotten worse over the previous ten years.

The worst spell had occurred two winters earlier. Her legs had felt like jelly. She had had to brace herself to hold herself up. It had felt good when she almost passed out. More recently, Mickey had experienced stresses with home, work, weather. Mickey found the cold dark of winter a dismal time of year and had a very difficult time dealing with it.

Obviously, Mickey felt that she needed to take control of her life, but she did not know how. She could not remember entire time frames, and suffered severe headaches that hurt for a week. Interestingly, Mickey had no trouble going to sleep. She could sleep like a log. Sometimes, if she woke in the middle of the night to go to the bathroom, she would start to worry. When she woke in the morning, the anxious feeling would not be there, but once she got up, it started. At fifty-one years of age she saw no future for herself continuing to live like this.

Mickey came to see me as a last resort. She didn't know where else to turn. All the doctors wanted to do, she said, was put her on drugs. She expressed great interest in metaphysics and had read books on various subjects, including near-death experiences and reincarnation. She hoped to get to the cause of her anxiety, to get rid of this feeling of being on overdrive, of being lost. She wanted to feel at peace.

As we began our session, Mickey stepped into the cause lifetime and found herself barefoot, with bare legs, and nothing on her upper body, totally naked, standing in a wooden cage.

Mickey: It's dark in front of me. It's crazy. I'm inside a cage. It is used to pull me. I'm terrified! I'm young . . . teenager . . . female. I'm on a dirt road. I'm the only one in the cage. Terrified feelings.

This scene started out intense, and her tension only increased from there. Her emotional state became extreme. Many of the questions asked of Mickey I have eliminated to increase the sense of flow.

Mickey: (Yells.) Let me out! ... scared. Don't know what's
            happening. Don't know why, where. There's a bright
            light, but it's dark. It's shining in my eyes. I don't
            have any clothes on ... humiliated. ... Nothing to
            cover with. People are watching. (Now Mickey
            described the very same symptoms she experienced in
            the present.) I feel terror. My head is spinning. Blood
            is pounding in my head. Feel hot. Chest hurts, feels
            tight. Hard to breathe.
Sam: Are you alone, or is someone with you?
Mickey: I don't see anybody. ... Man with a beard, has
            helmet on. I feel terror. He's big, big! Can't see!
            Getting ... I can't see. I'm scared to death! Where is
            he!!!! ... Can't. ... (Emotional intensity, crying,
            labored breathing.) My head is spinning. I don't
            know where he is. He is very terrifying. ... Light is
            there now, not as terrified. (This light provided the
            first subtle indication that a shift into another similar
            experience would be possible, into a time when she
            had felt these same or very similar feelings.)

Here I asked Mickey what she could tell me about the man
who wore the helmet.

Mickey: It's a steel helmet ... big, bushy beard ... big, ugly.
Sam: What does he want?
Mickey: *Don't know.* (The way Mickey responds says she does
            know.)
Sam: Yes, you do.
Mickey: I think he wants to do something to me. I can't think
            about it. ... I don't know. I don't know. I really don't
            know. (Crying.)
Sam: Yes, you do.
Mickey: He's on me. ... I don't know. ... *Leave me alone!*

She tried desperately to block her feelings. And here a truly traumatic shift from the past to the present childhood happened. She began breathing so heavily that she began to pant. I've seen some facilitators try to calm a person down when they enter such a heightened emotional state. I believe that calming someone is not the best choice in most instances. This intensity is old emotional yuck that the client has been carrying for a very long time. When it resurfaces, the client has an opportunity to release it. A facilitator's unease with this emotion should not be a factor. Of course, common sense is needed. But, the cathartic release of emotion is a dynamic and healing process. It needs to be allowed to take its course.

Mickey: I can't see him . . . blanket. (The blanket was a major clue that a shift had occurred.) Don't know . . . brown blanket. I see some light, but I don't want to see the light. *I don't want to know what's happened!* I can't feel it. (Said as if to convince herself.) Oh God! . . . I can't feel it! I won't feel it. I won't! I won't! I won't! You can't make me. I won't. . . . *Make the light go away. . . .*

Sam: What's happened?

Mickey: He's raped me. I don't want to feel it.

Sam: Who has raped you?

Mickey: I can't see him. I can't feel it. I won't feel it. I won't!!! (Screams.) I won't, I won't. Can't help it. Get off me!!!!!!! Go away!!! Leave me alone. Oh God, leave me alone, please. . . . I hate you, I hate you. Go away. (Her voice turned bitter and venomous.) I wished you'd died . . . died . . . died . . . died. . . . (Screaming.) DIED! . . . What are you doing? . . . Die. . . . Oh God, please make him die.

At this point Mickey lapsed into silence and her breathing gradually slowed. During this whole sequence she had been physically active in the chair, writhing in anguish and throwing her

head from side to side, but with her arms and hands always covering her face.

Sam: What are you aware of now?

Mickey: See the light. He must be gone. He's gone.

Sam: How does that make you feel?

Mickey: Feel lighter. . . . Feel lighter. (Crying.) I want to die. I
            want to die. Please let me die.

Sam: What are you feeling now?

Mickey: Feel peace . . . peace . . . peace . . . floating. . . . Must
            be dead. (Said with great relief.) See body on ground.
            Brown ragged dress on. Can't see face. Short, ragged
            dress. I'm above it. My body is dead. I'm glad it's
            dead.

Sam: Finish this sentence. I'm glad it's dead because . . .

Mickey: Because at peace. I've *never* been at peace. . . . Never.
            To be dead is to be peaceful. To be alive is not to be
            peaceful. *I don't know why.*

Sam: Now, I want you to go back to the rape. We need to
            work through this and see very clearly what hap-
            pened. Which direction did he come from?

Mickey: Just on top. Startles me. Opens door to cage. Takes
            me out of cage. On the ground, bare ground, dirt.
            (The light arrived and once again the scene shifted.)
            Don't want to see that light! It's daylight. I don't
            want to see light. When it's dark I can't see him . . .
            comes at night. I don't want to see the light, because
            I don't want to see who is there. (Screaming at the
            top of her lungs.) NO! NO! NO! NO! NO!!

Sam: Who is it?

Mickey: (Her voice dripped with denial.) I don't know. I *do
            not* know. No . . . No. I do not know who it is.

Sam: Yes, you do. And it's important for you to be aware of
            who it is.

Mickey: Oh God, it is not. It is not! (Repeats several times.) No,
            God, I won't let it be. Good Jesus, no! I can't live with

it. I cannot. I won't live with it. (She wadded herself up in one corner of the recliner, still with face covered, as her arms and hands held her trembling body, when suddenly she exploded with emotion.) God *NO!!* No he didn't, he didn't. (Weeping profusely.) No, no, no, God no! I'd rather die, than to be here. I know he didn't do this to me. No way on Earth. No way on Earth. Why would I see my daddy? No, no, this is crazy shit. It was the man with the beard. It was him. My daddy would never hurt me. This is not real. This is crazy shit! It's not real. Daddy, come here and tell me this is not real. It's not.

Mickey reported having no present memories of anything ever being amiss in her relationship with her father. She adored him.

Mickey: It's just because I've read this stuff. It's not real. Never going to be real. I don't care. I don't. If I drop dead, I don't care. It's not real.

Sam: Whether it is real or not, you just had this experience.

Mickey: If it's real I can't deal with it. I can't. I won't. My daddy was the most important person on Earth to me. There is no way. *I have never loved anybody more.*

Sam: What's happening?

Mickey: I just saw his face, but I don't think he did that to me. He didn't. It's got to be something else. If he did, I would see it and remember it. He didn't. . . . He didn't.

Sam: But, what if he did?

Mickey: It just can't be. It's insane. It can't be. Got to be something that came out of my stupid screwed-up mind. I'd rather be dead than have had him do something to me.

Sam: Well, now is the time to find out.

Mickey: I won't see. I won't see. I don't want to know. This is totally impossible.

Sam: Let's just see what comes up. Let's go back to where it happened, if indeed, it did.

Mickey: I see my house when I was a kid. White house, down the railroad tracks, between two hills. House, yard, well. I'm going to escape . . . in my mind. I'll just go away. This is crazy.

Sam: What are you feeling?

Mickey: I'm feeling nothing right now. Went somewhere inside where I can shut this off. (Pause.)

Sam: But you can't continue to shut it off anymore. It's in your consciousness now.

Mickey: I don't believe this. I don't want to do this anymore.

Sam: You need to do this now.

Mickey: Don't want anybody to look at me. Always been that way.

Sam: When was the first time you felt that way?

Mickey: I'm a little girl, four or five years old. . . . Can't breathe! (Here she started to clinch and release her hand, over and over, as we continued.) Brown blanket . . . see brown blanket.

Sam: What's happening?

Mickey: No . . . nothing is happening. . . . I see a head . . . that's all. Ohhh God! Dad's head . . . I don't know.

Sam: Yes, you do.

Mickey: No, I do not. (She said this in an emphatic, yet obviously *lying* voice.)

Sam: Yes, you do.

Mickey: My eyes are tight, making everything black.

Sam: You can feel.

Mickey: *No, I can't.* . . . The light again . . . is white undershirt, straps, open neck . . . Daddy's face, just one glimpse. That's not my daddy, that one's not him. . . . It's him, but not him. The way he looks, his face is red. Keep getting feeling like when I fade out. I just want to do that, just kind of drift off. See a white handkerchief . . . went over my face. He put it there. I don't know.

This constant saying of "I don't know" related to Mickey's feeling lost and having no sense of direction in her adult life.

From this point Mickey remained aware only of the light. So I asked her to go back to her past-life death and be aware of the cause. She said she had died because she couldn't live with it. Her final thoughts were, "It's over." When light came after her transition, she didn't want the light. I told her this was a different kind of light. A golden, healing, loving light that was bathing her entire being. In this light, with the help of her Higher Self, she could make the connections between the past life and the present.

The first thing she said was that the past had brought the light. The light seemed to be the key to her transition from the past-life rape into her present-life molestation. The intensity of her terror in the past-life situation, when she said, "I can't see him," flipped her right into the present-life similar circumstance.

Other connections between then and now included her feeling of being lost and having no sense of direction, as well as her feeling of panic at not knowing where she was, and not remembering or seeing. She began to perceive her feeling of overdrive that she experienced in the present as being directly related to her feeling of panic at being in the cage. Plus, the humiliation that she experienced at being naked carried over into her present feelings of not ever wanting anybody to look at her. Another connection was her need to escape, to drift off, as well as her always feeling dead inside.

This fading out, escaping that she did in her present life was certainly what she had done to *leave* what was happening to her when both Dad and the helmeted man were doing what they were doing. She so strongly stated throughout the session, "I won't see it; I won't feel it; it didn't happen." By refusing to see or feel it, she hoped that she would retain no memories of it. Interestingly, she had few memories of growing up.

Until this session, Mickey had done all she could to continue to keep this memory repressed. Her dad had died twelve years earlier. She began experiencing anxiety attacks about two years after his death. She emphasized, "I don't have anything but good memories of Dad. That's all." Mickey also described her emotions as fragile. "Say the word 'love' to me and I cry." She felt as if she were always spinning her wheels, not really going anywhere.

In today's session, she stated that she could not live if this were true. In the past-life situation, she didn't live. Now, she needed to. Mickey knew that. Toward the end of the session, I asked Mickey if perhaps her seeing her father's face had been a spontaneous recognition of his having been the helmeted man who had raped her in the past. She responded that she had seen her father's face in the present, which, of course, totally freaked her out. I realized that Mickey would find it difficult to deal with this, but now she knew the origin of her anxiety and panic attacks. Once we know the cause, then healing can begin.

The next day I made a relaxation tape for Mickey to listen to daily, knowing that she would need a place where she could go, especially since she was adamant about not ever telling another living soul. I also told her to feel free to call me, but I knew she wouldn't, even though she would want to. After almost two weeks, when I hadn't heard from her I decided to call. In our conversation she said she didn't know what to do, although, she felt that she was supposed to meet me and this was supposed to happen. "I can't deny that those emotions and feelings were real."

Approximately two months later Mickey finally came in for another session. She had tried to keep going, but stated that the time between these two visits had been absolute hell. Every day she felt nervous, anxious, and hateful, while simultaneously dealing with menopause.

Finally, at work it had all caught up with her. She had a stressful job and needed to meet a deadline. She lost it and felt as if she were going to fly apart. She found herself crying, hyperventilating, losing strength in her body, and feeling weak. She left work, got home, and cried and cried. She couldn't breathe. She got the notes of our session, put them in the sink, and burned them. Even though she hadn't consciously been thinking of these notes, she believed that she had to get rid of them. After that she took two tranquilizers. She had been feeling depressed and didn't think she was going to make it. She followed that statement by saying, "I don't even know what I mean."

During our discussion I learned more about Mickey and her father. Before he died he had said to her, "I've done things," but she never let him finish. In a dream, less than a year before she came to see me, her daddy had told her that this anxiety thing had come from him.

When Mickey had been twenty-one, she had married and was getting along well. Then she woke up one day and felt strange, disoriented. She went to the park on a picnic and found that she couldn't concentrate on anything. That night she couldn't sleep. The next morning she was worse. She started hyperventilating, had dry heaves, and her eyes rolled back in her head. The doctor said he thought she was worried about something. Her dad had just been diagnosed with black lung disease. Her family decided that it was this diagnosis that worried her. For a month she continued to be very sick. What had caused her illness was never known.

On another occasion, when she visited her parents for a week she became so sick that she was admitted to the hospital and fed intravenously for a week.

Mickey had always been a nervous person. For years she had been antisocial. She hated to go to parties or any other place with lots of people. These situations made her feel frozen in fear, afraid that she would fail, and that people wouldn't like her.

During a bad winter, she would grow severely depressed, stay tired all the time, and want to sleep as much as she could. She faded out, where she became only vaguely aware, and wanted this to happen because it felt good and so calm. (This fading out was the same feeling that she had experienced when she had seen her father's red, sweaty face.) For months her legs felt weak, as if they would not hold her up.

Her mother had always said, "You just don't know your daddy." He drank, ran around with other women. His buddies hung out at the house. "My dad did drink real bad. I know if he did this to me . . . so hard to even comprehend he could do it. With every day that goes by my life is more miserable." When Mickey was fifty years old, her mother told her that her father had a child somewhere. She also told Mickey that she had offered to take this child and raise it.

Her relationship with her mother had never been anything special. She had always resented her mother for telling her that her father wasn't perfect. . . . "To me he was. . . . When Dad died I hated my mother. I thought why him and not her. She didn't cry when Dad died. I didn't think she was good to him. She was hateful to him."

Her dad did try to kill himself as his disease worsened. He felt he was a burden. He went out behind the house and stabbed himself with a pocketknife. He didn't succeed. He punctured his lungs and was put on antidepressants, and then his kidneys failed. He wanted to go home. Mickey wanted him to come home with her so she could take care of him. Her father exclaimed, "How could a man do this to his family!"

In our next session we moved through, moment by moment, what had happened to Mickey with her father. It had happened on a Sunday, which made sense considering that Mickey always found the weekends depressing. She was dressed in her Sunday clothes, her dotted Swiss dress with the pretty lace collar and her patent leather shoes with the little strap. They had returned from her grandmother's house where they often went on Sundays for supper.

Once back at their house, Mickey's daddy took her into the bedroom to get undressed. We moved through the entire incident. At one point Mickey cried and wondered where her mother was, and why her mother would let her be in that room without her clothes on. This scene also goes a long way in explaining the hard feelings Mickey still felt toward her mom. A child believes that the mother should be there to protect her from any and all things. Mickey's mother wasn't.

Mickey: Back at home . . . someone pulls my shoes off and little dress. See little undershirt, but think it should be a slip . . . cotton panties. Hair in curls. Somebody

is taking me by the hand . . . Daddy. . . . Getting
scared. (Emotion.) Somebody has me by the
hand . . . in bed . . . don't let . . . shirt is being taken
off. He's pulling my pants off. (Crying.) Where's
Mom? Where is she?!! Why would she just let me be
in there with him without my clothes on? I'm on the
bed without my clothes on. It was him, his bed. He
put his mouth on me. He did it with his mouth.
(Screams.) God!!!

Sam: I'm going to count from one to three. When I get to
the number three, you are calm. Number one,
number two, number three.

Mickey: Oh, gee Lord. That's all he did. He didn't actually
rape me. He got up and left. He's gone. Feel relieved
he's gone . . . because it's over. . . . Did it, Jesus God,
feel good? This is the part of sex that I like. This is
when I can get an orgasm.

This last statement is a healthy one. I explained to Mickey
that even if it did feel good, none of this had been her fault. She
was a child and this was her parent, a person who was supposed to
protect her. We moved through the experience again, further releasing her from it. But this time she removed herself, hovering
above what was happening.

Mickey: Daddy says, "Come on and lay down on the bed and
I'll make you feel good." I feel like he lies down
beside me and pets me. He loves me. (God! That's
love?!) It's almost like in a loving way. It's not a
disgusting, ugly, drunk way. It makes me feel dirty. I
think I liked it. . . . The light is coming from the
window. I want it to be dark. The light is real bright.
It hurt my eyes. His white handkerchief is over my
face. I'm up above, not scared.

Sam: Go through it.

Mickey: His finger, after his mouth. I'm thinking he rapes me.

He almost gets on top of me, puts in me. See that part of him going into that little body, but I can't believe it. That's where the red sweaty face comes in. Saw him get up. I do. I want to know what the hell he felt! . . . I felt. I want to see his face. Maybe that's where all this anger is from. I'm not scared. He rubs me, pets me. Talking to me. "You're sweet. You're Daddy's little girl." (Mickey's hands covered her face the entire time.) He's kissing me on stomach, chest, down there, rubbing me. There's that light. I don't want to be able to see it. I don't want to see him.

Sam: What are your thoughts right now?

Mickey: This is my daddy. He won't hurt me. (Hands are clasped over her face.) I just can't get it dark enough! Clinch my eyes real tight. Where's Mom? Where is she? (Sighs.)

Sam: What's happening now?

Mickey: He's getting on top of me. I'm not feeling anything. I feel like he's saying he's going to put this little thing in me. See it doesn't hurt. "Doesn't" wouldn't be one of his words. I see him with his hand guiding it, and just aware of the window and me lying there on the bed. He's standing up. His back is to me. He's putting his pants on. . . . Still the window . . . light hurts my eyes. (It was this light that was so present during her reexperiencing of the past-life rape that had flipped her into the present. The subconscious was saying, "Look, yes, here, too.")

Even though Mickey avoided the emotion this second time through, I didn't push it, because I thought it was important for her to go through the memory, so that she could become consciously aware of what had happened. At this juncture I connected Mickey to her Higher Self. The first thing she wanted to know was, "Did Dad rape me?" The response was no. Mickey didn't want it to be rape. If she defined rape only as forced sex, then she might get away with her denial. But rape is forced sex without consent. Mickey certainly didn't say, "Sure, go ahead." Statutory rape is the crime of having sexual intercourse with a person below the age of consent. What Mickey appeared to feel here was that he hadn't been mean, ugly, drunk, and brutal; therefore, it couldn't have been rape, as experienced in the past-life encounter. Her Higher Self had answered truthfully what Mickey was asking.

The message she received from her Higher Self was one of Peace. Yes, she could forgive her dad and go on with her life. "I can. I can still love him." She also understood that it hadn't been Mom's fault that Mom hadn't been there to protect her. Mom didn't know.

Now, we segued into some hypnotherapy. I asked that the anxiety she had endured for so long now come forward and make itself known. I asked it how it was feeling.

Anxiety:	*Free*. My God, I'm free. I'm free. I'm free. (Crying. Mickey's hands are down for the *first time*.) I'm not ashamed. I've gone through my life ashamed.
Sam:	How do you feel toward Mickey?
Anxiety:	I think I love her. (Crying.) I never did, because I was ashamed of her.
Sam:	How do you function in Mickey's life?
Anxiety:	Not feeling. Don't feel anything. That way you can do.
Sam:	How has this affected Mickey?
Anxiety:	Been tough. Breathing heavy . . .
Sam:	What has been your positive intent for doing what you do?
Anxiety:	To survive . . . life.
Mickey:	I didn't kill myself. I didn't know I ever wanted to.
Anxiety:	The breathing heavy and all the rest . . . had to. She was feeling it at twenty-one.
Sam:	What are the negative consequences of doing what you do?
Anxiety:	Fat, for one thing. (Mickey had been overweight.)

Not loving people. Not loving herself. Mickey never
did anything wrong.

Immediately, Mickey stopped breathing heavily, something
she had been doing throughout both sessions.

Mickey: I feel calm. (Laughing.) Is this how this happens . . .
           easy?
Sam: What was the deeper need that you were trying to
           fulfill that motivated this behavior?

Here Mickey took over with the answers.

Mickey: Love. I wanted to be loved. Nobody could ever do it.
           Nobody could meet that need. I wouldn't let them,
           because then I would feel. If I would feel then I
           would know. Geez, my Lord, fifty-one years.
Sam: What is an alternative way to meet this need?
Mickey: Feeling, and loving, and needing. (Crying.) It hasn't
           been everybody else. It's been me. . . . Can I do that?
           Can I need people, love them, tell them, and will
           they love me? *They already do.*
Sam: Imagine yourself experiencing this behavior.
Mickey: I couldn't even feel God's love. I thought He was not
           there for me, that He did not love me. I never could
           find what everybody else did. Never could. Asked
           Him. Never could feel His Love. His Love is the Light
           of Love. (Here Mickey became deeply emotional,
           crying in a different way than before. It was a spiri-
           tual weeping.) Light coming through the window
           blocked Light of God's Love. I feel the need to say
           thank you to my daddy . . . for setting me *free.* Does
           God love him, too? . . . There's a Light. (Here
           Mickey had her very own spiritual experience. She
           saw and felt the Light of God. She wept profusely.) I
           am in the Light. I can take my hands down from my

face. I feel the Light of God. Thank you, God. Thank
you, God. Thank you, Sam.

Sam: Thank yourself for having the courage to do what
            you've done.

Mickey: I do. I never believed it. . . . I'm not going to breathe
            hard ever again. . . . I believe it might be peace I'm
            feeling. I want to open my eyes, so I can see light.
            Oh, I see my dad's face and he is smiling. He was so
            sad until now. His heart was broke. Now, he's happy,
            because I'm okay. I've never seen a smile like that on
            his face . . . ever. He's happy. He's happy. He's at
            peace, too. He's laughing. He's crazy. I can see him.
            (Here Mickey involuntarily put her hands up to her
            face, caught herself, and said that she didn't have to
            do that ever again.) That's why he's never been there
            when I've prayed and asked for him. He's happy now.
            Throwing back his head and laughing. I'm crying,
            "Why the hell are you laughing?" He never said he
            loved me while he was living. He just said it now. I
            always knew he loved me so much. "I love you,
            Mick," he just said. My God, he's really there. Come
            visit me Dad. Come visit me. I'm bathed in God's
            Love. I've got a lot of years to make up for. Bye-bye
            Daddy. He's leaving. He went into the Light. (She
            raised her voice.) He went into the Light. I was
            always afraid he didn't. So scared he did not go into
            the Light. I don't know where I thought he was.

Sam: Now, Mickey, I want you to envision yourself func-
            tioning in life at your highest potential, free and calm
            in all that you do. The anger is gone. The nervousness
            is gone. You breathe normally. And the neatest thing
            is that you are open to give and receive love. You feel.
            You need, and give, and receive.

Mickey: Feels different. It's like everything is surrounded by
            light.

Sam: You are now free to explore, experience, and partici-

	pate in life. The anxiety is gone forever. You are free. You know that, don't you?
Mickey:	I do. See, because my hand is down here (in her lap). I never thought I had a future, but I do.
Sam:	Is there any message from your Higher Self that would be beneficial for you to be aware of now?
Mickey:	I like this thing called *peace.* My Higher Self says, "Anything that would have come up in the past as anxiety is now replaced by peace. Allow that to be your response."
Sam:	How do you feel?
Mickey:	*I'm ready.* God loves me. Dad loves me. *I love me.* How am I supposed to go out there now? I feel like a totally different person.
Sam:	You look different, too. (And, she did!)

Naturally, the trick is to take such a transformative experience out of the office and put it to work in everyday life. Mickey began to do that. She called the next day, which she told me was a big step for her. She wanted reassurance that this spiritual experience had actually occurred. She said she felt that she had been healed. She had seen God; she had seen the Light.

A major step for Mickey was realizing that she hadn't been depressed all day. Also, that day was Thursday. Always she cleaned her house on Thursday, no matter what. On this Thursday she didn't. Mickey exclaimed, "I'm proud of myself. I've gone a hundred miles today. I'm having a wonderful time, and I now know why I was always hungry."

In listening to the tape that I had made for her, she finally realized that to love God, she must love herself. "It's on the tape, but today was the first time I heard it."

Then, she said, "Be quiet, be still, that's what the voice I kept hearing today, God's voice, kept saying. I'm realizing, *Wow! I can do this!!*"

About a week later Mickey called again. She had experienced heart palpitations for two days, but nothing else. When I asked her what was going on, she replied that only three out of five people had come to work the last two days. Mickey had a hard time delegating authority, so I asked her if she was trying to cover everyone's work. Of course, she was. So, I told her anyone would be having heart palpitations if they tried to do that. She needed to slow down. If the work didn't all get done, not to worry. It would still be there the next day.

Mickey also reported some good progress. She had found herself telling her husband not to worry when they had discussed finances. This attitude was so unlike her that it "blew his mind." Also, she and her husband had gone to a town an hour or so away on Sunday and had a great day. In another plus she had found herself cursing at work and for the first time realized that she didn't really care what people thought. "That is real progress," she said. I could hear in her voice that she was beaming. Mickey confessed that after our last session she thought she would leave and never be angry again. We talked about giving ourselves permission to not live a perfect life.

Some days, I'm sure, are better for Mickey than others, but now she can live each day knowing that she has made great strides and can continue to do so, one step at a time, if she so chooses. I would have liked to have one more session with Mickey to deal with her feelings toward the helmeted man in that past life. But, that session would not occur for about a year.

By the time Mickey called, she had taken major steps in her life. An opportunity had presented itself for her to take an early retirement. She jumped at the chance because she felt burned out from the stress and more than ready to get out of there. The first couple of weeks of her retirement were great, but then something started to happen. She found herself standing at her kitchen counter not knowing what to do, suddenly unable to relax. She felt miserable, all the while telling herself she was supposed to be enjoying this.

Now all the old symptoms started to resurface—the anxiety, feeling groggy in the morning, getting up in a fog, feeling nervous, unable to focus for five minutes on anything, experiencing headaches and heart palpitations, feeling extremely tired, her legs weak and rubbery. And she feared ending up like her mother, who had led an active life until she retired. Then she had sat down and stayed there, doing nothing.

Mickey now felt totally without purpose, lost and depressed. She no longer had the confidence that she had felt when she had worked, and she realized that she had always lacked the *courage* to go and do. All of these feelings had her frozen in fear. During our session I simply asked her to go to the cause of these feelings. I had a strong suspicion of where she would end up, and I was delighted that she would get the opportunity to complete her process of resolution, producing a true sense of closure.

Mickey: I'm outside, standing barefoot in the dirt, wearing a ragged dress. I'm a young female with long red hair. I'm watching people go by in wooden carts, like a parade, but not. I feel alone.

Sam: Move forward to the next significant moment.

Mickey: There's a flash of a helmet, a shiny helmet. They are going to pick me up. I feel fear, surprise. Two men, something with horses . . . I'm in something being pulled by horses. Feeling of some kind of shiny weapon. It belongs to a man on the right side of me. I feel scared. I'm the only one in this cart. (The cart is much like a cage on wheels.) It has a skin stretched over the top of it. My dress is skin. The man comes in the back, he's going to tear my dress. I'm really scared, tense and scared. He's tearing my clothes off.

Sam: How do you feel toward him?

Mickey: He's disgusting. I feel angry. I'm mad.

Sam: Tell him.

Mickey: "Leave me alone. Get away." He's tearing my clothes off. I want him to stop. "Get out!"

Sam: What's happening?

Mickey: He's touching me with his mouth. He rapes me. . . . I'm afraid I'll go back. (Meaning to the present life situation with her father. I told her to not worry about it, just to go with what was happening.) He rapes me and throws me out on the dirt. I feel total disgust and anger. I would like to kill him. He's laughing.

Sam: How do you feel about that?

Mickey: Makes me feel horribly angry. I want to kill him so bad. I don't know how but I want to kill him.

Sam: What's happening now?

Mickey: He left. There I am. I can't do anything. I feel totally *alone*. I have nobody in the world but me. All this anger. I'm just alone. I sit down and cry. I know I can't kill him. I can't do anything! Makes me feel devastated. I just lie down and give up. . . . A part of me wants to get up and kill somebody!

Sam: What are you feeling right now?

Mickey: I feel *rage*, absolute total *rage*. I just scream. I scream until I come into a thousand pieces—on and on. There's no end. I have *no control* . . . Jesus God, do I go mad? Do I go crazy?

Sam: What does happen?

Mickey: I kill myself with a knife. I stick a knife in my chest and kill myself. My final thoughts as I'm doing it are peace, rest, free. I have *no control*. I have such rage and I don't know what to do. All I know to do to make it stop is to kill myself.

Sam: Now move on through the death experience to the other side. How do you feel?

Mickey: I feel at peace.

Sam: Good. Now with the help of your Higher Self, scan that lifetime and make the connections between then and now.

Mickey: I took the rage inside of me. I still carry that feeling of no control and the feeling of being *alone*, terribly *alone*, always . . . forever and ever. That's why I have such a hard time accepting God.

Sam: How does that relate to what is going on with you now?

Mickey: I'm scared to death of being by myself. (Look what happened to her when she was alone, then and now.) That feeling of coming apart into a million pieces, that is how I felt at home, standing at the kitchen counter. . . . I feel such relief that I know. I'm in total awe because my entire life I have felt that "ALONE." I could never realize or understand what it was. Always afraid to go do things by myself. Scared to death to be by myself. I never had the courage to go out. *Courage.*

Sam: What would you like to do now?

Mickey: Tear him apart, claw his eyes, stick my fingernails in his eyes, scratch his face off. Let his eyes bulge out. Stab him in the guts.

Sam: Go ahead.

Mickey: You mean I can do that?

Sam: Sure.

Mickey: "You deserve this. This is what you did to me." Oh God, this *feels good.* I feel better. "Rot in hell! Because that is what you put me through—*hell.*" I stuck a knife in him. It felt good. . . . It's finished. He's dead and I'm glad. I set him on fire, burn him. He's burning. I feel really good, really free. It's okay now. I don't care anymore. It's over. That takes care of the rage.

It's always imperative to have clients work through their feelings. As Mickey's first regression had unfolded, she had flipped into her present life and we had never gotten to work through this past life completely. We had our hands full dealing with her father. Due to her lack of resolution in this past life, we had never dealt with her feelings of being alone, or of her lack of control. Now it was time.

Sam: Is there anything else you need to be aware of around this issue of No Control?

Mickey: That feeling of *No Control* was what was screaming at
          him, ripping at him. Oh, it's the same feeling as
          when I stand at the counter. . . . My husband is
          popping into my mind. He is total procrastination.
          He starts things and doesn't finish them. My house is
          full of unfinished projects that drive me crazy. I have
          no control, yet it's my house.

Obviously, since Mickey retired she had been surrounded by
these unfinished projects throughout every day. Being home all
the time only exacerbated her underlying feeling of having no control. After asking Mickey to tell me what some of these unfinished
projects were, and to list them in order as to the ones she would
like to have completed first, I asked her how all of these unfinished
projects made her feel.

Mickey: They physically make me sick, all of these unfinished
          projects everywhere I look.
Sam: Have you told your husband how they make you feel?
Mickey: I've tried to get him to complete them, but his
          defense is anger and then I feel guilty for bringing it
          up.
Sam: But have you told him how they make you *feel?*
Mickey: No, I guess I haven't. . . . I'm afraid of *confrontation.*
          I've never been able to handle it ever. (If Mickey
          could confront people she would have had to face
          what her father had done, which she had blanked
          from her mind.) I still resist taking control.
Sam: I would like to ask that part of you that resists taking
          control to come forward and make itself known. Give
          it permission to speak.
Mickey: I'm just a child.
Sam: How do you feel toward Mickey?
Mickey: When I was a child in this life, I had no control when
          Dad did that. A part of me feels responsible. That
          little child believed she had no control. She couldn't

stop it. I need to know why he did that. That's not
who I knew as my dad. I have no conscious memory
of it—none.

Sam: With the help of your Higher Self, I want you to be
aware now of why you resist taking control. Why your
dad behaved the way he did we don't know. What we
do know is that you are not responsible for his actions.

Mickey: It's because I wanted my dad to love me so bad and
when he did it was so wrong. Little girl wanted her
dad to love her so much and he did *that!* If I ask to be
loved to this day, if I confront someone, it's going to
come out wrong. I'm afraid.

Sam: What are you afraid of?

Mickey: I'm afraid there's going to be anger. I'm afraid of
people's anger, of them not liking me. If I don't
confront then I won't have to feel rejection, pain, or
worse, them not wanting to love me anymore. If I
confront him and stand up for myself then he won't
love me and will be angry with me. I need to believe
that I'm worthy. I need to know that I am.

Here again was the common malady of mankind—a lack of
self-worth. Often victims of abuse believe that they are unworthy,
otherwise this horrible thing would not have happened to them.
In their own mind it somehow becomes their fault.

Sam: What is keeping you from feeling worthy?

Mickey: Fear is keeping me from believing that I'm worthy.
There's still the little girl. She felt so horrible, so
nothing. . . . She was just a little girl.

Sam: What happened to the little girl?

Mickey: That little girl didn't have anywhere to put rage so
she keeps it inside . . . and she cannot feel it against
her father.

Sam: Says who?

Mickey: You mean I can?

Sam: Of course you can. Your father did a terrible thing to you. You have every right to tell him how you feel. Go ahead. (Make my day.)

Mickey: I hate you. I hate you! I don't know why you did it to me. I hate you. Oh God, I hate you! *How could you say you love me and do that to me?* How could you? I hate you! I hate you! I wish that part of you was dead.

At this point, the little girl killed him, releasing all the rage she had to swallow. Remember this was the young woman who had visited her parents and had to be hospitalized rather than confront her father. On a subconscious level she knew, on a cellular level she remembered what he had done; although on a conscious level all she could do would be to come undone physically. The doctors never found anything physically wrong with her.

Mickey: My dad tried to kill himself before he died.

Sam: What would you like to do now?

Mickey: That part of him that was ugly, dirty, nasty, I need to separate that part from him. . . . All that fear, all that aloneness, all that rage . . . I killed that part of him. That part of him is dead. That part of him is gone. His eyes are closed. He's dead . . . wasn't worth burning. . . . I stood on top of his chest. . . . I feel like I have control. . . . I feel *courageous*. I do! . . . That feeling of aloneness is *gone!* . . . I can go home, sit in my house, and be alone, and feel totally at peace. . . . Oh God, yes, it feels good. . . . *I'm free.*

At this point I gave Mickey suggestions to reinforce our work, telling her that every day in every way from this day forward she would honor that little girl. Every day in every way she would be stronger and more courageous. She now knew deep within herself that nobody was ever going to push her around again, to which Mickey added, "*Nobody!*"

Mickey now confirmed for me that she perceived within herself no resistance to this, and that all her symptoms were gone.

Mickey:　God said to me when you accept what God has to give, you will be free. I know I am free. I needed to accept His help to get through it. He was trying to help me. That's why when I finally said in meditation, if I am to go see Sam I need a sign. I want my right arm to raise up off the chair. I don't know if I thought anything would happen or not, but when my arm started to raise all my itself, and I swear to you I was doing nothing, I knew I had to call you. The reason it took so long is because I felt like I had failed because the symptoms came back and I was embarrassed to tell you.

We had a good talk about expecting so much of ourselves, about loving and nurturing and being gentle with ourselves, about acceptance of who we are and that is a part of God. We are all children of God and are in a constant process of learning, of becoming. If we look at ourselves in this way, then it's easy to stop being so hard on ourselves.

Now we took time to envision Mickey's husband receiving what she said to him, and receiving it in a new receptive way, without the anger that is born out of his not feeling good about all of his unfinished projects. He would be able to take a load off himself as he finished the uncompleted projects one after the other.

Sam:　Envision yourself in the not too distant future as a courageous, strong, in control, worthy person, stating your truth in a way that confronts without being confrontational, knowing deep within yourself that the aloneness is now an absolute thing of the past.

Mickey:　I see the little girl and she's smiling. I want to hug the little girl.

Sam: Go ahead.

Mickey: It feels fantastic!

Sam: You know you can do whatever it takes to stand up
            for that little girl from this day forward.

Mickey: Yes, I do know that. I *do* know that I'm worthy. *I am.*
            Mom's situation brought it up again. (Her mother
            was suffering from dementia and depression. This
            coupled with her mother's own negativity, lack of self-
            worth, and stubbornness had made it almost impos-
            sible for Mickey to deal with her.) I can be of more
            help to her now. I was so afraid of ending up like her.
            She has a little girl inside of her, too.

Sam: Envision helping Mom in the most positive way
            possible, knowing that everything you do makes you
            feel freer.

Mickey: It feels good. I can do it now.

Sam: What about those feelings of being totally without
            purpose, lost, depressed?

Mickey: Gone.

In closing, I guided Mickey to get in touch with her Higher
Self, feeling herself embraced and enveloped in that golden light,
in that part of her that is God, melding as One energy, knowing in
every fiber of her being that she is Love. Mickey's message from
her Higher Self was the following: "You are so loved and you are
never alone, *never.*"

Mickey: I feel such incredible peace.

After anchoring that feeling of incredible peace with neuro-
linguistic programming, we closed our session, having finished
our unfinished business. Neuro-linguistic programming offers specific techniques that a facilitator can employ to organize or reorga-
nize a subjective experience in order to secure a desired behavioral
outcome.

The following week Mickey kept popping into my mind. I knew my intuitive self was telling me to call her. When I did call, she told me she couldn't understand it, but she had had a really rough time all week and felt depressed. I simply asked her what was going on. Had she confronted her husband about finishing up the first project that we had decided needed to get done? When she said no she hadn't, I explained to her that she was not doing what she had said she was going to do. She had to take the steps. She had to follow through on the commitments she had made to herself. If she hadn't done that, then no wonder she felt depressed. She couldn't come in and have a session, feel great, and then leave and do nothing. That kind of behavior would open the floodgates for a huge bath of guilt, negativity, and low self-esteem.

Our conversation served as a revelation to Mickey. It's vital to do something, rather than merely to think about it and procrastinate. In the doing comes the affirmation. Two weeks later Mickey called to tell me that she had just spent a week with her mother and had taken steps to get her out of her rocking chair and active. Our visualizing and meditating on her mother's being cooperative had paid off.

Lo and behold, her husband had finished the first of the unfinished projects on Mickey's list. It was done! She had begun to put together a schedule for the rest, and felt really good, and now appreciated not having to go to work. All the things she had been waiting to do until she retired were on her own list, and she had begun to take action. She realized she is personally responsible for creating the life she wants.

Mickey has grown in leaps and bounds since our first session, and I thoroughly enjoy watching the blossoming of a wonderful human being, and a good friend, as she discovers her own inner strength and spirituality.

X

Passion Flower

Truth, oh Stranger,
is a fair and desirable thing,
but it is a thing of which
it is hard to persuade men.
— Plato

My memory of my first encounter with Violet remains very distinct, after nine years. She had arrived after work one evening for an astrological reading. Throughout the evening I found myself watching myself watching her, catching glimpses of this striking, "other" personality that flipped through occasionally. Violet oozed a vitality, an aliveness that lay underneath her outer persona, and this other personality darted and danced about her as she talked. I could almost see the colors of the energies that played about her.

She dressed quite nicely, in her own definite style, dressed for business but with a flair. As I got to know her over the years, I noticed that this flair remained consistent with Violet. A scarf, a pin, some dangling earrings, a bright color, whatever it was, she always carried a sense of daring about her; yet she dressed appropriately for the situation. She was European, and worked for her country's local consulate. Violet was charming, poised, culturally engaging, gracious, and attractive. Most catching about her demeanor was a *joie de vivre*, an intense love of life, of fun, and of a good, even raucous time, that threatened to bubble to the surface with a startling force.

As I read her astrological chart we talked about her love life and the karmic implications of her present relationship with a Greek man with whom she had been involved in an on-again off-again relationship for the past fifteen to sixteen years. She was forty-eight years of age and had never married. We decided to get together soon for a past-life regression.

At the beginning of our session, in describing her relationship with him Violet used certain key phrases—"hanging on when I shouldn't," "I hit the wall," "sick and tired of it," "can't get out of the box." She didn't understand why she hung onto his shirtsleeves. She wanted to take a step forward. She sought a past-life regression to know whether she should let go of him, or if the two of them had more to work out in this lifetime.

With Violet's abundance of key phrases, I decided to use the method of letting the repetition of a key phrase guide her into a past-life experience. As she repeated the key phrase she moved back through a tunnel of time. The image of a tunnel is often used in guided visualization to move the client back to the cause life-time. As Violet emerged from the tunnel she found herself in darkness. She felt happy, then started crying. When asked the cause of this crying, she responded, "Sadness, sadness of the heart." I asked her to repeat the phrase "hit the wall," and she started laughing. She felt as if she were floating. There was nothing. She felt light, felt like laughing, then crying, both of which she did. I asked her to repeat the phrase, "hanging on when I shouldn't" . . . nothing. I ask if she felt afraid. She responded, "I don't think so . . . a little bit."

Even though she experienced emotion, that emotion didn't take us further. I let it run its course and we found ourselves back at square one. Recognizing obvious resistance to what might be seen here, I took her back into the tunnel to try again.

On the second entrance into this past life, she said she was still searching . . . blocking . . . "can't come through." I asked her to relate that statement to her relationship. She said that in the present when she was with him she felt relaxed, but always watching herself, "so doesn't get thrown back to me in a negative way. Always have to weigh my words." Now she started to cry. "Many times I want to have my true self come through, but don't."

Violet began to feel cold, though we were in a warm room on a balmy summer night.

Violet: So dark. My bones are cold.
Sam: Where are you?
Violet: I don't know, but cold. My feet, top of my body, my
           face, my hands, all cold.
Sam: How do you feel?
Violet: Calm.
Sam: Why are you crying?
Violet: I don't know.

At this point Violet grew hot, and her whole body tingled. She felt hot, yet she stated that she's always cold, referring to her present life. When I asked the reason, she laughed and said poor blood circulation. "That's funny. Seems hilarious." She described herself as warming from the inside and said that she felt tense, and continued to laugh, but didn't know what was so funny.

Now I told her she was going to see her feet. She saw nothing, but I told her she would just have to use her imagination and make up the story. (This is a good tool to use to get a client started when encountering resistance, or as in Violet's case, strong intellectual analyzing. Once a client has gotten a foothold, the subconscious memory takes over. This was all that Violet needed.)

Violet told me she had on blue shoes, women's, that looked flat and dressy. She wore a white dress that felt long. She felt warm in the dress. She had pearls in her hair, which was long and up on her head. She found herself sad and crying.

Violet: I'm looking out of a window. It is high up. There is
           no glass. My dress is Roman style, tied on top of
           shoulder. I feel sick to my stomach . . . pressure in

chest . . . feel locked up. Maybe I've been locked up
all my life. It's foggy. I feel this is why I want to go to
the ocean in the present, to feel free. Costas (Her
Greek lover in the present life is her past-life husband, but she is referring to him by his present-life
name.) did lock me up. He's jealous because I'm
fooling around.

She made this last statement while laughing. As I watched,
the personality, mannerisms, and voice of this woman in the blue
shoes took over my client's behavior, in a more complete version of
the behavior that had mesmerized me at our first meeting.

Violet: *Lots* of other men. It's a relief to laugh. . . . Christ . . .
          Christ, I feel cynical, very cynical.
Sam: How long have you been locked up?
Violet: Seems like a long time. Don't know why I don't want
          to say it, but he's my husband. (Crying.) It's silly, I'm
          dead, can't cry if I'm dead. . . . Maybe my heart
          broke . . . feeling of jumping, running away . . .
          always run away.
Sam: What happens?
Violet: Water, there are stones . . . cliffs. I'm very high up . . .
          and I'm falling. (Crying, very emotional.) I don't
          want to . . . out the window . . . onto the stones. I see
          my white dress. People running . . . running. They're
          upset.
Sam: What is happening now?
Violet: There's an old boat, Viking ship, half out of the
          water, like going ashore. Round wheels along side of
          boat, light wood. (As it turns out, Vikings carried
          their circular shields hooked to the sides of the ship.)
          . . . Funny feeling in chest.
Sam: Did your chest hit the stones?
Violet: I feel sick to my stomach.
Sam: What else could make you feel sick to your stomach?

It then dawned on her that she was pregnant.

Sam: Now, let's go back to what was going on to cause you to fall out of the window.

Violet: I'm standing up in the window . . . he was behind me.

Sam: What happens next?

Violet: Not sure, maybe he frightened me. You can walk around the house on it, like a balcony. There are columns, so can look out. Nothing on floor. . . . So empty. He's holding my shoulders. He's mad at me.

Sam: He's mad at you because . . . ?

Violet: He's telling me I'm lying. . . . My arms hurt. I'm telling him I'm not lying. (Laughing.) *He can have it.* I feel like cheating on him. He's beating me up mentally. He puts his hands around my upper arms. He's crazy! I'm nice now. I'm not going to tell him I've been fooling around with his brother. It's his brother's baby. I'm pregnant and I don't want to die. I can't tell him . . . I love him. I want it to be his baby.

Sam: Is it?

Violet: No.

Sam: If you love him, why did you have other relationships?

Violet: (Laughing uproariously.) Because his brother is cute! . . . Others are cute. . . . I don't think he knows. . . . Not all of them . . . I don't want to, but it's like a challenge. I want to see if I can get out and cheat on him. Men come to the house for business, have affairs with some of them, if they're cute. Meet them some other time, other place. *I want to get back at him.* (Long pause.) He killed me and my baby! How could he do that? . . . The Viking, man on the ship, I had an affair with him. Costas was furious.

Sam: What is Costas' name in this time?

Violet:	Victor.
Sam:	What did Victor do to you? (She avoids the question.)
Violet:	Maybe I'm hurting myself. He's a good husband. He's boring. There is a daughter, but I want to have a son.
Sam:	How young is your daughter?
Violet:	She's not very tall. (Crying.) I feel so sad, because I didn't want to die, because he's a good husband. . . . I'm so mean! I have to have everything I see! . . . Spoiled rotten. He loves me, but it's his brother's baby . . . this is a disaster.
Sam:	Does he know the baby is not his?
Violet:	No . . . So much fighting, one moment nice and quiet, one moment shouting and screaming. He's screaming that it is his brother's baby, but I didn't tell him. I don't think he means to push me, but he's very mad. I don't want to die. (More crying.)
Sam:	Do you try to reason with him?
Violet:	Yes, but he doesn't want to listen to me saying it *is* his baby. . . . I'm lying. . . . Christ . . .
Sam:	What is the next thing that happens?
Violet:	His eyes are black, pitch black. *I deserve to die*, he's saying. (Crying, she is very emotional through all of this.) We have a daughter. What's going to happen to her, if I'm not there? Please, oh please, I don't want to die. *How can you kill me when you love me?*

This question was so emotionally charged that I had her repeat it several times until the emotion had drained out of it.

Violet:	He doesn't believe that I love him. He's had enough of it. He doesn't want to kill me, but he gets so angry that he shakes me and I go over. He tells me he wants to kill me, but he doesn't really. He's just angry. . . . He killed me and that's it.

I now asked her Higher Self what it could tell her about her present situation. One word: "Caution."

Sam:	Are you able to let this go?
Violet:	(Still crying.) I still don't want to, but I think I must.
Sam:	Has Costas been able to forgive you?
Violet:	No. He won't let me make it up to him. He's afraid. He doesn't trust himself.
Sam:	Does he frighten you?
Violet:	I get nervous when he raises his voice, I get hysterical, I start to laugh. (The connection dawned on her, as she further realized.) He wants to get back at me. We can go on doing this . . . getting back at each other.
Sam:	Can you resolve it?
Violet:	Don't think so.
Sam:	Is it to your higher spiritual good to continue the relationship with Costas?
Violet:	For now. To do it would be almost to erase myself, and I don't want to do that. I can still manipulate him, but then he backs off. It was then I could make him dance to my music. (She twirled the forefinger of her right hand in the air, as she said this very defiantly, sarcastically, cynically, flippantly.) In the present life, when we get that close, he turns off to me, he drops me. He is a little jealous of his brother who has three children. His brother fell in love with an ex-lover of Costas. They have three little daughters and are happily married. Costas has one daughter who will be eighteen in October. She doesn't stay with him.
Sam:	Do you know the entity who was your daughter from the past life in the present?
Violet:	It's Melanie. His daughter. He doesn't want me to see her. She lives with his other ex. . . . He has been married three times. The first marriage ended after seven months and produced Melanie. I met Melanie when she was two years old.

Sam:	Have you ever asked Costas why he keeps coming back to you?
Violet:	No.

At this point I asked Violet's Higher Self if we had explored enough for this evening. The answer was yes. I also asked if it would be to Violet's benefit to pursue this work further. Again she answered in the affirmative.

After Violet returned totally to the present, she felt sarcastic and unsatisfied. Then, she said in much the same way that the lady in the white dress had spoken, "I want to see him crawl, see him on his knees."

She recently consulted a doctor to see if she could still get pregnant. She had turned forty-eight years old that week. The doctor said there would be some problems to overcome, but yes. Costas had to be tested, too. He agreed to it. His tests came up negative. He could no longer produce a child. She had not yet told him. When I asked her why, she saw how this behavior of hers continued to play into the old patterns.

A week later we met for our second session. Her reason for doing the session was to answer three questions: "Why do I want to get back at him? Why doesn't our relationship become anything and why doesn't it end?"

She emerged from the tunnel, finding it warm and herself alone on a beach.

Sam:	What are you doing?
Violet:	Floating. (I get her to place her feet on the ground.) It would be nice to be barefoot.
Sam:	Do you have on shoes?
Violet:	No. It is daytime, light, the sun is shining. I'm walking along the beach, the ocean is very blue. I have a white scarf on my head.
Sam:	What kind of clothes do you have on?
Violet:	Cotton, blue dress, long, white apron on top, long full skirt fitted to the waist . . . almost like washing

clothes. . . . I'm walking, no clothes with me. I'm thinking about the clothing that you wash, and it's blue, the water is so blue, and it's so beautiful. It's like I'm on an island. There are mountains on the island.

Sam: What kind of mountains?

At this point Violet brought in another life. Often this will happen when the subconscious wants to avoid a traumatic situation that is forthcoming.

Violet: Dark, dry lava. I see other islands. My island is not that big.

Sam: Are there other people on the island with you?

Violet: I don't see any.

Sam: Do you know how you got there?

Violet: No . . . Maybe I don't live here . . . just visit.

Sam: What's happening?

Violet: Not much. (Laughing.) I'm floating.

Sam: Go to your home.

Violet: I can't really see it.

Sam: Are you there?

Violet: Yes, think so.

Sam: Anyone else there?

Violet: No.

Now, she went back to the island. She expressed resistance to wanting to be "home."

Violet: Green, green trees, flowers, all growing up the mountain, but it's so strange, like the island was deserted.

Sam: How do you feel about being alone?

Violet: It's all right. . . . Running, running along the beach . . . but I don't always have heavy clothes on me. It's so quiet . . . looks like my skin is darker.

For a while she talked about this other existence. Oftentimes when the lifetime that a person needs to reexperience is a traumatic one, he or she will go off to another life or place that is more pleasant, to escape the pain associated with the cause lifetime. I let her stay on the island until it became clear this choice of hers was a tactic of resistance.

Sam: Do you know how long you've been on the island?

Violet: Feels comfortable . . . don't know. . . . There isn't another soul.

Sam: How did you get there?

Violet: I don't know.

Sam: What do you eat?

Violet: Vegetable, mutton . . . sheep.

Sam: Are they wild . . . do you raise them?

Violet: I don't see them.

Sam: Go to where you sleep at night.

Violet: It's funny. It's like a hut . . . on bamboo mats, or something. I'm colored . . . Negroes' curly hair. I'm watching two things and it's confusing. It's like one is watching the other. I'm in the dress watching the black one running.

Sam: Let's move forward in time to when they meet. Do they?

Violet: The black man is offering me fish from the sea. I'm at the harbor with many people. . . . Black caps on heads . . . white men.

Sam: Are you white or black?

Violet: White woman in scarf at market by ocean, standing where they sell fish. There are ships. . . . Feels okay, good to be there. I'm mingling. I buy fish. The people are friendly.

Sam: Do you take the fish home?

Violet: Yes . . . Open fireplace. I'm boiling it in big black kettle. I can't see him, but there should be somebody . . . with *big black boots*.

Sam:	Is there someone there?
Violet:	No . . . Strange . . . I feel that way. Big kitchen, stone walls. I'm trying to find out what the house looks like. There is a fire in kitchen . . . cooking in fireplace almost.
Sam:	Do you live with anyone else?
Violet:	Yes, but he's not here.
Sam:	Move forward to when he comes home.
Violet:	He's very tall.
Sam:	Who is he to you?
Violet:	I want to say he's my husband.
Sam:	How do you feel about him?
Violet:	Not sure. I feel happy seeing him. Want to rush toward him, but I don't. He looks nice, is friendly. I'm just standing there by fire. It's like he's taking his hat off, sitting in wooden chair, hands on knees, all dressed in black. . . . What does he do? No, more like he comes from the mountains.
Sam:	What does he do in the mountains?
Violet:	Could be a farmer.

At this point Violet said that she had felt a tingling sensation in her arms since we had started. I asked her if she was uncomfortable. She answered no.

Sam:	Do you recognize the soul?
Violet:	Yes.
Sam:	Who is it?
Violet:	I'm not sure. . . . I'm looking at Costas.
Sam:	Move forward.
Violet:	My heart is beating fast. . . . My heart is upset. The left side of my face is paralyzed.
Sam:	Do you know how that happened to you?
Violet:	It's like he hit me with a hot thing from this fire . . . hurts me . . . paralyzed . . . leaves a scar.
Sam:	Why does he hit you?

Violet: I don't understand. When I saw him, I wanted to take
            iron and hit him . . . like a quarrel.
Sam: Can you hear the words?
Violet: No . . . Hurts also in the abdomen. I have a pain. He
            kicked me and I feel like vomiting.
Sam: Why did he kick you there?
Violet: Drunk.
Sam: Does this happen often?
Violet: No . . . No . . . Not always.
Sam: But more than once?
Violet: Seems like it. My left arm is burning on inside. I have
            feeling he burnt me with a stick. He's rude and
            yelling and screaming. I don't understand why he
            wants to hurt me. . . . Maybe he likes to. Whatever I
            do it's not good enough. . . . And he is so tall. He's so
            big. . . . And he scares me. He's turning his back. I'm
            still standing by the open fireplace. It's like I don't
            move. I don't say anything. . . . I don't understand.
Sam: Move forward to the next significant event.
Violet: It's like I'm moving out . . . but I don't understand.
            I'm leaving the house.
Sam: Where do you go?
Violet: I'm on the street . . . to see an older woman.
Sam: What's your purpose for seeing her?
Violet: Abortion.
Sam: Why?
Violet: I don't want the baby. (Here I asked if that was why
            he had been mad. Violet didn't answer.) There are no
            other children.
Sam: What's the reason *you* don't want the baby?
Violet: Because he's drunk all the time. Thought would be
            better without. Get abortion. Yes.
Sam: Does he know you're pregnant?
Violet: No, not when I go to see the woman. He finds out,
            gets very mad.
Sam: Mad because you had the abortion?

Violet:	Yes, he wanted the baby. . . . I'm afraid of him. . . . He kicks me in the stomach. He doesn't think I'm worth anything because I could do that. He's turning his back because he's crying. And, I don't (cry). I don't want him to see me cry, because then he gets even worse and he hits me more. If I can just keep my face straight he will stop. He's walking out.
Sam:	Does he come back?
Violet:	Yes.
Sam:	And what happens?
Violet:	He starts a fire.
Sam:	Where are you?
Violet:	In the kitchen.
Sam:	What's happening?
Violet:	I'm burning. He's doing that, but I don't understand . . . I don't want to see it. Don't understand why I'm burning and the house is not. I'm screaming.

She grew quite emotional and appeared to be in a great deal of pain as this was being done to her. As I started to tell her to move through the pain, I found myself fascinated by a most interesting phenomenon taking place. Her arm in the present began to grow red and looked as if it were being burned. As we moved forward beyond the incident, this redness subsided. (Similar situations have occurred with other clients.)

Sam:	Where is he? What's he doing?
Violet:	He's taking wood from the kitchen fire and placing it on my arms because he's going to *mark* me. . . . Taking burning wood in front of my face.
Sam:	Does he burn your face?
Violet:	He just wants to tickle my face with it. He throws those things back into the fire. He's laughing. He looks mean. He brushes his hands like he's finished his work.
Sam:	Move to the time of your death.

Violet: Heart is beating faster. Like excitement. I'm outside
            my body. Brown coffin . . . women all dressed in
            black with black heavy scarves over head, like shawls
            almost.
Sam: Where is this taking place, what country?
Violet: I would say *Greece*. . . . I feel very peaceful.

At this point Violet showed some resistance to reexperiencing
her death. I asked, "How did you die?"

Violet: My jaws feel different somehow. Why does it have to
            be violent? Somebody is squeezing my head with
            their hands. . . . It's almost like there is a knife in my
            heart. It's like he wants to carve my heart out because
            I killed the baby. I'm in the kitchen. I'm sitting on
            the chair. He's squeezing my face in his hands. He
            crushes my jaw . . . that's why it feels so stiff. I'm
            falling to the floor and he just kicks me. But, it's like
            it doesn't bother me. I don't care.
Sam: Who finds you?
Violet: His mother and his sister. Sister takes knife out of my
            chest. It's like she's killing him. Stabs him.
Sam: Does he die?
Violet: I think so. That's maybe why I didn't see him at my
            funeral. Sister and mother are there. It's because all
            the men are with him.
Sam: Do the townspeople know what happened?
Violet: No. Maybe that's why my heart is beating so . . .
            because they don't know.
Sam: What do they know?
Violet: That we killed each other . . . but we didn't. We
            didn't do that.
Sam: How does that make you feel?
Violet: I'm upset. Sister killed him because she is angry,
            because he killed me.
Sam: Do you know this sister in this present life?

Violet: I've never met her. Today Costas has a sister in a
           convent.

Sam: We'll ask your Higher Self if this is the same sister as
           in the past life we are exploring.

Violet: Yes, the Higher Self says yes. . . . I want to get back at
           him. But, it really doesn't matter anymore. That's
           probably why I don't talk to him. Probably why I
           haven't confronted him.

Sam: Is he violent in this life as Costas?

Violet: No.

Sam: Never hit you?

Violet: No . . . Once his eyes were cold, were burning
           cold . . . so black. We were making love and he shook
           my shoulders and he said, "I could kill you."

Sam: Was this in the heat of passion?

Violet: Yes.

I then asked Violet's Higher Self if we had done enough for this evening. The answer was yes. I believed that more remained here to uncover. For instance, what original situation in the past had set up this cycle of inflicting pain on each other? It would certainly be beneficial and interesting to explore further.

It is of interest to note that in both of these lifetimes Violet met a violent death at the hands of her present lover, who in both lives had been her husband. Their present relationship has continued for years with a great deal of passion, but he has remained unwilling to take that step again. Perhaps his reluctance is healthier for Violet, since in the act of lovemaking he has stated, "I could kill you." Also of note is that Violet has no children and has not married in the present, not even once.

A correlation exists also between her feeling the need to watch herself now and her statement in the past that if she could just keep her face straight, he wouldn't be as angry. This connection to the past has kept her from being able to speak of how she really feels in the present relationship. It is always so amazing to see the hold that a past-life situation can have over the present, and how gratifying it is to see that grip finally be released.

After these two past-life regressions, Costas and Violet gradually stopped trying. Their passion dissipated. He has since married someone else, and she has gone on to other relationships, still not married, but has experienced a deep and gentle love that is not based on a volatile, dangerous passion that had been rooted in the past.

XI

Vietnam through the Eyes of a Child . . .
the Value of Remote Healing

Children being born now
need to be around
people with open hearts.
— Baba Hari Dass

Normally, I don't see children in my practice. Jesse was a special case. He was eleven years old and very much looking forward to spending the following week with his class at what had become a traditional fifth grade outing known as Outdoor Education. This program took the students out into nature for a week, instead of keeping them stuck in the classroom!

The problem was that Jesse was well on his way to assuring that he would be too sick to go. He already had a clear runny nose and a cough that produced lots of phlegm. Jesse had a history of asthma and upper respiratory complications. Since infancy, whenever he caught a virus he would go into a bout of asthma. He would produce the classic symptoms of glassy eyes, fever, congestion, tummy ache, sometimes headache, and generally feeling very ill, which would climax with the onset of vomiting phlegm almost continually. This cycle would peak for seventy-two hours, and then the heavy, belabored asthmatic breathing would cease. Just like that. Other times and on a consistent basis, his ailments would mushroom into bronchitis or pneumonia.

Jesse's mother had suspected psychological implications of his illness when he was still just a baby. She found it extremely painful just to watch his little, worn-out body as it struggled to breathe. His mother took him to bed with her early one morning after her husband had left for work. She was holding Jesse and soothing him, telling him how very much she loved him, when suddenly his breathing returned to normal. She knew that this change had everything to do with the love she was giving him. Metaphysically, she knew the reasons for asthma—*a fear of life* and a feeling of not wanting to be here. In her caressing and expressing her deep love for him, Jesse's mother gave him exactly what he needed. And at that time, he was able to receive it.

Through the years this recurring pattern had worn down both Jesse and his mother. He had never been able to have a simple cold. Whenever it started he would usually get sick on one weekend and not be well until the Monday after the following weekend. Thus he missed a week of school with every virus that came his way. Interestingly, Jesse had become a strong and determined boy who loved to play outside, and who worked very hard at anything he set his mind to. He had been known to work for hours digging a hole just because he found it fun. He did not fit the description of a physically compromised child. But his asthma attacks had caused him to miss out on several neat things that he wanted to do.

Naturally, when the telltale signs appeared the week before his scheduled departure, something needed to be done, and quickly. His mother and I determined that we should try hypnotherapy by simply asking that part of Jesse to come forward that felt the need to make him sick. We soon discovered that Jesse felt uneasy about the process of hypnosis and the idea of losing control. He resisted the relaxation process, fighting it every step of the way, and then moved into it so deeply that he found it difficult to respond verbally. It became a precarious balance.

As I asked that part of Jesse to come forward that felt the need to make him sick, he started a choking cough that continued for some time, and brought up so much phlegm that we started rapidly going through a box of tissue. Nothing was being said in words, but reams could be heard in the coughing. Jesse described the image of a snake that said its function was to make Jesse sick. It claimed to eat the bad stuff, to get rid of the bad stuff. The snake said it did this because Jesse felt sad. A snake carries many esoteric meanings, often having to do with wisdom and healing, and often associated with Scorpio, Jesse's astrological sun sign.

Instructed to go back to the cause of the sickness, Jesse suddenly screamed, *"It's a WAR!"* With this he sat bolt upright, opening bloodshot, glazed eyes in abject terror as he stated emphatically, "I don't want to do this!" At this point, I placed my hand firmly on his chest and gently pushed him back down on the recliner, admonishing him to close his eyes and tell me what he was aware of. When something like this happens, the facilitator often wants to acquiesce and bring the subject up immediately. This I did not do. I knew the child very well, having known him since birth, and felt that it was important to continue. We had obviously begun to discover a vital key to unlock this pattern that had held him prisoner all of his young life. I told him that this war was something that had already happened, and it was important for him to reexperience it one last time so he could be forever free of it. It was of the past, and he was now okay.

After his confirming to me that this was indeed the case, we continued. I advised him to be aware of his physical body, to tell me what he was wearing. He said they were wearing green uniforms . . . camouflage. When asked to describe his surroundings he said, "It is bushy. There are vines, *the* river, marshes, trees." With this description, he grew visibly irritated as he suddenly blurted out . . . "It's Vietnam!" Jesse again resisted going further, saying he didn't want to do this. But we couldn't stop now. It would not be in Jesse's best interests. I told him we had to go on.

Then, in a deeper, older voice, dripping with contempt, I heard him say, "Why do the governments have their guys just go over and get messed up in it when two sides go against each other? In every instance, it has nothing to do with us." Stunned by the volumes unspoken in the sound of his voice, I asked him how he felt about that. He said he felt angry and sad. I then asked him to go back to just moments before his death and share with me what was happening. He said he got killed. There were bullets flying everywhere. His friend got shot. That made him really angry, so he stood up and started shooting, yelling, and cursing at the supposed enemy. When he did this, he was shot in the chest. "Blood comes pouring out. I'm dead. I'm not alone. We're all dead. There are bodies all over the place." When I asked him how dying this way made him feel, he responded by saying that he felt sad, angry, and mad, and he regretted joining the Army—he and his friend were both killed. When I asked him to let his *sadness* speak, he said that before he died there was something there, something scary, not the enemy, but something. This entity attachment we would deal with later.

At this point I asked Jesse to move on through the death experience to the other side of life, and with the aid of his Higher Self, to tell me why he kept himself unhealthy in his present life. He answered, "So I won't have to go into the army and die in another war." We then spent time making sure that he made the connections between his anger and sickness in the present, and his recent past-life experience in Vietnam. When told that he could leave his anger, sadness, regret, and his feeling the need to be unhealthy in the past, he decided to bury all of it.

Then I had him reenvision the past with a different ending, which I don't often do in my work. In this instance, with Jesse being so young, I felt it was important to do this. In his new scenario, both he and his friend got out alive. "A helicopter came down and blew up the bad guys, and then we went home." Since Jesse was so young and didn't like to do this work, I hoped that we had done enough to resolve his problem. Actually, we were very successful in the short term, in that Jesse did not get ill as had been his usual pattern, and he was able to go away the following week with his classmates. Also, he stopped having nightmares as often.

We did, I believe, break his pattern of illness, but he remained resistant to giving up control to do this type of work, as the process was an unknown for him and seemed to frighten him, so we agreed not to pursue it at that time.

Since this session, in conjunction with Jesse's beginning to drink the Manchurian Mushroom Tea widely known as Kombucha, he has not suffered a single bout of asthma. He has had two colds, and not only did they not turn into asthma, but they proved to be just colds. Jesse did not miss a day of school. This result was quite an accomplishment for him. Before his mother discovered the mushroom tea, she had taken him to the Maharishi Ayurveda Center in Los Angeles and had found that the prescribed herbs, if taken early enough, could lessen the severity of an illness by helping him to strengthen his immune system. The aromatherapy that she stills uses in his room at night seems to soothe him.

There is no one way to the mountain, and there is not necessarily only one way to emotional freedom and good health. We live in a time where thankfully we have options other than the medical profession and their use of synthetic drugs to treat symptoms. We now have a renewal of the more natural ways to bring ourselves back into balance, and we can take this opportunity to try them out, letting each one be of service in the healing of the body, mind, and soul.

Perhaps in our lifetime, doctors will be trained as healers and see each patient as the whole being that he is. We still have a long way to go, but as more and more people turn away from the medical profession's narrow viewpoint, because they are getting true results elsewhere, change will come. When money walks, they *will* listen.

Here a little more background information regarding Jesse is helpful. This child had experienced nightmares from the time he was around three years of age. When his mother would ask what was wrong, he would always reply that monsters were about to get him. His closet always had to be checked at bedtime, as he feared monsters hid in his room. He always appeared to be doing battle in his dreams, and found it difficult to relax enough to go to sleep at night.

As he grew older, he began talking more in his sleep, and started sleepwalking. He always seemed to be trying to get somewhere and he acted extremely agitated. His mother became a light sleeper, and would wake as he passed her bedroom door. However, on two occasions she found the back door ajar the following morning, and once Jesse's feet looked as if he had been outside during the night. His parents started putting barriers in front of the doors at night, so they could hear him if he tried to go outside.

Jesse's parents had never bought toy guns for their children, but had watched in fascination as their children managed very creatively to make weapons out of whatever they found available. Naturally, part of this phenomenon is the human nature of the male-thrusting warrior drive that male children need to express. In Jesse's case he would want to take his weapons to bed at night "for protection," and had always felt safer wearing a hat to bed, as a soldier might do in a foxhole or when sleeping outside in the open.

After Jesse fell asleep, his mother would go in and check his bed and remove whatever he had taken to bed with him. There under the covers she would find some handmade weapon. A hat of some fashion would be on his head, his favorite being an old, black, wide-brim hippie hat of his mother's, and his large collection of stuffed animals would be arrayed all around him to keep him safe. He was fiercely loyal to his stuffed animals. When he traveled, he filled his suitcase so full of stuffed animals—because he couldn't choose just one to take with him, or even two or three—that he had no room for his clothes. Often his parents would find another bag loaded in the car with nothing but stuffed animals in it.

Another interesting point is that Jesse was a deep sleeper and very difficult to wake, but if someone entered his room at night to straighten his covers, he would often startle awake, with a look of absolute terror in his eyes. If he couldn't pull the covers up over his head, he would throw his arms over his face and head as if trying to protect himself. Often he fell asleep with his head tightly wrapped, like a mummy, with the covers tucked in at his sides. When his mother tried to loosen the covers, she would find him drenched with sweat.

Jesse had always been very competitive and literally could not stand to lose. He always became combative and emotional. When he had been younger, his family had allowed him to win because it meant so much to him, but as he grew older they continually tried to teach him about playing for fun, doing the best you can, and enjoying the doing. This one lesson he never managed, although once he reached puberty he did start to improve.

Throughout his childhood, he showed a bravery beyond his years in various situations when hurt or ill, but he disliked the sight of blood and could overreact. He explicitly didn't want to see it, but he did want to know how badly he might be hurt. Jesse was a child who carried a heavier load than most young-sters his age, due I feel, to having died so violently in Vietnam, and not so long ago. He had been young and had died in a war, and more importantly a war he did not believe in. He had died angry, scared, and saddened. These young soldiers do not accept death easily; often, I believe, as with Jesse, they come back into a body way too soon.

Actually I have a theory, or perhaps more correctly called an intuitive feeling, that a large number of the children born, espe-cially in the early eighties, are young soldiers who had died in Vietnam. Often young soldiers who die on the field of battle find it difficult to accept their death. They are young and the young have always felt themselves immortal, although I'm sure most are scared to death. They died violently and in heightened states of emotion. But, due to their youth, they often jump back into a body as soon as they can, instead of giving themselves more heal-ing time on the Other Side.

A swarm of these souls, I believe, came in specifically in 1981-1982. Their outlook on life is basically that of anarchy. They need a tremendous amount of love and patience to help them heal the wounds of their recent past. We owe them that. Very few of them chose to go to Vietnam. They were forced to go by a government that was making choices for reasons other than what was best for the people or the country—reasons that had more to do with money, greed, and politics as usual.

In Jesse's case I wanted to deal with an entity he had referred to as being there with all the dead and dying. I wanted to try a procedure I had studied in my hypnotherapy training called "remote releasing of an unwanted influence." This remote release can be achieved when a person, while in trance, is guided in the releasing work on behalf of another person who is not present. I wanted to do remote healing on Jesse to remove this entity, if indeed it had attached to him. I felt fairly certain that it had, and I thought it would be well worth the effort if we were successful, because we could do it without requiring Jesse to participate.

Once I entered a deep state of relaxation I was told by James, my facilitator, to focus on Jesse's face, to look into his eyes and be aware of what was there. I saw a pair of shiny black eyes. I was instructed to reach out with my consciousness to Jesse's Higher Self and gain permission to do releasement. It was granted.

James:	Look deep into the eyes. Is there something else looking out?
Sam:	The eyes are angry. . . . Something else is there other than Jesse.
James:	Say, "I refuse you permission to touch my body or use my voice. I will repeat your words." (My colleague had me repeat this twice.)
Sam:	It's a *big* monster. Just growls.
James:	What is your purpose or function in Jesse's life? What is your role in these explosions of anger?
Sam:	It's sort of confusing.
James:	If confusion could speak, what would it say? Let it speak.
Sam:	"I punish him. I keep him scared."
James:	Why?
Sam:	(Venomously, it blurts out.) "Because I want to!!!" It's so big and dark, red and black.
James:	There's a place where you can get even more power. Look right into the core of your being to that spark of light, right in the core of your being. Look deep inside.

Sam: It's very sly. It's onto your tricks.

James: Then you visualize light within its core. Call upon
            other Light Beings to help. Project a beam of light
            into it, from you into it. There is an atomic explosion
            of light, massive explosions of light. Rescue spirits are
            ushering it up into the Light.

Sam: It's screaming. It doesn't want to go. It's being taken
            up under its arms. It's resisting. But, it's in the air.

James: Send it another spark of light right into the center of
            its being. There are explosions of light again, and
            again, and again shattering all dark forces. It is being
            taken up into the Light.

Sam: It's higher, and limp, but still there.

James: Who, or what, is it that is inside of it, slowing down
            its progress into the Light?

Sam: Something about a war. He died in a war . . . the
            spirit. It's dark and smaller, but dark . . . really dark.
            No wonder Jesse sees monsters.

James: If the dark one could speak, what would it say?

Sam: (Instead of hearing the dark one speak, I started to
            describe what I was seeing.) Battlefield . . . dead
            bodies . . . dead body . . . Jesse's. A murky, dark force
            is settling into it. It's got these eyes, like really
            sad . . . big ovals. Its arms are really long.

James: Let the sadness speak.

Sam: (Screaming in a really guttural, yet high-pitched
            strangely different voice.) "I want to live! I want to
            live! I want to live! I want to live!"

James: Look to the Light. Move into the Light now!

Sam: It's changing color, from black to a deep red. "I don't
            know if I can trust this."

James: Just put a part of yourself into the Light . . . testing
            out the Light, seeing how good it feels.

Sam: It's moaning. In a little, young voice I hear, "Leave me
            alone . . . I want my mommy."

James: There are forces of Light helping you move into the

Light. Move into the Light.

Sam: In that moaning, raspy voice, "The Light feels like my mommy."

James: Look in the Light. See Mommy waiting there for you.

Sam: "Feels better in Light with Mommy."

James: You're invited to step deeper into the Light. What is that like?

Sam: "My body has changed color again. It is now a golden yellow. . . . (Said with great relief.) I'm not seeking anymore."

James: Share with me what you've found.

Sam: "Mommy . . . I've found my mommy. But, I'm not quite in the Light. I'm below it."

James: Call down all available helpers from the Light to push you up totally into the Light.

Sam: "I'm totally in the Light, like in a hammock. I'm pulled into the Light. But, a part of me is afraid of light."

James: The Light is safe and secure. Feel into it. Experience what it feels like. Share with us what you are experiencing.

Sam: "It's like I don't have to do battle. I'm so tired of doing battle. . . . That monster doesn't know what to do without me though."

James: Pull it into the Light with you, where it can be totally restored in the Light and find peace.

Sam: "He's smaller and scared. He's sitting on me."

James: Tell him about the goodness of the Light.

Sam: "Mommy is there. You don't have to be scared, even little monsters have mommies." It's been in dark existence for so long. It's just so hard to lift up.

James: I'm going to count from one to three. When I get to the number three, you will feel a buoyancy, a lightness. All the weight is gone. Number one, number two, number three. Now, experience the comfort of being with Mommy in the Light.

Sam: "Mommy! Been without Mommy for so long." (Here
          there are some guttural sounds, like explosions of air,
          as the monster is being released.)

James: Share with us what you are experiencing.

Sam: "Getting free . . . Mommy. (Crying.) Mommy is with
          me in the Light."

James: Who are you?

Sam: "I lost my soul a long time ago . . . and it got darker
          and darker and darker."

James: Let it all be behind you. You are now in the Light
          with your mommy, in peace and joy and profound
          well-being.

Sam: "I'm walking off as a little boy holding Mommy's
          hand into the Light. Bye-bye."

James:.   Bye-bye. Now, Samantha, direct your attention back
          to Jesse. Visualize a miniature sun in Jesse's solar
          plexus filling him up with light. . . .

Sam: There's a little bitty black and red monster over there
          to my right.

James: Focus on him. Let it speak.

Sam: It says bye-bye as legions of Light Beings usher it into
          the Light.

James: Good. Now, picture that sun, growing, spreading
          out, filling up Jesse's entire being with bright white
          light. There is an aura of brilliant light all around
          him, helping him to release all of that anger.

Sam: He's beautiful.

James: Look once again into Jesse's eyes. What do you see?

Sam: Light.

James: Experience his life force filling up all of that space
          that had been occupied. See him optimizing his
          capabilities, having his emotions balanced, experienc-
          ing a sense of well-being, living a happier, more
          contented, peaceful life.

Sam: I see him with his arms and legs spread out from him
          just bathed in white golden light.

Jesse had indeed been carrying a heavy load. His mother had received the distinct impression that he had been a warrior many times, and she felt that he was a very strong soul who knew that he wanted help but didn't know how to ask. We all believe that this session of remote healing proved helpful to Jesse and insightful for all of us.

A further step in Jesse's progress occurred when Jesse reached age fourteen. His mother, Elizabeth, felt Jesse would benefit from visiting the Vietnam War Memorial in Washington, D.C. This thought had come to her in such a way that she knew to take heed. The two of them traveled to Washington. As soon as they checked into their hotel, they walked to the war memorial.

Elizabeth let Jesse approach the memorial by himself. Not very far in, he stopped at one particular panel, placed his hand on it, and leaned into it bowing his head. He then discreetly placed something at the base of the panel and slowly moved on. His mother followed, looking down to see what he had left as an offering. To her surprise, it was a cigar. Obviously, Jesse had put some thought into coming here. He didn't smoke. So, he had to have bought the cigar, intending to leave it at the wall. That action on his part was extremely moving for his mom. She needed to gather herself before she moved to catch up with him. Together they walked along in silence. After some time, Elizabeth asked Jesse if he wanted to share what he had felt. He said no, that he didn't want to talk about it. It was private.

When they reached the name registry, Jesse's mother had an odd spelling of a name that Jesse, at the end of our session, claimed had been his last name. This name hadn't made much sense to me, but Jesse had been young, names are often difficult, and this information had emerged at the end of the session, when he was in a much lighter state of relaxation. However, he had also said that he had lived in a climate much like either California or Florida.

The name started with the letter "D." The spelling he had given did not show up in the registry. A friend of Jesse's mom had also died in Vietnam and his last name also started with a "D." She had begun to look it up when Jesse came up to her and promptly slid his hand down the page, stopping at a specific name. The spelling was unusual and the person had lived in California. Jesse's mom looked at him, he gave her a shrug, she wrote down the name, and they set off to find these two names on the panels. Elizabeth's friend came up first. It was on a panel much closer to the name registry.

The other name turned out to be on the very same panel that Jesse had leaned against and where he had left the cigar. Coincidence? Well, I don't happen to believe in coincidence, but a little Cosmic synchronicity was certainly at work. Jesse knew something was up. He sighed, softly shook his head, and silently leaned into the panel. It was a moment of quiet release. Jesse had made peace with some of his feelings.

His mom has noticed a difference, a lightness, more like an absence of weight. Each step he takes brings him closer to wholeness.

XII

A Wild Irish Rose

*The greatest victory man can obtain
is over himself.*
— Amenhotep IV

Shannon O'Connor presented herself as an aggressive personality, one quick to anger and slow to forget, with flaming red hair and cheeks. Yet, she had soft green eyes that belied her behavior, giving me glimpses into the depth of her sensitivity. Still, with other people she acted much like the proverbial bull in the china shop. Always ready to speak her mind, and doing so with very little tact, she often hurt herself in the process by driving people away. Aside from her aggressiveness, she seemed to harbor something, an uneasiness, as if she trusted no one and lay waiting for the ax to fall.

Shannon came to see me because she needed to lose weight . . . lots of it. She weighed two hundred and fifty-plus pounds. When I asked her why she wanted to lose weight, she said because she was unhappy. Her excess weight hurt her ability to get roles as an actor, and also hurt her social life. She wanted to be pretty again, not feel so heavy and tired. She had a problem with depression. Shannon found it easier to pull herself out of it when she could be more active, but being hit by a car had damaged her knees. This injury had provided a valid excuse, although none was needed since she had and still did strongly resist doing exercise.

Being overweight first became a problem about fifteen years earlier, when a man with whom she had been living broke up with her. At the time, she had been only about ten pounds overweight. Not only had she felt emotionally dependent in that she loved him, but she had been financially dependent on him as well. When the break-up occurred, she went on "automatic pilot." She felt intense rejection, even though she knew the relationship hadn't worked, and that he was the wrong person for her. But she also knew she couldn't go through it again.

She took a desk job, squashing any opportunity to get an acting role and she started to party. However, this was the early to mid-eighties, not the sixties. Shannon had been a *child of the sixties* and she described herself as a party girl. She had done a lot of drugs and alcohol, at one period shooting speed along with smoking marijuana, going out to bars and getting loaded. But these were much more dangerous times. Still she found herself going to bars, getting stoned out of her mind and leaving with men. For three months she did this, until she found herself waking up in apartments on Avenue C on New York's Lower East Side with guys who didn't even speak English. She knew then that this behavior had to stop. From that point she ate more so that she would not look good and therefore would not get picked up. Then she started to eat food for companionship.

When I asked her what emotional need eating fulfilled, she simply stated that her eating had now gone out of control. Her daily routine with eating had become totally helter-skelter. She grabbed what she could, fast food, anything cheap and easy. She said that she kept losing control with it. "I would like to eat like other people eat. I most want to eat at night and I eat when I'm not even hungry. I eat on automatic pilot. I look at my hand and discover food that I've been shoving into my mouth unconsciously. I'm eating and I don't know I'm eating. What am I trying to feed?"

When I asked Shannon why she ate, she responded with, "I have no choice." This response provided a very interesting key as we will see later. It's always so important to note how a client answers questions, including the tone of voice, the intonation. All of these aspects can provide valuable keys to the truth of what is really going on.

For instance, when I asked Shannon if she was willing to lose weight she hesitated in answering and looked at me like a young frightened girl. Her eyes filled up with tears and quietly she said, "I really want to on some level, but when you asked, it struck terror in my heart." I immediately asked if that terror could speak what would it say, and a deeply pained voice said, "Go away." The next moment she felt sick to her stomach. A moment later she flashed a smile as she said, "My comedy response is here trying to push this down BIG TIME. . . . There's a lot of pain here."

We were ready to work. I asked her if she knew the meta-physical reason for being overweight. She said no. I said listen. . . . Fear, naturally, and a need to protect oneself. It's about running away from your feelings—oversensitivity, insecurity, trying to find fulfillment. The fear can also be a cover for hidden anger and an unwillingness to forgive. To this she simply said, "Yeah."

We asked to go to the cause lifetime of her present problem of being overweight, of the feeling that she "has no choice," to go to the lifetime that would give her the most insight, awareness and resolution. When she stepped through the light and planted her feet firmly on the earth, I ask her where she found herself.

Shannon: A lot of water.

Sam: Where is the water in relation to you?

Shannon: All around me.

Sam: Are you on the water?

Shannon: On top of the water . . . I don't know if I like it. Floating.

Sam: How do you feel toward the water?

Shannon: I'm afraid of it.

Sam: What color is the water?

Shannon: Blue-grey . . . grey-blue water.

Sam: Is it a sunny day or an overcast day?

Shannon: I don't know.

Sam: Are you face up or face down in the water?

Shannon: Face down in the water . . . I think the body is dead. I don't know why I'm there.

Sam: Are you a younger person or an older person?

Shannon: I'm a young person. I don't know where everybody was. . . . I'm sinking. My body is so heavy. *Nothing I can do.* (I sensed this was a key phrase relating to her statement, "I have no choice.") . . . I can't move my hands.

Sam: Where are your hands in relation to your body?

Shannon: They are next to my body. My hands are tied to my body.

Sam: What's binding your hands?

Shannon: Something tight . . . a sheet.

Sam: Does the sheet cover your entire body except your face and head?

Shannon: Just my head and feet are out of the sheet. Why would they do that?

Sam: We are going to go back to before they wrapped you in the sheet, to before you were in the water. I'm going to count from one to three and when I get to the number three, you will be there. One . . . going back . . . two . . . back . . . three . . . there. Go with your very first impression. Where do you find yourself?

Shannon: Some mountains that go down to some water.

Sam: Where are you in relation to the water?

Shannon: I'm looking out over the water. I'm confused.

Sam: I want you to focus on your body. Tell me are you sitting, standing, or lying down?

Shannon: I'm sitting down.

Here we determined she was barefoot, wearing some kind of long skirt, a blouse, and she felt her hair on the back of her neck.

Sam: What are your thoughts or feelings as you are sitting there looking out over the water?

Shannon: I'm confused. I don't know why they're doing that. I can't figure it out.

Sam: What is it that they're doing that you can't figure out?

Shannon: They keep grabbing my hands. I'm a woman, a young woman, thirteen, maybe fourteen years old. I don't understand it. Two guys are trying to grab my hands. . . . I know them.

Sam: Who are they to you?

Shannon: They're friends. Oh, my God! (Emotion.) They're going to kill me. They're going to rape me and kill me. I can't move my hands. They're holding them down. . . . (She was crying now.) . . . I really liked them. I can't believe this!

Sam: What's happening?

Shannon: One is on top of me. The other is making these awful sounds, real guttural, laughing . . . I don't understand it. I don't know why they are doing this.

Sam: What are you doing?

Shannon: I'm telling them to stop.

Sam: What are you feeling?

Shannon: I'm sick to my stomach. (Shannon had told me earlier that one reason she ate was to make the sick feeling in her stomach go away.) . . . Oh God that hurts!!

Sam: What hurts?

Shannon: What he's doing to me. . . . I've never done that before. . . . He's fucking me. The other one is hurting my arm. . . . I'm really fighting.

Sam: Is it helping?

Shannon: It's helping a little. I know they are going to kill me. I'm afraid. I've got to get out of here. I'm really fighting. (Shannon was very combative in her dealings with others in the present.) I'm yelling. I don't think anybody hears me. I'm too far from home. (She started to cry more now.) I want my mommy. (She sounded just like a very scared little girl.)

Sam: You want your mommy because . . . ?

Shannon: Because I'm afraid. I can't breathe. I can't see. Some
           hands are on my face. . . . I think they killed me. I
           can't see anything. I can't feel anything. . . . Nobody
           will ever know.

Sam: What brought you out here so far from home?

Shannon: I wanted to see the water . . . never seen it before.

Sam: Did you come by yourself?

Shannon: Uh-huh. I met them there. I had met them before.
           Knew them . . . seen them around. I thought they
           were nice. . . . Nobody is going to know where I'm at.
           We were talking. . . . They're acting weird.

Sam: How are they acting weird?

Shannon: It's just not like before. Think they are older than me,
           in their twenties. They live in the same area as me.
           I've seen them on the road. There's a lot of water,
           must be an island.

Sam: What else can you tell me about them?

Shannon: One has on a rough shirt. It scratches when they're
           doing what they do.

Sam: What is your last conscious thought before you make
           your transition?

Shannon: My family doesn't know where I'm at. . . . I'm
           getting sick . . . in my stomach. (At this point I asked
           her if this was the same sickness in her stomach that
           she felt in the present. She realized that it was.) *I
           can't control it.* It happens when I'm afraid.

Sam: If this sick feeling could speak what would it say?

Shannon: "Get the fuck off me!" (Here I asked her to repeat this a
           couple of times until the emotion dissipated. Sounding
           tired and worn out she said . . .) "Why don't you just
           leave me alone?" . . . Why don't they just go away? I
           didn't do anything to them. . . . *I don't want to die.*

Shannon made her transition as I watched her face release
and relax, losing the tension and fear as it became calm. I asked

her how she felt and she said she felt tired, didn't feel anything, didn't feel any pain, paused, and said it was actually calming.

As I started to put a golden light around her connecting her with her Higher Self, I knew there was more, so I again asked her how she felt. This time we got there.

Shannon: *I feel angry.* I just can't let it go. They shouldn't have done that. I'd like to kill them! (She welled up, full of emotion.) I'd like to make them feel how they made me feel.

Sam: How did they make you feel?

Shannon: They hurt me, made me feel disgusting. They betrayed me. I didn't do anything to them. I trusted them. . . . I don't know if my family ever knew what happened. . . . They never knew. I don't think the body was ever found.

Sam: Had you told anyone where you were going?

Shannon: No, I just left. I was allowed to.

Sam: Who did you live with?

Shannon: My mother, a brother, I think a father. We lived in a village. It had a lot of nice people. The temperature was always cool.

In the present life, Shannon had a hard time with the heat. She was extremely fair. The heat flushed her cheeks and made her very uncomfortable.

Sam: What was your name?

Shannon: My name starts with an "M." I don't understand it. It's another language other than English.

In this instance, as in most, I did not pursue this detail by telling her that she could speak and understand the language. That would be interesting, but not the reason we were here. The session had been going on for some time and we still had much to do. I now asked her to make the connections between then and now.

Sam: What did you bring forward with you from that past
            life that is affecting you in the present?

Shannon: Anger . . . mistrust . . . pain—right smack dab in the
            middle of me. I seem always to mistrust, even drawn
            to people who can't be trusted. Makes for pretty
            shitty relationships. This way can validate my feel-
            ings. I can do this or that because I knew all along
            you couldn't be trusted. Just get on with it. I'll get
            over it. . . . I was pretty pissed off then.

She now realized she no longer had to attract this type of person.
Shannon saw the connection. She had been so overwhelmed then
that they could have done this . . . friends . . . betrayed her, and now
in the present she had been playing this out in relationships.

Shannon: It wasn't a sheet, was some part of my clothing. I was
            slim, very pretty with light—colored hair. . . . You
            have to be careful with that type of body. *It's a
            dangerous world.* There are good people and bad
            people.

At this point Shannon came to some realizations about her
anger.

Shannon: I don't think I knew why I was angry, confused,
            trying to make things right. . . . It's a different time. I
            died yelling and angry. I was smothered. They choked
            me and so my anger got pushed back in.

Here I gave Shannon some time to leave her anger in the past.
She gave it to the Light. Then she left all the confusion in the
water. When I asked her about the tiredness she felt after her transition, she said:

Shannon: It was just the anger. It seemed to consume me. . . . I
            don't feel heavy now. . . . Maybe they wouldn't have

raped me if I'd been heavier. Maybe I could have
fought them off.

Sam: Do you really feel that would have made a difference,
            you a female and there being two of them?

Shannon: No . . . The weight is to keep people away. That
            makes me unhappy. I don't want to keep people away.

Sam: And you now know you don't have to keep people
            away to stay alive.

Shannon: Yes . . . I don't need to keep people away to stay alive.
            I no longer need the weight.

Sam: And what about the sick feeling in your stomach?

Shannon: It doesn't have anything to do with me eating. It has
            to do with emotions that happened a long time ago.
            Fear, when I'm afraid, nervous, uncomfortable, then I
            eat to make it go away. Stress, too.

Sam: How do you feel now about the statement you made
            when I asked you why do you eat and you said . . . "I
            have no choice?"

Shannon: No one is holding my hands now. I do have a choice
            now. Before I'd go on automatic pilot . . . you have to
            try and save yourself the best way you can. I no
            longer have to do that.

Sam: Yes, because now from this day forward you are in
            control of your life. And you can now open your life
            up to abundance, knowing that you deserve it. You
            are now able to feel really good about yourself. You
            are in control and conscious, making choices for your
            highest good, and that feels really good. You know
            now all of that protection manifesting as weight is no
            longer needed.

At this point I asked Shannon to envision herself in the not
too distant future feeling good about herself on all levels of her
being, looking good, and in conscious control of her life. She related, "I look good, costume looks good, energy is good. I'm dealing with stress. . . . I never thought I could deal this way." (Said

with intense pleasure.) After a pause Shannon said, "I know I can do it . . . I'm doing it."

Here I surrounded Shannon in a golden healing light as we reconnected to the Higher Self, that part of ourselves that is all-knowing, that has all the answers. The golden light filled her body, every cell, every atom, every molecule of her being with love and reinforcement, as she continued to envision her life unfolding at its highest potential, while I made a weight loss tape for her to listen to at least once every day for the next month.

After our session, I did not hear from Shannon for quite some time. When we finally spoke, she said the session had been so powerful that it had "scared the shit" out of her. She had found herself questioning why she had never realized this before on her own. Her feeling that loss of control and an inability to keep herself safe had been very scary. Where the session took her really worked. She did end up losing a lot of weight. However, to continue in this vein meant going into some uncharted territory she had avoided all of her life. Therefore, in the interim since our work, she had put all her weight back on. Shannon affirmed that listening to the tape also really worked, but she just let it all slip away. "I just lost the way. I just couldn't stay on the path."

In the course of our conversation, I reminded Shannon that in this life, she is a person who has willingly walked the edge. Once she has stepped beyond, even though she is in over her head, she will continue on that downward spiral, until at last she comes to her senses and begins the long journey out of the quagmire. Then, comes the rehab period when she recuperates and tries to heal, or as she puts it, "nurses the burns." This *living dangerously* keeps her convoluted and divided, split against herself, trying to remain open, while becoming more cynical and paranoid, as if this self-imposed being out of control is her way of regaining control.

When I averred that this kind of behavior and the time spent dealing with it steals a lot of her creative time and energy, Shannon said quietly, "It's easier to take the short cut through the woods . . . in the shade. I've done a lot of drugs and drink to forget it, to keep it pushed back behind me. I know I need to pass through it, but it's a *rough* walk."

I hope there will come a time when this powerhouse of a woman will be willing to take that walk. I want to be there with her when she does.

XIII

Not for Gold

*Persecution does not make
the just man to suffer,
nor does oppression destroy him
if he is on the right side of Truth.
Socrates smiled as he took poison,
and Stephen smiled as he was stoned.
What truly hurts is our conscience
that aches when we oppose it,
and dies when we betray it.*
— Kahlil Gibran

"If things are going too well then something has to be done. I can't be too successful, then I might have money. So, don't worry, I'll manage to sabotage myself in some way. No doubt. I always do. All my life I have felt apocalyptic, therefore there really is no point to my achieving physical success. Besides, my comfort zone with money isn't very high. Different opportunities have come and I've stayed with them until it was obvious I was doing well or the potential for a future was there. Then of course, it would be time to do myself in. I only allow a certain amount of success and a little bit of money. I need to uncover the cause of this seeming inability to come into my own."

The above were the feelings of Hiram William Sloane. He was forty years old and once again trying to overcome this oft-repeated pattern. Considered successful in his profession, he nevertheless constantly found himself in situations that disintegrated before his eyes in one way or another. He had evolved enough to know that he was the reason this continued to happen. But, he had also reached a point in his life where he knew he had to break the pattern once and for all.

Hiram was a philosophical, spiritual man whom one might easily think of as a mystic. He had meditated for over twenty years and had studied and read much in his metaphysical, philosophical, and mythological pursuits. He was an interesting man with a gentle yet large presence.

Once again, I've left out my obvious questions so as to give the regression transcript more of a flow. As you continue to read, remember Hiram's relationship to money in the present.

Hiram: I'm in a waterfall, behind it. . . . I'm hiding. . . . I feel tense. . . . I have on some kind of shoes . . . metal armor, whole body in armor. I'm male, twenty-five to thirty years old. . . . I'm waiting for someone. . . . I'm waiting for a man. . . . I hear someone coming. I pick up my sword. . . . It's a cardinal, bishop, priest with red outlines on black dress. . . .

Sam: How do you feel toward this person?

Hiram: I'm suspicious. . . . I've liked him before, known him. He wants to work out some kind of deal.

Sam: Who is he to you?

Hiram: He's my brother. He's my father in this lifetime. (These kind of spontaneous connections to individuals in the present life are quite common. Often we are together with the same people, but in different relationships from life to life, always working to balance the karma.) He's with the Vatican. He wants to know where the gold is. I have a long beard. . . . He wants to give me a promise of safety if I tell him where the gold is. I'm being hunted . . . heresy. . . . It's us . . . an order of knights. It's not me in particular. We had too much power. (The emotion started to build here.) It's a trick! He didn't come alone. I won't tell where the gold is. It belongs to the Order. . . . The Crusades are over. It's after that.

Sam: What is the name of the Order?

Hiram: The Order of the Temple of St. John. They're taking me prisoner. My brother betrayed me. I can't believe it!

Sam: What's happening now?

Hiram: We are on horseback now. My hands are tied behind my back. There's rope tied around my chest. Person behind me on a horse is holding it.

Sam: What are your feelings right now?

Hiram: Feeling it is all over . . . the Order.

Sam: What is the purpose of the Order?

Hiram: The purpose of the Order is to protect. The Order fought in the Crusades. . . . We are coming to a castle.

Sam: Where is this castle located?

Hiram: In France. I've seen it before. They pull me off the horse. I'm thrown down dark steps into a very small, muddy, wet room. . . . I take off my armor. . . . There's an emaciated body and I think he's dead. . . . Footsteps coming down the steps. They're taking me back up. The sun is out now.

Sam: What's the next thing that happens?

Hiram: I'm inside now looking up at the ceiling . . . sort of rounded . . . big room. . . . Bunch of men in black are here. I'm in the middle of the room with them around me . . . facing a throne. . . . A male on the throne . . . He must be a bishop, not the pope . . . not black, dressed in pale white with golden embroidery . . . . They want to know where the *gold* is. I'm not telling. I think my brother is outside the room. I don't think he can face me.

Sam: What's the very next thing you are aware of?

Hiram: They're going to torture me. I'm angry at the world. I believe in the Order . . . . I hate these people.

Sam: What's happening now?

Hiram: I'm locked in a little cell. I can't even sit down. It's just big enough for me to stand . . . pressing against my shoulders. They come to get me. I was there while they were preparing something. . . . It's the Order of the Temple of Solomon, not St. John . . . . They're stretching me out, on a rack, feet and hands are tied . . . pulling in opposite directions . . . . A man is pushing on the wheel that tightens . . . . I'm just wearing something like a burlap brown cloak, or something . . . . I feel pain in lower back and . . . shoulders, right shoulder. They're loosening it . . . . I didn't say anything. They're putting something on my feet. They're doing something so I cannot move . . . all my limbs locked in, my head, too. They're bringing AAAAHHHHH!!

Sam: What are they bringing? What's happening?

Hiram: It's red hot, a piece of metal on a longer pole of metal. It's red hot. They're branding me on my right side . . . burning flesh. I scream out, pass out . . . . It makes no sense . . . . It's all *greed*. . . . It's supposed to be about justice, order, maintaining peace. It's the church. It's all political now.

Sam: What's the next thing you're aware of?

Hiram: I'm back in a dungeon. He comes to visit—my brother. He's explaining it's all for the best. The Order is finished. Serves no purpose anymore, he says.

Sam: What do you say?

Hiram: I won't speak to him.

In his work with affirmations to try to give voice to his resistance to money and success in the present, Hiram was told that it had to do with his father, who died two months before this regression, and who had been his brother in this particular past life. His relationship with his father had been difficult. Hiram had found it hard to talk with him about anything personal. It would make them both uncomfortable. Hiram said he loved his father more than anyone else on the planet but you would never know it.

His present-life brother said that Hiram and his dad had "a thing." His father had not been well and Hiram and his young daughter lived with his father and took care of him in his final years. The father had undergone bypass surgery with all kinds of complications and had almost died twice. He had been hospitalized for six weeks.

At that time Hiram determined that he would take care of his father. With this decision, suddenly they opened up and started talking. They grew to be very close. As Hiram put it, *spoken close.* When he did die it was perfect. With his father's death came a release. Hiram felt a big upsurging of energy and realized that his fear of success or failure—he wasn't sure which it was—had started to recede.

Sam: What is your reason for not speaking to your brother?
Hiram: They're not interested in me as a heretic. They are not interested in me repenting anything. *It's the gold.* My brother left. I know if I tell them they will kill me. I think they might kill me anyway.
Sam: What do you do?
Hiram: I pray.
Sam   What happens next?
Hiram: They take me up the stairs, but I can't straighten up. Two of them are sort of carrying me, not gently though . . . . Take me back to the chamber . . . . There's a body hanging on a hook. He has a long beard like me. It was a trait of our Order. It's my brother in the present life. He was a member of the Order . . . . Now I know they are going to kill me.
Sam: What makes you say that?
Hiram: He had been with me before the waterfall. They came

and got some of us. They knew where we were. We were out in the forest somewhere . . . seven of us . . . but I had gone off, scouting or something. It's the afternoon, but they were sleeping. I was up on a ridge. I couldn't see them from there. I was going to the bathroom . . . . Then, I did my prayers. I put on this mantle, white with a red cross over my armor . . . . I came back and they were dead. They killed them sleeping, but the one on the hook is not there. They took him. They took someone else, too. There are only four dead. I know I have to get out of there. I don't have time to bury them. I take off the mantle. I'm on horseback. It's night. I come to this church. I know somebody here. I go around to the side entrance. It's a friend of my brother, the cardinal. He knows him. I ask him to send a message to him to meet me behind the waterfall. (Now he moves on his own, back to the chamber.) That guy cut off my left hand!! . . . a big ax, not too big. They don't even ask me ANYTHING! They just put me down, pulled my arm out and chopped it off . . . . I'm getting very weak . . . . I'm sick of them. I'm not going to tell them, not because I care about the gold, but I'm not going to give them the satisfaction.

Sam: What are your thoughts or feelings right now?

Hiram: It all went wrong. I never believed it would end this way. They're putting me in a hanging cage and they leave. I covered it hard with my right hand to keep it from shooting out blood. It's pretty much stopped now . . . . They are just going to let me die there . . . . I'm dying. . . . *"What did it all mean?"* We were important. We protected the roads. The work of the Order is *Sacred*. We are not just warriors. We were taught things . . . they had brought back from Jerusalem . . . the Middle East . . . breathing techniques. We are meditators. . . . *"What did it all mean?"* There was something like glory and now it's all gone. . . . *All greed* . . . But, I still love my brother. They would have killed him if he didn't do it.

Sam: What's happening with you now?

Hiram: I'm all scrunched up in this cage. My left arm is throbbing. My back is killing me . . . I'm dead.

Sam: What is your final thought, your last conscious thought before you made your transition?

Hiram: I don't want anything to do with politics, or money, or Orders. It's all a waste. I just want peace.

Sam: Now, that you've made your transition, what are you aware of?

Hiram: It's all bright . . . . Feel good. There are lots of Beings all around me. From here it makes sense, all that happened to me, and it's okay. It's almost like looking at a play. There's a Light Being showing that to me, that this is how it's written. I see her. She's all Light. . . . It's me. . . . She's the one . . . she's blonde . . . . Oh, I've dreamed of her. It was like I was coming to her, but that's what I was. That's my Higher Self. . . . *You are within and One with your Higher Self.* Feels great . . . kind of emotional, but great. Can always at any time connect with your Higher Self.

Sam: Is there a message that your Higher Self has for you at this time?

Hiram: "There's no fear." Even that this day had to wait until this day. It's right that it's NOW. The strength from that life was the dedication to a spiritual life. That was the good that came out of it.

Sam: Now feel this energy that is the Higher Self descend upon you and within you like a mantle. From this perspective become aware of the attachments and connections to this past life that you brought with you into the present.

Hiram: I was the treasurer and was connected with the gold, kept it in a castle, but they moved it when the Order was done away with. A bunch of the knights got it. It was put on a ship heading for Scotland. . . . Now, I don't want to be around too much of it, even your brother will betray you.

Sam: Good. Now leave that thought form in the past. You can do anything you want to with it. (Hiram decides he will put it in the river.) What else?

Hiram: I can be spiritual and have funds needed to function in a spiritual incarnation.

Sam: Excellent. Next?

Hiram: My brother, who is my father now, I see why I was here with him in his final months. . . . I didn't want him to feel bad then. It was bigger than him. I wanted him to feel forgiven, but I never got to talk to him. . . . I now see why it was difficult to talk until close to the end in the present.

Sam: Any other attachments?

Hiram: Yes . . . that feeling in the present of "What does it all mean?" . . . That was my dying thought then.

Sam: Leave it in the past.

Hiram: Also, my stiff lower back.

Sam: Okay. Now you know you can let it go. Anything else?

Hiram: Yeah, I can't join a society or group. I've always had deep antagonism toward groups. . . . And, these jobs I didn't get . . . they were too much of a group thing.

Sam: Do you now realize this will no longer be a problem?

Hiram: Yes . . . Also, when I was twenty-one years old a car radiator blew up and hit me on my right side. It was so painful. I was immediately aware of the karmic connection.

Sam: Great. Now I want you to envision a time in the not too distant future when you are functioning at your highest potential, free to be all that you are capable of being.

After a few minutes to allow him to do this, I then asked him to once again feel that connection to his Higher Self and any further message his Higher Self would like him to have.

Hiram: "Be free."

With that our work was finished and Hiram is now moving forward in his life, released from the fear that had kept him from being a successful human being.

For further edification, it is known that the Knights Templar of Solomon were so named because they had occupied quarters near the site of Solomon's Temple in Jerusalem. They were a military religious order of Crusaders established in the early twelfth century under the direct authority of the Pope. This meant they were exempt from royal and episcopal control. The knights often received lavish gifts of land and money and sometimes grew wealthy enough to act as bankers of kings.

In 1307, Philip the IV, known as the Fair of France, suddenly ordered the arrest of all Templars in his dominions. Torture was used to extract confessions of innumerable crimes, including heresy, and witchcraft. The king, it appears, fell desperately short of money and needed an excuse to seize the *gold* and wealth of the Knights Templar. The knights were totally suppressed in a few years time.

It's intriguing to ponder if this was historically the situation in which Hiram found himself so many years ago.

XIV

Guilt, Guilt, and More Guilt

*What you see and feel
is your own creation.*
— Baba Hari Dass

Guilt is an insidious and dangerous weapon that people in large numbers wield against themselves and each other. Those in our society often spout, "God will punish you for that," but it isn't really God who does the punishing. It is ourselves. We feel the need to balance the scales, to do penance, to make amends by torturing ourselves for our past misdeeds.

Such was the case with Nancy Dugan, guilt being the driving force that set her up to spend most of her life in two abusive marriages. She had earlier been sexually abused by an older brother from the time she was eleven years old and had her first menses. In the beginning, the rape hadn't occurred that often, but then it got to be once a day, sometimes more. This brother's violent behavior hurt Nancy. She soon realized that if she didn't fight him, he wouldn't act as mean. The sexual abuse continued for four years, until she became pregnant.

At this point she told her mother, who had to have known what was going on but who had chosen not to help her. When confronted with the pregnancy, her mother told Nancy's oldest brother, who then came to the house. The abusive brother threat-

ened to kill Nancy for telling, and did beat her up "pretty good."
Telling obviously hadn't helped her. So Nancy started having sex
with other boys. Her oldest brother then tried to have sex with
her. Nancy's father had died when her mother was pregnant with
Nancy. Her stepfather had divorced her mother. So there were no
other authority figures to step in.

Once Nancy became pregnant, social services removed her
from the house and placed her with a Mormon family. There she
had the baby and gave it up for adoption. After this, her brother
joined the Air Force, behaved with extreme violence, and was eventually thrown out for raping a girl. Later he kidnapped and raped
another young woman and was committed finally to a mental hospital.

Nancy married this brother's friend for "protection" and continued to endure a life of verbal and mental abuse that had begun
with this same brother when she had been very young. Her brother
had tortured animals and made her watch, had built her a playhouse so he could burn it down, had made her stay outside freezing in the snow, and when she became pregnant he had become so
angry that he had tried to kill the baby, beating her stomach as he
raped her.

Nancy's divorce from her first husband had been traumatic
after twenty years of marriage. She had not been able to face that
first divorce. But with her second divorce, everything came back,
including all the years of abuse. She remembered that when her
brother had tried to rape her younger stepsister Nancy had
screamed, but no one had come. Her mother had ignored anything in life that she couldn't handle, just staying put in her warped
dream world. Nancy hated her mother for a long time for letting
this abuse go on. Once she had left home, she never went back
until after her mother had died. Amazingly, Nancy still felt guilty
about that, that she didn't go back at the end of her mother's life,
when her mother was suffering. She felt she should have gone back,
but she didn't. She couldn't.

Now, after a lifetime of abuse, Nancy wanted to know why
she let herself remain the victim. Why did she feel so weak that she

let herself be used? What did she ever do to deserve the punishment that she had endured? This punishment never stopped. She had had lots of encounters with men since her early abuse by her brother. She continued to let men use her. The last one took total advantage of her, even after she had bailed him out of jail. He stole her car. She found herself four house payments behind.

She herself saw the pattern. Her first husband had been very domineering, as both her mother and her second husband had been. She was afraid of them and kept repeating the same pattern, letting them run her life, self-sacrificing, giving a lot and getting very little back.

Nancy sought help because she found herself having trouble functioning at work after a particular man became her boss. As she put it, he sickened her. She saw him as evil, and without any known cause she felt that she hated him. After about fifteen months of enduring this man, she finally had all she could stand. Symptoms started to manifest one day when she entered his office. He asked her if she shouldn't go lie down. As she left the room, she felt as though a knife were going through her back and out her chest. Her feet and hands went numb. Her supervisor called Nancy's daughters. Her heart was skipping beats. The doctor told her she had experienced a panic attack.

One of the hardest things she ever had to do was to go back to work. She was terrified of it happening again, this feeling that had come over her, closing in on her chest, then tightening up, and climaxing with a pain in her back.

As his secretary, Nancy had told this man that he was a vengeful person, always trying to get back at people, seeing everyone as the enemy. To make it worse, he seemed to enjoy telling her the bad things he was doing, but he told her in a nice sort of way.

With all of this background information, we were now ready to begin our work. We humans are utterly amazing. We go to such great lengths in order to punish ourselves. Nancy is certainly a prime example of this tendency. When we came through the tunnel, approaching the light at the end through which we would step into the cause lifetime, Nancy immediately stated that she was not allowed to see the light. When I asked why, she said that she had not prayed hard enough, that she wasn't as holy as she should be. There were times home in bed when she could see the light and connect to it. But she was afraid of it, because the light would take her to a place that frightened her, so she would dismiss it.

Next, I told her she was standing in front of a door through which she would step into the cause lifetime of this guilt that she carried. She described the door as yellow. It was a house door. She stood barefoot and her feet were cold. She felt grass down there, swampy grass, dark and muddy and wet. It didn't feel good on her bare legs. She saw nothing, but she was aware of her body. It did not feel right. It was not shaped like her body. She described it as weird up and down, white in different spots, not formed. Her arms felt too long. It was an old person's body. She couldn't see the head, but dark spots with pink in them. The arms looked weak and the body concave.

When something like this starts to happen it's important to realize that this is the way the subconscious mind imparts information at this point. Just let it unfold. A good technique to use is simply to ask, "If that body could speak, what would it say?" When I did this, she responded that it was not human or dead. It remained stuck in the mud and unable to move. (This could certainly be seen as a true metaphor for her present life.) She continued to describe this body as spindly with no face. She perceived the shape of a head with white hairs sticking out. The body was brown and the head was brown.

She now declared, "It's me. I'm different now. There is a light shining out of me, a light shining away from me. The light is coming back to me. It's coming out of something, a hole in front of me." When I asked her what this light represented, she stated that it meant energy.

I now asked her the reason for being here in this swampy, muddy, dark place. She replied that it didn't feel good at all being here. At first, she thought she could be a being from another planet. She felt she had been here for a long time and said that it didn't seem to bother her that much because she could see something else, kind of yellow, kind of orange, kind of like the sky all around her, kind of like a planet or something, other than Earth, something dark yellow and brown and with things sticking up, tubes, which were part of the planet. She described spots on it, like craters. "I'm there . . . on the dark side of it." Metaphorically, we might say that her subconscious had given her a picture of how she perceived herself. Now we could see her unable to come through as who she really was as she took on the identity of the victim. In this way she found herself able to tap into the problem lifetime.

Nancy:	I've tried to get out of the mud and my feet won't come up. They feel stuck. I've lifted up my foot and stepped out . . . walked. I can see my boots. They are mine. (Here is a clue that they may not be hers.) I'm a little girl. I've got boots on, black and big . . . heavy. They fit me.

She wanted the boots she saw to be the little girl's as she wanted herself to be the little girl. She had spent her present life being the little girl.

Nancy:	I have a dress on. It's full; it sticks out. There's an apron on it. The dress is brown plaid, brown with a white apron.
Sam:	How old are you?
Nancy:	I'm five years old.
Sam:	Where are you? Are you inside or outside?
Nancy:	Inside . . . I don't think I like it here. I'm by myself. There are things on the wall, black harness, things for the heat, for the stove. The floor is wood. The walls are wood. I'm sitting down on the floor. I'm a happy child. (Starts to cry.) I'm so cute. I have curls, a bonnet; my hair is brown. I have brown eyes, black eyelashes.
Sam:	What are you doing?

Nancy: I'm sitting there. Spoons, chain . . . the room is
            smaller than it ought to be. Big room in a house, but
            seems to get smaller. There's a coal bin, cellar maybe.
            Not there long.

    Now she needed to do another switch. We were getting too
close.

Sam: What's happening now?
Nancy: I've grown big. I'm a young woman.
Sam: Where are you?
Nancy: I'm outside, in a carriage, sitting down on a piece of
            wood. No horse. I'm alone. I feel shut out. I've been
            locked out. . . . This man . . . (Immediately starts
            moaning.) Oh, noooo. (Crying.) I don't like that
            man. I don't like that man. (She is very emotional.) I
            see his boot. He's got high riding boots on. (Here is
            the real owner of the boots.)
Sam: Yes, and what else?
Nancy: Brown hair and long sideburns, mustache, brown
            eyes . . . He's John, my husband. (Now, she flips back
            to the little girl.) We were in a room together . . . a
            riding stick . . . I saw it before. He had it in his hand.

    Here she hesitated. I asked her to move forward to the next
important event and she once again left the little girl.

Nancy: I love John . . . I'm young. I don't think I've been
            married very long. I can see John standing there,
            taking the whip and hitting it in his hand. . . . He
            keeps doing that. (This is greatly upsetting her.) I
            know he's angry. I don't know why.
Sam: Ask him why he's angry.
Nancy: (In a thick Southern accent, very unlike her current
            voice, Nancy speaks.) "John, why are you angry at
            me? Why won't you tell me? You know you could tell

me. . . . John, please tell me. John, why won't you tell me something? John!"

Throughout this pleading with John, Nancy became extremely emotional. Here something dramatic happened. John spoke in a deeper, different voice, very emotionally. "You know I can't tell you anything!"

Nancy: "Please, please, please tell me what is it? What is it?!"

At this point, the boundaries broke down. With deep, deep emotion Nancy realized John's identity.

Nancy: *I'm John! I'm John!* (This realization terrified Nancy.)
Sam: Get in touch with why you are so afraid.

Nancy began to emit a deep whine that slowly moved into wailing that continued for a while. I let this old pent-up emotion come out and I again asked her why she felt so afraid. She at first claimed that she was numb and that she didn't know. I told her that yes she did know and it was time to face it.

Nancy: (Reluctantly.) I'm John. . . . I'm this terrible man. I'm so bad.
Sam: What have you, John, done that makes you so terrible?

Nancy's head started to move from side to side, as if trying to push the truth away. Finally, she managed to utter:

Nancy: I killed somebody.

Then she immediately refused to believe it.

Nancy: No, no, surely I didn't kill anybody. Surely . . . I didn't do that . . . no way.

Here Nancy went through classic denial. She was battling the horrific truth that she on some level knew she had to face. Yet, refusing to accept, she continued to move in and out of denial, edging closer each time to the ultimate reality that had haunted her, the reality for which she had punished herself over and over again in the present life, by choosing to come into her present-life circumstances and by refusing to honor herself. For how can she honor someone who has done such a foul deed? Now, she had to face herself and her past actions, and forgive herself.

Sam:	If, indeed, you did kill someone, who would it have been?
Nancy:	There's a picture in my mind, a child, lying down near the grave.
Sam:	Who is this child to you?
Nancy:	I don't know this child. I don't have a clue.

She said this with the inflection of one caught with her hand in the cookie jar and yet denying that a cookie jar existed. I waited. Slowly, gradually, the truth rose to the surface, emotion growing with each repetition.

Nancy:	It's dead. . . . It's dead! . . . It's dead!!
Sam:	How did the child die?
Nancy:	Not me. (Said very quickly.)
Sam:	Do you believe in God?

My intuition prompted me to say this, due to the way she had started the session. It worked.

Nancy:	I believe in God. (Crying.)

Now, all the guilt that she had held within her cellular memory all this time came pouring out.

Nancy: Dear Lord, help me. Please, help me God. Oh God, I
           need you so. Please help me. Forgive me, Lord God,
           please forgive me of my sins.

Sam: It's not God who needs to forgive you. God doesn't
           judge you. It's you. You need to forgive yourself.

Nancy: (Here she flipped back into total denial.) I don't
           know what I've done. I don't know what I've done.

This was like watching two very distinct personalities battle
for control.

Sam: Yes, you do. You know.
Nancy: I keep thinking about a well.
Sam: What about the well?
Nancy: I have two daughters.

Nancy moved back and forth between time frames, now in
the present, when her children were small like the little girl.

Sam: How old are they?
Nancy: Three years old . . . (She again switched, adamantly
           stating . . .) I don't know anything!!!

The most difficult part of this memory for Nancy to deal with
was that a child's life had been taken, and by her.

Sam: Let's move forward to your death, to the death of
           John.

Nancy: I'm in the woods. I've been here a long time . . . since
           the death of the child.

Sam: How do you feel?
Nancy: I feel all right. I don't feel like I'm going to die.
Sam: What are you doing?
Nancy: Walking down a path. I had a little house there. It's a
           beautiful day. The sun is shining . . . I'm afraid to
           die. I don't want to die. It will hurt.

Sam: Let's move forward to the moments right before your
          death.
Nancy: Wind is blowing. I'm lying down and John is lying
          down.

She obviously needed to separate from John and so she stopped
speaking in first person.

Nancy: He's cold. The snow and the frost . . . lying down,
          outside, by a tree . . . I don't want to be John. . . . I
          don't want to be a man who . . . died with something
          on his mind.
Sam: Was that something guilt?
Nancy: (Very emotional.) YES! YES!! . . . Father forgive
          me . . . *I HURT SOMEBODY!!!* I'm sorry, Father. I
          hurt a child, in the chest, right at the solar plexus.
          The pain . . . I've carried it with me. I hurt her.

Nancy released all of this information in a state of high emotion. Then, speaking as Nancy she said, "I love children so much."
     John wanted to be forgiven. He was very, very sorry. He was
never punished for it. He put the child in a well. She was already
dead. And, no, he did not sexually abuse the child.

Sam: What happened? How did you hurt her?
Nancy: The child was playing by the fire in the room. She
          had a little thing. She was playing with a ball or
          something. She was playing quietly. There's some
          kind of stick, brown, round on end.

     Reliving this scene proved extremely emotional for Nancy
and not in her best interests. Normally, I would have the client
go through step by step whatever the situation might be, since
great release can occur in the reexperiencing. But in this particular situation such reexperiencing did not feel appropriate, so
I asked Nancy's Higher Self if it was necessary for Nancy to

reexperience the actual death of the child. The answer was as I suspected.

We then dealt with Nancy's attachments to that life, the connections that affected the present. Guilt was an enormous issue. We spent time understanding that John did not deliberately try to kill the child and that the time had come to forgive John, to forgive herself. She realized that she had chosen this hellacious present-life circumstance because she had somehow hurt a child whom she had loved, and so chose to suffer as a child in the present, so she could feel punished for her past misdeed. It seemed that she may have overshot the mark, choosing a punishment so severe, and yet chosen by herself for herself, due to her overwhelming sense of *guilt*. When Nancy felt ready, when she had released all the emotion around this past life, she decided to shove all of her guilt into a box and leave it in the past, knowing she would never open it or look at it again.

Another connection to the past was all the pain that Nancy had carried in the present life, particularly in her solar plexus, which naturally is the seat of emotion. She chose to put all of this pain in a trunk that had a key and lock, leaving it in the past, knowing this, too, she would never open again.

It remained difficult for Nancy to get rid of the suffering, to let it go. She had suffered her whole life in a futile effort to make amends. Finally, she could place this suffering in a drawer, in a cupboard in the past.

Nancy realized that part of the reason her boss had set off the panic attack was that he looked a lot like John. It's no wonder she felt the urgent need to get away from him. She also felt that she was the only one who saw his evil. Knowing that it would not be in her best interests to leave her job, I asked Nancy to let her Higher Self be her guide. Her Higher Self told her she needed to be strong, to find a way to leave, or allow herself not to be bothered anymore. She needed to deal with his evil, yet not let it affect her.

Nancy: I need to be able to look at him in a different type of light, as not evil, but as a human being who has lost his soul. I've known all along that I could help this man, but I thought that he was so evil that he didn't deserve that. I never said or did anything that would let him know that I was on to him, that I *understood* him. I knew what made him that way—*self-hatred.*

We now, with the help of Nancy's Higher Self, worked to see him in a different light. We spent time having Nancy envision the not too distant future, seeing herself dealing with him in a way that could free them both into the light of love and acceptance.

Sixteen days later I received a call from Nancy telling me about an amazing change that had taken place. That horrible feeling had lifted. She could talk to her boss without it bothering her. And, because a director stepped into her department, her boss planned to leave! Before our session, she had been job hunting. Now, not only could she tolerate her boss, but she could stay right where she was. The panic attacks were gone, and she was very grateful for the work we were able to do together.

It's always so amazing how a person will step into our lives to jog a memory loose from our subconscious, a memory that then allows us to let go of the past and heal. I often wonder who that boss might have been in Nancy's past. What kind of karma did he owe her to come into her life as he did, setting this guilt in motion so that it could be healed, and she could finally move beyond it?

Cosmic threads bind us one to the other. We are all a part of this incredible fabric, interwoven in such complex patterns. I've often thought how insightful it would be to see the patterns, the web of our being, our Akashic record. Perhaps we can see this pattern from another dimension, as I'm sure we do on the other side. But to do so now, in an Earth incarnation, would take away our freedom of choice. If we could, I can assure you that if our intent here is to evolve, we would all be rushing about making peace with whomever for whatever, using our Akashic record as a road map of our life's choices. But, that's not the way it's meant to be. We need to act from a state of *being* in the Now.

XV

Where Comes Courage

As the Druids know,
it is the belief of mankind
which shapes the world,
and all of reality.
— Merlin, *The Mists of Avalon*

Katie Harrison came to see me because she felt displaced and inadequate, with an overwhelming sense of dread with which she woke daily. She described this sense of dread as a Capricorn feeling, meaning morose and dark, that made it hard for her to get out of bed. "Just let me die in the night. I want to run, to bail out . . . I feel no joy in my life. . . . Why don't I trust myself . . . love myself? Why don't I have the confidence and courage to be myself?" She expressed a need to find her own identity. In her family situation she felt as though she had to choose. "I choose me or I choose them," she said. "I don't want it to be that way." She hinted at another important issue when she stated, "I've always resented having to depend on men . . . always looking for someone else for my source, for my happiness."

Interestingly, Katie appeared to be a bouncy, vibrant ball of energy and considered herself unconventional. Metaphysically oriented, she sought to grow as a spiritual person. She had been in her second marriage for eight years and felt as though her husband was living his life, but she had been left out. She had a young child with whom she felt a deep soul connection, and she devoted much of her energy to him.

Katie experienced headaches and jaw discomfort that had escalated to the point of being chronic and debilitating. She believed that these pains gave her an out for not being herself, representing a pattern of maxing herself out and then using her physical pain as an excuse for not doing. Problems with her jaw had started at age eighteen. According to Louise Hay's great little book *Heal Your Body*, the metaphysical reasons behind jaw problems are anger, resentment, and the desire for revenge. Headaches relate to invalidating the self, criticism and fear. Both issues speak to the need to love and approve of the self, to be willing to break the pattern that is creating the condition, and to allow oneself to feel safe.

We are going to look at two past-life regressions that Katie experienced. Katie proved to be an excellent subject, being very present in the past, both emotionally and physically. Information poured forth from her with little prompting. The first regression happened chronologically after the second, but linear time is irrelevant in this regard. We are simply going to the cause lifetime, the lifetime that can give us the most insight, awareness, and resolution around a particular issue. However, both lifetimes share some of the same issues.

Katie found herself outside, standing on the corner of a city street in front of an old apartment building, looking across the street at a building being built, a hospital. She felt like exploring. She then saw herself inside big glass doors at the front of this building. The number above the doors read 623. She commented that she was reading it backward. She saw the entrance as wood with a marble floor and wooden staircase. She thought it was the 1930s. Here she started to cry.

Katie: I don't know why I'm here, but it makes me feel
            sad. . . . Something keeps drawing me outside, but I
            want to stay in. . . .

Sam:	What is it that's making you sad?
Katie:	It's new, it's changing. It's making my life change. I think we are going to have to leave because the new building is going to take over our place. I just keep looking at the front of the building. I have to say goodbye. It's like a moment I just don't want to let go of. I keep telling myself it will be all right.
Sam:	Are you alone or is someone with you?
Katie:	I don't see anybody. . . . The new building has a wooden fence around it.

Katie started to go back and forth in linear time. At times she seemingly had already made her transition, and at others she spoke from before her death. She originally looked at this building at some point after her transition, noting its construction as a hospital.

Sam:	And who are you in relation to this building?
Katie:	I'm a child. (Crying.) I'm about ten. I don't know that anyone is in this building anymore. I just came back to look at this building. The floor is not marble. It's those little white and black checkerboard squares. . . . I think I'll go upstairs.
Sam:	What are your thoughts or feelings about going up the stairs?
Katie:	Thoughts are I'm not supposed to go up the stairs, but stay in this room that's like a big parlor. It's on the left as you go in the door. It has a big fireplace, still furniture in there. . . . The *sadness* is just in the hall. It's winter. I have a coat and hat on. It feels hard to breathe for some reason. (More tears, coughing.)
Sam:	What's making it difficult for you to breathe?
Katie:	I'm just standing here. I'm not waiting for anyone. I just feel so alone, but I want to be here with me. I want to stay here. They're destroying the building and I can't breathe because of all the plaster filling the

air. I don't want to go. I don't want to leave because this is my home. . . . I feel very anxious, and I'm not going to have time to say goodbye, to finish what I'm doing . . . I'm very tense. I've got to decide. I want to hide, but I know I'm not supposed to go in the house. *My left jaw is feeling very tight.* . . . I'm . . . tension . . . I'm moving out of my body. I'm sitting down on the steps, clutching my knees, all tingling . . . feel release. I'm all alone, looking out the front, see trees with no leaves on them, and other houses across the street that are different from my house. They have round balls that are decorative. They're all two-story. . . . I feel scared.

Sam: What's causing you to feel scared?

Katie: I'm going to have to go. . . . I'm going to have to go out. I'm going to have to leave . . . I just know I have to! It's so empty. It's like an evacuation or something. I know I'm not supposed to go in the house. They won't see me if I go in the house. (She is extremely anxious and feels pulled in two directions.)

Sam: Who are "*they*"?

Katie: Soldiers. (Cries.) . . . I didn't want to say that. The building across the street has been bombed and they just put those boards up to keep everybody out. . . . This is a nice house. I'm afraid. . . . I feel this heaviness in my chest. I'm afraid to go on. I just want to stay here where I feel safe. But, I don't want to hide. I know this is a wealthy home . . . really nice home. I feel like they might come marching around the window any minute. I don't want to hide.

Sam: What are you feeling right now?

Katie: I just want to be here. I'm afraid of what I'll find. I feel like I'm ready to say goodbye. (Sobbing.) I don't want this house destroyed. I want to hold on to it. It's not even the memories, it's the *security*.

Sam: Okay, now I want you to move forward to the next

significant moment.

Katie: It was a lot of white light, and it started in my head
           and chest. It's coming back. It's cold on my
           mouth . . . the air . . . it's external . . . it's on my
           neck, too, and it's going up to my eyes. It's freezing
           me, my hands, am I freezing? It's . . . my hands are
           all . . . I don't have any protection . . . I can't breathe.
           It's from my chest, my eyes, it's suffocating . . . it's
           choking me. I'm very scared. I feel it moving down
           into my chest. It's a big vibration in my chest . . . my
           eyes and face . . . it's all . . .

This experience of Katie's was both intense and confusing. She
didn't know what was happening to her.

Katie: It's in my throat. It might be from behind. I feel very
           tense. I'm fighting it. I'm getting warmer. That
           feeling is gone. It's . . . shall I die? Whiteness is still
           there. Tense in shoulders and body. I'm tingling. I
           fought, but I didn't win. Why would someone want
           to kill me?

Sam: Who killed you?

Katie: The man killed me. He had white gloves on. He was
           choking me. (The man neither did the choking nor
           the killing as we see later.) I'm vibrating now . . . my
           arms. I'm in my house. I'm looking at my body. It's
           in a little pile by the stairs right where I was. It's just
           a little clump, just humped over in a little ball. He
           has a uniform on. It looks like a marine uniform . . .
           hat with black rim, real hard . . . little gold tassels,
           that cross in front. He is there. He's looking down on
           me and he's sad. I don't understand. Who are you? I
           don't know him well. He's not my brother. He's my
           friend. He's going to take the little girl . . . her
           hands . . . pick her up. I don't think she's dead. I
           don't know if he did it. He was on the stairs walking

down in front of me, picks me up, carrying me, head on his shoulder. He's a big man. There's stuff on the floor, plaster and stuff. He's having to walk over it carefully. He has on white gloves. I'm not bleeding or anything. I'm ready to go with him, but I'm still watching him carry me. He's right at the door.

Sam: I want you to go back to the trauma. Be aware of what happened to you.

Katie: (Tears.) I want to say a bomb . . . the glass. I'm afraid the glass is going to hit me. It's going to come in. It's going to break. I didn't want it to. I don't want my house (her security) to be ruined. I want to scream, but I can't, because I can't breathe! It's in the air. It's light, flashing in the light, and it's blowing up everything! (High emotion.) Everybody is running down the street. They're running onto the truck. . . . I'm alone. I'm by myself. I feel it coming, but I don't know what to do. I'm afraid to go upstairs. It's white. It's light again. It's cold . . . my face, my lips. The heat from the explosion. I don't think it's the . . . It's coming down the street . . . the bomb . . . it consumes everything as it comes. I can feel it around the corner down the street, but I can't see it. It's going to come. I'm already gone when it happens. Everything is falling apart. So much dust and plaster in the air. I can't breathe. Oh, my God, so many fears I have this time (referring to present life). I'm holding it back. I can feel it in my shoulder. I need to let it come—the destruction. It's like I'm holding it back. It's like a ball about two stories high. That's what . . . was waiting for, not the soldiers. I can't do anything . . . the light, the tingling on my hands, my face. I'm resisting it. I have clothes on everywhere else, but my hands and face. It's the glass, tiny pieces of glass on my eyes, face, and hands. It's tingling and it's cold. The light goes from my head and I'm out of my body. I'm out. But, I still feel my eyes and tingling hands. It's gone by. It's such a heavy vibration. It was trucks. They were firing into the buildings. They're destroying everything. I'm afraid to look. It's the red cross, the swastika, on the front doors of big cattle trucks. They're just standing in the back shooting everything. The bomb is me. It's the fear . . . but I *stayed* there, I didn't run. It was my right. I had a right. It's my home. I wanted to be there.

In actuality there was a bomb, but Katie also referred to her fear as if it were a bomb. At this point Katie moved backward in time.

Katie: My neighbors are running. My mother is screaming. "Run!! Faster!" They're starting to pull out. She's in the truck, but I don't want to go. I don't know what I want. I want to stay in my home. I made a choice to stay. I'm sad to see my mommy go. She's screaming, but someone is holding her. She's in the middle of the truck. I have this feeling like really bad indiges-tion. A man is holding her. It's not my father. My father is not here. He left before. Why did Daddy go? There's no other children. *My jaw is hurting now.* Chest is cold. My mommy is gone. My daddy had to go before. It's *very bad* when he leaves. It's very emotional. They're making him leave.

Sam: Who's making him leave?

Katie: Soldiers. I'm watching him from the same place I was *before* (on the stairs, in the hall, with the sadness). He's a professor, a very prominent man. He knows something. He's a scientist. He's my daddy. (Crying.) He's telling me he'll be back for me. *That's why I stayed.* That's why I had to wait in front. He wouldn't be able to find me if I left. He said, "I'll be back for you." My knees are warm and my hands are tingling. I feel funny. I feel . . . I feel

sad. I love you Daddy. I love you, Daddy. They're
making him go. They are tearing him away. That's why
I can't trust men! My daddy *never* came back. (Spontaneous realizations like this are common in the course of
a regression.) It wasn't his fault. He loves me very much.
I just wish I could see him one more time. I'm by
myself. My mom isn't even there. She's not even
consoling me. She's so wrapped up in her own grief.
She's fighting. She's hitting the soldiers. My granny and
grandpa are holding her back. My daddy . . . It's
nighttime. They take him. "I love you Daddy." He
wants to come and hold me now more than anything in
the whole world. It's like the love my daddy has for me
is what keeps me going. Let's me know it's going to be
all right. He didn't want to go. I can feel his heart and
my heart. It's Willy. (Willy is Katie's young son in the
present life.) Our eyes are connected until they drag
him around the corner.

Sam: He does come back to you, as soon as he could, as
         your son, Willy, in your very next life.

Katie: (Really pleased.) We always give each other energy
         through our eyes. Willy is six years old now.

Sam: How much time passes between your daddy being
         taken away and your dying?

Katie: Eighteen months between Daddy leaving and me
         dying in the hall. I was about eight when he left. In
         this present life, I've had nightmares all my life of
         trucks, and planes, and bombs, one reason why I'm
         scared of earthquakes. (Katie lives, not easily, in
         California.)

Katie later realized that the nightmares about war had actually started when her family moved to a *new* house when she was
eight years old and in the third grade.

Here I asked Katie to connect with her Higher Self and make
the connections she needed to make between then and now. As is

often the case, Katie experienced trauma in the present life at the same age as that of her death in the past life. At age ten she fell on her neck while tumbling and was paralyzed for three minutes. She also experienced air raid drills during the Kennedy years when she was ten years old. She had a bomb shelter for the family under her bed, so she felt she wouldn't have to go through that again.

Katie realized her feeling of being displaced in the present came from her experience of a threat being right around the corner—the bomb, the trucks, the soldiers . . . death. "I died when I was all alone and I believed in that power of love so much." Expecting her daddy to return even though he couldn't had fueled her feeling of resentment toward men.

Katie: The reason I can't trust myself now is that I did then what I felt was right and it killed me. I made a choice to stay. . . . I probably was more quickly reunited with my father in this life because I did die. The soldier who came to get me was Daddy. He was perfect. That's why he had white gloves. He couldn't come before because he was dead. But he was there for me as soon as I died. That's why when the marine picked me up there was so much light in my head and neck area. I made the best choice I could. Worse things would have happened in the truck.

Sam: Do you see the connection between then and now regarding your jaw?

Katie: Yes, I was so tense, so anxious, fighting so hard to hold it back. When I died still carried that tension, and brought it into the present life, still manifesting it in my jaw.

Sam: What other attachments are there?

Katie: We were different, our family. Our religion, Jewish, made us different. It was hard because everybody wasn't. People made fun of me and I knew it, which made me feel isolated. I was an only child. We had different rules, different because we were richer. We had a live-in nanny. Everybody else didn't. It was our house. The other buildings were apartment buildings mostly.

Sam: What do you need to let go of around this?

Katie: I need to let go of feelings of being different and isolated. I don't feel love because I'm different, feel rejected. I need to let go of the deep sadness of dying so young—so much to give and I never had the chance. Our house was a fortress. It kept me in and them out. I lived alone and isolated with four adults, not a lot of joy or play. So much sadness. My mother was locked in fear. I did learn the violin. My grandfather taught me that.

But after Katie's father had been taken away, while her mother and grandmother were out trying to buy food, her grandfather molested her. A member of the family, he had been her music teacher, a man whom she could trust, one with whom she could supposedly be safe. After that one incident she never let him give her another music lesson and she made sure never to be alone with him again. She didn't trust him or want to get close to him, yet he was the only man in the house. The *man* is supposed to provide a feeling of protection and security.

Sam: Is there anything around your grandfather's actions toward you that you need to be aware of?

Katie: Yes. Men just want what they want and do what they need to do to get it. They are not to be trusted with my emotions.

In the present life, this same soul had been her first husband, who constantly insisted on having sex.

Sam: I want you to leave those feelings in the past.

Katie: I won't bury them. I'm going to burn them.

Sam: What else do you need to let go of?

Katie: Every day waking up dreading that day, because it
            may be the last day. I hear the adults talk at night
            time, when they think I'm asleep. Everything could
            have died every day. I'll just keep filling up that grave
            in the backyard. (This is where she has been leaving
            the things of the past.)
Sam: Anything else?
Katie: Allegiance to religion. (In the present life her father is
            a Protestant minister.) Family is the thorn that causes
            the division from what you really want. The connec-
            tion to this life is that now I feel if I do for the family,
            I can't do for me. . . . There was very little freedom in
            that life. Maybe that is why I am so unconventional
            now.

At this point I asked her if she needed to let go of anything
else in this past-life experience. We scanned that lifetime once again
to be sure. We then determined that her name had been Nadia
and that she had lived in Strausberg, Germany. Strausberg is almost halfway between Berlin and the Polish border.

When the client is guided into memories of the present-life
prenatal period, birthing experience, and early childhood, triggers
to particular past-life issues need to be discovered and acknowl-
edged. One might ask why it is that we have these specific issues
to deal with in the present lifetime as opposed to other issues. It
seems that this decision is determined by what the soul is exposed
to during the time it is carried in its mother's womb. These expo-
sures restimulate particular patterns, certain past-life issues from
among the many karmic avenues that may yet remain unresolved.
In Katie's case, while in the womb she was exposed to a television
or radio show about the holocaust.

Also, she heard her maternal grandfather ask her pregnant
mother if she was sure she really wanted this child so soon after
getting married. Katie responded to this question with a strong
feeling of *disappointing father*, and of again having men in control.
She started wondering why she was coming into this life, and sec-

ond guessing whether she should. Her mother harbored a fear of the "end times," due to her religion, and felt a sense of *dread* about bringing in a new life. Naturally, Katie picked up this sense of dread. Toward the end of the pregnancy she also felt very confined and started to really dread coming out. Katie said the way she felt right before being born was the way she wakes up every morning, with a dread of the day, wishing she could just stay asleep and not be born. This is a very common feeling, prevalent when the soul feels unwanted or dreads coming in.

The birthing experience proved to be hard and long. Her *jaw* was hurting on both sides. She found herself facing another choice. Should I go forward, should I go back? Experiencing some problems with breathing, she couldn't catch her breath. She fought to stay in the womb, just as she had fought with herself to stay in the building. She immediately made a connection of not being able to breathe when the bomb had hit. After the regression Katie asked her mother about her birth and discovered that the sudden jaw pain was a result of forceps being used during the final throes of her delivery.

Katie also realized that she still isolated herself when upset. In her early childhood, around age seven, she saw a war scene on TV and asked her dad if it could happen here. "Well, it could," he said, which to Katie meant it would. Also, she remembered that due to her parents' right-wing religion at age ten she had been forced to watch a film of children torturing their parents.

These connections are important to make, and they help in furthering a resolution of those particular issues. An astrological reading is also helpful, as a natal chart provides a way to get in touch with karmic residue from the past. Often just being made aware of this residue stimulates all kinds of realizations and awareness.

For Katie, this past-life regression proved to be a profound experience. A few days after the session, she called to say that her relationships with both her husband and child were deepening. She had written a lullaby for her son around the concept that she would love him forever. Her husband felt that she had become softer. Katie said that she had opened up to this *man* who had loved her for a long time. She believed that the regression had helped to release her from the petty stuff. Most important, when she woke each morning she felt like a different person. She described feeling lots of freedom, everything having much more meaning. "The whole dread thing still comes up, but this regression work has transformed my life in many, many ways. Thank you."

This sense of dread we then addressed in a second session about four months later. The dread had grown more specific. Katie said that living in California felt almost like living in survival mode. She felt she needed to have peace about where she was to be. "I'm not at peace with the now. I always feel that I need to be somewhere else, doing something different. I want to work with children. I feel that if I could just live in the country I would be okay. Then I would be fulfilled, like bringing my destiny to me."

Katie also felt that she had both invested and enabled in her present marriage, and she wanted to know when it would be her turn. She did not feel that her turn would happen. Her turn would never come. Again, she perceived a choice between what she needed—her path—or her family.

Before we began the regression itself, I thought it would be good for Katie to get in touch with her Inner Guide, that energy that is wise and loving and always there to support her from within herself. She then experienced a very powerful meeting with her Inner Guide, who told her to let Katie's way be flowing like her. "Be fluid and allow *self* to be. Be flexible." After this regression Katie spoke of how wonderful it would be to have the strength and energy of her Inner Guide, "Violet," in their continuing communication. Now we were ready to begin.

Katie found herself wearing a long white apron. She was with a man in a western hat. She described lots of wagons around—Old West—eight wagons. (There had been more wagons when they first started out, but not everyone was traveling as far as she and her husband.)

Katie: There's a fire in front of me. It's almost going out, just cinders.

Sam: What are you feeling as you watch the fire?

Katie: The feeling is the feeling of the present. When are we ever going to be there? (When am I ever going to be doing what I want to be doing?)

Sam: What's the next significant moment?

Katie: A couple of kids run up. Grab onto my legs. We are all very close. I miss that now. Don't have my *family.* (Here Katie grew emotional because she had left her own family in Tennessee to come West with her new husband.) I don't want this part to end because I love these people so much. Children aren't mine. Just playing . . . I feel like I'm guarding myself, afraid to move forward, to see what happened. I feel like I'm in a shadow . . . like looking out from a cave. It's really a protection because it's so hot. (Emotional.) It's so hard for these kids. *I feel like it was wrong to make this choice.* For the kids, it's so hard. Then, always push back my feelings. They say the kids don't know the difference. Little boy is six. Little girl is eight. Don't feel burden from them.

Sam: What is the next thing you are aware of?

Katie: It's morning. The leader, a man with a hat . . . we're moving. My legs hurt so bad from walking. Damn shoes . . . You know you still have to be a lady. Black shoes, lace up . . . I'm riding, legs still hurt. I'm controlling the horses. I've got two horses . . . a lot of bluffs . . . real red . . . dirt is red . . . think I'm pregnant.

Sam: How far along are you?

Katie: About seven and a half months.

Sam: How do you feel about being pregnant?

Katie: That's a happy feeling.

Sam: How is the trip going?

Katie: We're pretty organized. Goat is behind the wagon. My husband is riding another horse. Feels like my left arm is in my right shoulder. Hands aren't working right. They're like tongs. No one in the wagon.

Sam: What's the matter?

Katie: I'm anxious to get there. I'm just so uptight. The
            baby is coming.

Sam: Okay. What is the next significant moment?

Katie: It's night. There's a fire. So tired. I want to go to
            sleep. I just want to have sex with my husband . . . it
            doesn't matter how tired I am.

Sam: Just move forward to the next moment?

Katie: Want to change it. Things just never are what they seem
            like they are. Don't know we made a good choice to
            come. So hard, so hot. So different to what we're used
            to. Is it ever going to end? Are we ever going to be there?
            Is it ever going to be what we wanted it to be? Always
            hoping and believing in something, but not knowing if
            it's ever going to happen. Feel so hopeless. Can't go
            back . . . would die . . . can't stay . . . just have to go on
            even though . . . go on when no hope, nothing green,
            no water . . . no sign of anything. Every day I wake up
            to the same thing, but worry more.

Sam: What are you worrying about?

Katie: About the water supply . . . no food to eat. I just wish
            I was back on the farm where I knew where every-
            thing was. . . . It's green. I knew what to do. So
            secure. I knew if I put seeds in the ground, they
            would grow. There's no way to survive out here. I'm a
            bigger woman than I am now . . . red hair . . .
            Quaker cap on.

Here Katie made an interesting statement.

Katie: *I'd rather be in the desert than here in the present.*
            Everything was spelled out. At least I knew what I was
            supposed to do. . . . There's no place to hide, it's so hot.
            There are these cliffs . . . feel like could just go up,
            get into, but there's no place. It's never going to be
            any greener. Probably never going to be any water

	either. I don't feel like we're going to be chased by anything. . . . There are lots of snakes, makes me want to stay on the wagon. . . . Foreign, too. Nothing here for me.
Sam:	Surely there is something positive. What about the people you are traveling with?
Katie:	Yes, the singing, the people, the love I share with my husband is really good. But, my body is dead, put it there and just go each day, eat and breathe and move as little as possible.
Sam:	What's happening now?
Katie:	Huge thunderstorm. Ball of orange light. It's dusk. Huge canyon. We have to stop. Can't go anywhere. Have to find a way around. Cliffs . . . looks like we're trapped. Feel like I just want to give up . . . that's it . . . have it be over. I'd rather die, except I have this baby to think about. It's so scary to have a baby without your mother. I think I'm a teacher.

Earlier in this past life Katie had taken a teaching position in North Carolina where she had met her husband. She enjoyed teaching, and she felt uprooted from her work as well as her family back in Tennessee when her husband had decided they should go West. Her wanting to work with children in the present life was certainly due in great part to the attachment she felt to teaching the children in this past situation.

Sam:	Move forward to the next significant moment.
Katie:	Huge storm front coming . . . canyons . . . trapped. So, I guess we'll have to go north.
Sam:	What are you doing?
Katie:	Just out looking at it by myself. At least it's water. We're on a bluff, a lookout. It's *desert*. I'm so tired. I just want to lie down and go to sleep and never wake up again. How long do I have to do this? It's like being in prison.

Sam: What's the very next thing that is happening?

Katie: It's later. I can't see, feeling my way. Windstorm. I
          have something tied over my eyes . . . to protect my
          eyes. It's day . . . feel like just going to sleep. Trying
          to go on. The wind is making us stay here. . . . I can't
          go on. I'm behind the wagon. I'd really like to kill
          myself, I think. My husband is there with me. I feel a
          refuge with him. Our relationship is really different
          from anything I've known (referring to the present).
          It's really good. . . . I can't go on. I have to rest. The
          winds won't let us.

Sam: What's happening now?

Katie: We're sleeping together in the back of the wagon. Sun
          is coming up. The wind has stopped. Feels better, but
          worried about having enough nourishment to feed
          my baby. Water is low. We've got enough rice. Men
          are hunting, just rabbits. Sun is up. Got to get going.
          Just keep believing in a place where we can be a
          family.

Katie expressed a realization that the constant going to that
place and never getting there related to her present need to keep
moving because she's not there yet.

Katie: This baby is going to come before we get there. I
          didn't know I was pregnant when we started. Been
          traveling about five months. I'm feeling really heavy,
          restricted. Damn bench is hard to sit on. I just don't
          know if it's worth it. Keep feeling I want to go to
          sleep.

Sam: I want you to move forward to when the baby is
          coming.

Katie: It's night. The baby is coming. It's scary. We're
          outside. I don't like that. Feel exposed. But there's not
          enough room anywhere else. They've got me squat-
          ting to push. About four moms are there. Throat is

really sore. It's hard to breathe. We're close to some cliffs again. There's a quilt under me. I'm looking at it from above. It's so dark. I just want to see that baby. I want to be with my husband. I don't want to have it. I don't have enough energy. I don't know if I can. This labor is just like this trip, going on and on. *Men* always rushing us, telling us what to do. Woman telling them to shut up. Big woman delivering. It's going to happen. I'm afraid of ruining this quilt, because my great grandmother made it, but we don't have anything else.

Sam: How's the baby doing?

Katie: Baby is okay. . . . Coming down . . . hard . . . okay . . . going to be okay . . . pushing . . . feels so good. It's still really dark. Baby's head seems so big. It's crying now. It's weird. The baby's head is so big. . . . Baby is out.

Sam: Good. So, what is the next thing you are aware of?

Katie: I'm having a lot of pain now, in my abdomen. Baby is okay, I think. It's so dark. I can't move. I want to see my baby. The baby looks dark. I'm crying. I'm afraid. I don't think the baby is alive! I just want to die. Oh God, let me die! I don't want to go on living like this. Baby is a boy . . . dead. The pain is so *bad*. I don't want to live. My baby's not alive. They won't let me hold the baby. They're paying attention to me. I'm screaming. I can hear my voice echoing against the rocks. Angry. There's no one to blame. Just agony . . . I hate it. It's hell. I don't want to be here. My husband is trying to console me. "It's all right." I don't believe him. Just let me die. I'm just going to die. I just want to go to sleep and not feel anything. I don't want to be here. He's promised me there will be another time. I don't believe him. *I don't trust him.* It's all hopeless. I just want to die, but I don't think I'm going to. I don't. (Disappointed.) They load me in back of the wagon. One of the kids is there with me. They bury the baby on the side of the hill. It will have some shade there. It's hard to dig—rocks.

Sam: How are you faring?

Katie: I'm so weak. I'll just wither away to nothing. I can barely stand up. I'm not sure why I'm still alive. I'm a vegetable. I'm in the way. I'm a bother. I'm just a burden. I can't cook, can't drive. I'm dead emotionally, just shut off. I can't hate, love, hope, fear. I'm like a board. I'm *stuck* out here in the desert.

Sam: All right, now I want you to move forward to your death.

Katie: There's a tree. That's hopeful. Still outside. It's peaceful, not green, but a little shade. It's about three in the afternoon. I'm not going to make it. My husband is holding me. I'm not worried about him because he is young and strong. I'm happy for me . . . go on to something better. I just never made it. There's a lot of blood, not too long after the baby. He's so sad. I'm so weak. I can't do anything, can't even whisper. I'm just going to be *stuck* out in this damn place forever. First, my baby, now me. I'm like a mad woman. I'm mentally insane. I'm totally deranged. I just can't talk any sense. Stagger around. I'm a burden. I'm dying. Just going to be here . . . bury me out here in the middle of the desert by myself. *Alone.*

Sam: What are your dying thoughts?

Katie: Husband will be okay. I love him. I just slip away. I'm in a white gown. I just float away, into this cave. I'm in the heavens. My husband is sitting there. Everyone has gathered around. I'm not that pretty.

Sam: As you look back over that life, what are your feelings?

Katie: Makes me sad to look back. Fighting for nothing. All that way, that agony. For what? What cause? To die in the desert, be buried there. Have it steal my child

	from me. Baby never got to breathe a breath of air. Bouncing up and down in that old wagon. For what? Going to the Promised Land. It's green there, could farm there, gold there. Someone went before us. Husband was going to be a rancher out there.
Sam:	And what was this place called?
Katie:	It was CALIFORNIA (very emotional). I hate California. (They had been heading for Tulare, California.)
Sam:	Tell California why you hate it.
Katie:	I hate it. Every day, the boredom.
Sam:	Tell it how you feel.
Katie:	You stole my baby . . . my life. You robbed me of my family and friends. I hate you, California! You took my whole life away. My beautiful country, my security. You separated me from the people I loved. *You stole my will to live.* You made me doubt myself and my own abilities. You killed my hope, faith, my body—I hate California.

To accompany her husband to this new land, Katie had left the green, green valleys of Tennessee, the family farm, her security, a place she truly loved, where she had felt safe. She had left it all, friends, family, all of whom she would probably never see again, to go with her husband, *a man.* Katie also realized that this decision involved the choice of *my path* or *my family.*

If, she surmised, *I take his path* (referring to her present husband, and staying in California), *as I did in this past life, my life will once again end in death and agony.* Katie associated family with the farm, the "Garden of Eden." However, in her first past-life regression she chose to stay at home and also died. But, in that life, too, she had left the family. In this pioneer life, she left home, lost everything and died.

In her present life, it had seemed impossible to settle in California and have a family and be happy. She had been living in a state of dread fueled by her past-life experiences. As a result, Katie had been obsessed with the feeling that she needed to leave, needed to dread each day, because any day now she wouldn't make it. *She would die.* Now she understood the source of those feelings of dread and could begin to live in California with a proper perspective of the present, having resolved that sense of dread from the past.

In Katie's situation, I asked her to envision a new ending. In this new scenario she gave birth to the baby inside the wagon. Her husband held her head. She nursed the baby immediately. The baby gave them new hope. They sang to the baby. As they came down over the mountains, the terrain changed. From a bluff they saw greenery off in a valley. They kissed each other deeply, knowing this was their beginning. They still had dry goods. Everything would be okay. They descended the mountain and staked out land. People who had made the journey with them settled close. The wind blew her hair as the sun set. She cried with happiness as her husband held the baby.

We then anchored this wonderful feeling of belonging and love by having her place her left hand over her heart. Next, we envisioned the future, feeling a peacefulness in the present. Katie saw her present-life family at a cabin on the river. She lay in the hammock. A gentle breeze moved through the fir trees. Her young son and husband fished in the river. There were sunlight, beautiful flowers and a little family of raccoons. The three of them had started a family project to build a raft to take downstream. They could stay in one place and be a family. It felt really good not to have to go anywhere.

When I asked Katie if she had any attachments to this past life, she recognized her beloved husband who had taken her to California. He is now a person with whom she enjoys a deep bond of love and friendship. Katie also recognized her attachment to that beautiful green Tennessee land. As she put it, "The land is so gorgeous, the greenery, the air, the rain, the embrace of the land, the valley, plowed, overcast." I asked her to realize how the farm had become much too important. There now existed an imbalance that she needed to balance by realizing that wherever she is can be the "Garden of Eden."

Katie also realized from this past-life regression that she needed to be more responsible for herself. Her present husband would be who he needed to be, and she was the one who needed to change. The time had come for her to start her own path. She now saw her future as bright, with lots of color. She understood it was up to her to keep to her creative path and follow the joy. In closing, Katie asked her Higher Self what direction to take in her work. She was told to follow the children, to relax and it would all come together.

When I heard from Katie a few days later, she described herself as very much attuned with the Eagle spirit in the *Medicine Cards*, a wonderful Native American deck of cards created by Jamie Sams and David Carson, that help us discover our power through the ways of animals. Katie felt that through our work she had connected with her own personal power and had gathered her courage to soar above the mundane parts of her life. She had conquered her fear and gained her freedom. As the Eagle card says, "If you have been walking in the shadows of former realities, the Eagle brings illumination."

Several years after our work together Katie had this to say about the benefits of her past-life regression work: "Having explored many different methodologies of 'inner work' toward a deeper understanding of self, my spiritual connection and purpose on the planet at this time, I must say *the* number one most profound experience of my life was the past-life regression work with Samantha. The process led to profound shifts in my perspective that facilitated greater freedom in all areas of my life. Experiencing the process of dying has allowed me to detach from the emotional, mental and physical bodies and freed me of the illusion that we ARE our bodies. The moment of death in my past lives was precluded by fear, great sadness and conflict, but once I had made my transition I was released into states of profound peace, warmth and love. After experiencing something like that, how can you ever live life the same? The experience of dying in my dreams has even changed. There is now a surrender instead of the struggle to fight for life. My mental conversations of self-judgment have ceased along with the feelings of inertia, depression and the desire to die—all that seems remote and detached from me. I feel free to find joy in each moment. I now find myself living more in the NOW."

XVI

Ties That Bind

The expense of spirit in a waste of shame
Is lust in action; and till action, lust
Is perjured, murderous, bloody, full of blame,
Savage, extreme, rude, cruel, not to trust,
Enjoy'd no sooner but despised straight,
Past reason hunted, and no sooner had
Past reason hated, as a swallow'd bait
On purpose laid to make the taker mad;
Mad in pursuit and in possession so;
Had, having, and in quest to have, extreme;
A bliss in proof, and proved, a very woe;
Before, a joy proposed; behind, a dream.
All this the world well knows; yet none
Knows well. To shun the heaven
That leads men to this hell.
— William Shakespeare

The ties that bind are a reality. We never know exactly when we will send a flare up that attracts to us that particular someone with whom we have gone around before. Rarely does a facilitator have the opportunity to work with both parties involved in this mysterious dance. But, in the case of Patricia and Roy I did, and it was an extremely intriguing unfoldment.

Patricia, a single mother of two young children, worked as a cashier at a local discount store. She found it hard to make ends meet . . . until Roy stepped into her life. He held a good job, made a good living and wanted to help Patricia. He actually wanted to marry her. He was the answer to her prayers. It didn't make sense to Patricia not to marry him, but something major held her back from this commitment. She expressed her reason for wanting to do a past-life regression by stating: "Why can't I love him the way I want to? I can't stand him, but I love him. I'm afraid to be tied down. There's no space."

As she sat there on the chair, Patricia seemed small and somehow fragile, although in actuality she was a good-sized, sturdy young woman who could stand to shed a few pounds. She mentioned her weight as something she would like to deal with. She also mentioned that she had no women friends, saying that women don't like her. Patricia then said, "If I go to a man, I always get what I want. . . . I want all men to find me attractive, give me attention, but do not approach. Roy is smothering me . . . always pushing me."

Patricia appeared a little nervous, but anxious to get on with it. She proved to be an easy subject as she entered the cause lifetime:

Patricia: Feel like a fat woman. . . . Feel like got something all over me . . . it's fat.
Sam: How do you feel about the fat?
Patricia: Feels okay. I'm laughing and happy.
Sam: What are you doing?
Patricia: Serving beer to men in a drinking place . . . All men (she says very pleased). I feel like one of the guys.

She enjoyed doing what she was doing for a while, then I asked her to move forward to an important event.

Sam: What's happening?
Patricia: I'm getting married. (From her tone of voice she

could have been saying she had polio.)

Sam: What's the matter?

Patricia: I feel sad and depressed because I have to look at
            myself . . . all fat for my wedding. . . . I can't be with
            my friends (the men in the drinking establishment).

Sam: What happens next?

Patricia: Well, he's a farmer; he works in the fields. I didn't
            want to get married, but I loved him. We're living on
            the farm. It's in England, but not on the coast.

Sam: How do you like being there?

Patricia: I'm bored, being nothing. No one to talk to . . . feel
            ugly . . . fat.

Sam: What do you do about it?

Patricia: I'm trying to lose weight, so I can go back and see
            everybody. I want their attention.

Sam: What's the next significant thing that happens?

Patricia: I go back, but it's not the same. Before I was happy,
            just one of the guys. Now . . . I lose weight and they
            all want me.

Sam: What happens?

Patricia: I leave my husband . . . felt good for a little while . . .
            but really uncomfortable now. Feel confused, going
            back and forth. He's not what I want. They are not
            what I want. I feel very lost, miserable.

Sam: Move forward to the next significant moment

Patricia: I died.

Sam: What happened?

Patricia: I'm buried alive in wood box. The box is being
            covered with dirt.

Sam: Who is doing this to you?

Patricia: My husband, with a shovel. I'm tied up. Can't say
            anything. I'm upset, real nervous.

Sam: What happened to cause him to do this?

Patricia: Last time I came home, he said I should stay home,
            be like other wives. He's real angry, hits me. I wake
            up in the box.

Sam: What are you experiencing?

Patricia: My chest is heavy . . . my chest hurts . . . I start to go
            away . . . I'm dead now.

Sam: What makes you say that?

Patricia: I'm floating above the box, tingling, feel rested. . . .
            He's leaving. Box is buried in field. . . . *He tried to
            smother me, wanted me to be there all the time.*

As I began to bring Patricia back into the present, an interesting thing happened. In a flash she saw herself, in a hot pink, saloon-type dress that she described as what might have been worn
during the time of Jack the Ripper. I explained to her that it was
probably a past-life fragment from another time associated with
this issue, and that we would have to explore it at a later date. This
brief image impressed Patricia and caused her to confide that she
felt guilt about sex in the present life.

We then talked about the regression. She confessed that she
loved to go out on weekends, be happy, have fun, much as Molly
(her name in the past life) enjoyed being in the pub with the guys.
Her past-life husband smothering her to death, both figuratively
and literally, obviously related to her feelings of having "no space"
with Roy. Her hesitancy about marrying Roy connected to the
subconscious memory that the fun had stopped when she had
married in the past. She also realized that when she had been fat,
in the pub, she had been happy, and that was why she carried the
excess weight now . . . to somehow help her to be happy.

At the end of the session, Patricia said that Roy also wanted to
have a past-life regression about their problem. Great! But I agreed
on one condition, that she promise to say nothing to him about
her session, until after he had been regressed. She promised.

The very next morning Roy called and wanted to come over
right then. The earliest I could see him was the next evening. I
reminded him that it was to his benefit not to know anything
about Patricia's regression until after we had worked. He said that
would be difficult, because he was dying to know what happened,
but he did agree.

The next evening Roy arrived at my door looking rather ominous in a black long-sleeved shirt. This attire struck me as odd, since it was a warm summer night. It had not yet grown dark outside, so I had not yet switched on the light in the foyer when I opened the screen door to let him in. The design work in the door created shadows across his face, adding to his somewhat sinister appearance. I had the distinct impression that our session had already started. It also seemed unusual that he deliberately avoided direct eye contact, as if he did not want me to see him just yet. He was clearly nervous. Hoping to make him feel more at ease, I commented on his black shirt, to which he replied that he thought he looked "devilishly" handsome in black—an interesting statement. As it turned out he had dressed for the part.

The following words expressed Roy's position in the relationship: "I want to find out why we are unable to be together. What is keeping us apart? It's either bliss or hell. It's been more medium lately. I feel I'll just wait a little bit longer. I feel like I just don't fit . . . put off. Offer, don't make me ask. I just don't know what it would take. Every time I try to be with her, something happens . . . tired, no babysitter. I hurt Patricia just recently by trying to help her, when I told her I could have sex with anyone at any time. It didn't matter who it was. Instead of it making her try harder to be with me, it made her feel guilt and shame at being with me. (As I learned later, this issue had to do with the sadomasochistic sexual practices in which they had engaged at his behest.) How can we feel perfect for each other and yet be so far apart?"

Roy was a young man, around twenty-nine years of age, with so many medical problems one had to wonder what he had been doing. He suffered from arthritis, ulcers, high blood pressure, an enlarged liver, and ran the risk of having a stroke. He described his health problems as stress-related, and he listed the names of all the medications he was taking.

As we began the session, he seemed extremely nervous. As the induction continued, and I suggested that we enter a tunnel of time, his body language revealed fear. He trembled visibly, and his hands shook. When I asked him how he was doing, he told me he tingled with fear. In the tunnel, he felt as if he were floating, falling. "Does this feeling of falling scare you?" I then asked him, to which he replied, "Something is saying no." At this point, I enlisted his Higher Self to tell us if we should continue. The Higher Self responded that there was something Roy needed to see. So we continued to move toward the light at the end of the tunnel, stepped through it, and planted our feet in the cause lifetime.

Roy proved to be quite a talker, so I just let him go. To enhance the flow, I also have removed some of my questions.

Roy: It's like Tom Sawyer days. Country town, meadows, rolling hills, trees, old houses. I keep seeing a little girl with blonde hair, ribbon in hair, in a bow. Smiling, laughing. She's outside playing by herself around a rope . . . something . . . a game.

Sam: How is she dressed?

Roy: Dress . . . old type, pretty though.

Sam: Where is she playing?

Roy: This is Illinois, Tom Sawyer times, not really western either. Townspeople walking by me. Rows of men with round-type hats, farmers, workers. I'm just looking. The house next to where the girl is playing is a shack. Poor, I'm almost smirking at it. . . . I think only of these people. I feel like I'm an old man. My suit is old, out of fashion. I'm real proper, cane, top hat, on a dusty road. I'm looking at my watch, feel old, admiring it. I like my money. I'm wondering if that little girl is mine. Not legitimate. Something bad. Weird feeling. I'm fond of her, but not used to admitting it. I'm wondering if that's why I feel so bad. I love her, but I can't be with her. It's the same thing with Patricia. Jesus! There's nothing, no feelings. I feel the little girl putting her arms around me, right around the waist. She loves me. She adores me. I can see it in her face. She just keeps smiling. I feel disgusted with myself because of what I'm not doing.

I'm not being with her. I'm not with her. It's like there's a wall between us, which is my face. Feelings I feel never show through. I feel like I'm not even from here.

Sam: Where are you from?

Roy: England . . . Old England, real dirty, real dark, old England . . . real dark. I fit with her. Nothing strange there. But, I don't belong here. I'm very solemn, white-faced. She's just a bundle of love, more like the ultimate of a little girl, seven years old. Eyes are bright. See Patricia's eyes. She's now crying. She looks real sad. I'm not a very friendly man. I don't know if I rejected her. She's walking away from me to the house. I upset her because I didn't hug her. She knew who I was.

Sam: Who is she to you?

Roy: Think she is my son's daughter. (This identity later proved incorrect, but at this point he didn't want to realize who she really was.) Inside my heart, I love the little girl, but I don't approve, and I'm hurting her right now. They're poor. It's a poor ugly shack. The girl doesn't fit. It's wretched. There's a plain woman, long apron, hair tied back, cooking. I feel real disgust. There's nothing for me not to like, but I don't like them. I'm prejudiced. The only thing I don't like is that they are beneath me. Woman is sweet and warm and gentle. She cares, but I don't like her. The little girl likes her. They feel safe together. She's her aunt. The girl's mother is not there.

Sam: What do you know of the mother?

Roy: She is *beautiful.* WILD! She is wild, fancy dresses, fancy hat. I sense that she is a cheap woman, and she doesn't fit there. She's a singer in a saloon. She's very *slim* . . . red dress, extremely gorgeous. (This proved to be the same "hot pink" dress that Patricia had seen at the end of her session.) Magnetism toward men is almost evil . . . black hair. Way she is looking at me, teasing me, makes me feel mad. The girl's mom has her. arms around me. I don't like it, but I do like it. She's making fun of me. *I feel like I own her.* She's doing this to hurt me, because I own her. I pay for everything. It would have to be sex. I don't feel sex. I'm a sucker. She tells me I'm just an old man. But, she needs my money. She's wild, she's evil, she uses me. That's why I don't go to the little girl. That mother I hate . . . because I want her, can't have her. I pay her when I want her, but I can't have her. I want her, but she disgusts me. I'm too much of a gentleman for this. She's a tramp. Amazing she could have such a beautiful little girl.

Sam: Who is the little girl's father? (This question he ignored.)

Roy: She's lying on a bed naked. I'm standing there watching. My body is flabby, white, grey hairs, overweight, not heavy, ugly. She's beautiful, but wicked. She's laughing, drinking, waiting . . . for me. I'm going in bed with her. She's getting on, but I'm nothing special. I'm stiff, like an old sack of potatoes. She's going nuts, all spread out all over the place. She's just passing time. I'm really stiff, don't really feel like I'm doing anything. Lying on top of her, hands by my sides. Oh no, I'm in there . . . feels good, when put in like going into a deep hole. I did. I put it there. I don't feel very happy. I do, but it's not the way you should feel when making love . . . making me mad. She's laughing at me. I'm slapping her. . . . This is embarrassing, but it makes me feel strong, powerful, not stiff. I'm moving around, still slapping her. She's looking at me different now, afraid but not. I think she likes it. I'm more shocked that she likes it. It makes me feel like I'm ten years younger. She's tamed down now. Now, I'm in control.

She's tied to the bed. I tied her. That's the way we make sex, both enjoy it. Old brass bed, just like the one I have now. This is the way Patricia and I like to make love, too. I was like this when I was a little kid, had that want, always liked tying girls up. I'm a kinky old bastard. I feel like it's a duplicated life carried on to here. There's been two me's all this time, and now I see this man and I understand that part.

Sam: What's happening now?

Roy: Standing there looking, this is part of it, admiring the work. I'm smiling, doesn't seem to be anything wrong. Seems real natural. I'm almost laughing, but I'm younger. Still bald, stronger, bigger arms. I sure feel powerful. Rich, old bastard. Long sideburns, not very handsome, solid, have beer belly. I'm very big, hairy arms, hairy back, big back.

Sam: What do you do?

Roy: Banking. This seems very proper. Sex seems like that's the way it's supposed to be, like having dinner. It's a different time now with same woman. More solid room, like a hotel, feel like I'm in the West, San Francisco. We met again here in the West. Big city boom, a visit. I move around quite a bit, only come here for business. It's a long trip. Wonder if that's why I never see the little girl ... I sure hate that woman.

Sam: Why do you continue to have sex with her?

Roy: Don't know. . . . It's real fun. I feel like I made her this way. That's why she hates me so much. I turned her into a whore. That's why she hates me. She was something sweet. Dressed real plain. Pure, Quaker-like, bonnet, flowery dress, collar up to neck, closed in, flowers in her hands, walking down the street. When I first see her I'm ... I feel shifty, dark eyes, dark eyebrows, not very nice man, smirky, face of an evil man. I'm all in grey, suit, top hat. Everything's dusty. She's a sweet young girl. Introduce myself. She's going into the General Store. She's very impressed with me. I'm a sweet talker. I'm not someone to be afraid of. She never goes in store. We're walking away, back down where I was originally. She's wholesome and pretty, very pure. Bonnet is strange, makes her look angel-like, the way she keeps looking at me, wide-eyed, clean.

Here I asked Roy to move to the next significant moment.

Roy: I feel like I'm raping her. She's confused. I feel like she's hurting more than anything . . . more than the rape. It's the way she feels about me. She doesn't understand. It's love at first sight for her. We're outside, not far from town. I feel her struggling. She's real hurt.

Sam: How do you feel?

Roy: It bothers me. I get the feeling I used to do this quite a bit. I know I did. A trail of rapes.

Sam: Why does this one bother you?

Roy: *I love her.* But, I don't know how I could feel love. I'm a *bad* person. Felt like "Jack the Ripper" type trail. (Interesting descriptive choice.) I'm feeling very evil, very definite . . . not a killer. This is the business I'm in, think I'm a slave trader. I do whatever I want.

Sam: What do you want to do?

Roy: I see myself in dirty clothes. I think I'm a slave trader. I have a whip. I do what I want with anyone, frown on face, lot of power. I'm a mean man, and so evil. . . . I can't feel love for her. I think it's Patricia. Rape is over, get up, get dressed, walk back. I tell her I'm going to take care of her. Something feels different about her, and that bothers me. For the first time I feel like I've done something *wrong*, of everything I've ever done. I'm telling her it's okay. She's pretty shook up, but she's like a western girl, holds everything inside. Bounce back to saloon and she hates me. They look so different, real long pretty hair, but bonnet is still on. She dyed her hair, lot of make-up. Painted woman, dark red lipstick. I almost feel like she still loves me as much as she hates me. I'm really upset at what I did to her because I love her. I can't turn it back.

Sam: What's the next significant thing that happens?

Roy: I'm looking at two faces. I want to be with her now, but I can't. She's a whore. I'm a banker now. She does love me. She hates me. I love her. I can't take her. This is Patricia. She's a saloon girl, a whore, runs it. Maybe thirty, forty. The feeling in this place is that nobody wants to mess with me. They act like she's not laughing at me. She stops laughing then, takes me upstairs.

Sam: What's the next significant moment?

Roy kept moving back and forth in chronological time as he reexperienced this past life. What he had become aware of now was what had happened to Patricia after the first time they met. At first, he expressed some confusion as to what he was seeing.

Roy: See us like a regular family . . . young . . . shortly after the rape. She's cooking. I even feel there's children around, not the little girl. I don't think I married her. I feel like I'm there, but I'm not. I look too nice, like a farmer . . . can't be me. I get a feeling the man is her husband. Those are her kids. Plates on kitchen table. Not too bad, clean cut, sandy hair, young, suspenders, muddy boots, worker pants, hard-working man. This is a couple of years after the rape. She might have been engaged. He doesn't know about it. Feel like I'm looking in their window. I have a right to be there. I own the property. I feel like I own everything. I think I own everything. Not just there. I'm just passing through. She sees me. She wants me. She doesn't say anything. I want her. She wants me . . . I don't know. It's a weird feeling with her. It's always a weird feeling with her. I'm so wealthy. I don't deserve her. She doesn't fit in my life. I'm a very corrupt person. I'm into a whole bunch of things. I feel like I'm the dark side of power. I deal with senators. I take care of what they don't want to take care of. I think most of my money is illegal.

Sam: What happens with Patricia?

Roy: Don't see her for a long time. I feel like I've been looking for her. Think they're all dead. Killed by Indians. They're all dead. That tore her up. She had nowhere to go. I think she hates me because she couldn't find me. Blaming myself. She blames me because I should have taken her then, when we first met. I didn't take her because she was good. I started to rape her, but then *I made love to her*. She did something to me. She made me good. I didn't like that because I can't do what I've got to do. She won't fit into my life. I spend time with her. She's starting to change me. I leave. I don't want to be changed. I don't want that life. I think my past would come to get me. I can't settle down. She wants family, kids. I don't feel like I deserve it. It feels too good. I started my life this way. I have to finish it. Hurts to leave her. She's crying. I'm leaving. I don't deserve her. She doesn't understand why I'm leaving. Neither do I. Impulse . . . I just do it. Don't put that much thought into those things.

Sam: When do you see her again?

Roy: Next time, I see her in the saloon. A lot of time has passed, twenty years. I've changed a lot. She knows me. She would know that I was coming. I knew where she was and didn't come. It's almost like we never had a chance. I finally became the man that could, and now she's this. I don't want this. It's killing me. I can't have her. Everything is reversed. We've changed places. I'm so upset . . . poetic justice. I can't bring her to my place because of who she is. Now I want that straight life. And, before, I couldn't for the other reasons.

Sam: What happens?

Roy: The sad looks go in between the hate looks. She's gotten hard over the years. Never loved anybody but me. I'm pretty sad now. The kid happens then. I'm real emotionally screwed up right now. We both don't know what to do anymore. We're upstairs. We don't know what to do. We can only love each other in the room. Can't take her as my wife. Going in that room is killing us. I just leave.

Sam: Move to the last time you ever see her.

Roy: That was it. I'm in England, after I saw the little girl. (He is referring to the very beginning of the regression.) Her mom died in childbirth. I knew where the little girl was. I had my ways. I always had my ways. I wanted to see her before I died. Now, just memories. Thinking about everything. I feel worn and tired, feel like I've lived four or five lives in one and this is the only part that made sense, the time with her mom and seeing our little girl. I came home to die.

Sam: Where is home?

Roy: In England. Looks like slum area, dingy, dirty room, cold, fireplace, room is real small. It's where I grew up. Sure is ugly. Dim lighting. Counter type thing next to window, a bay window. I lie down on it. Die of a broken heart. I just wanted to die. I see these people looking at me, concerned. They were looking for me. They don't know why I'm here. Brought a doctor. They don't know why I'm dying. I won't

speak. I just lie there and look out the window. I'm
thinking about her. My last thought is about her.

Sam: Where are you now?

Roy: I'm up above, just looking at me. Now, I'm starting
to move away. I go through the roof. Everything is
white.

Sam: How do you feel?

Roy: Feel okay, feel confused. Can't believe I'm there.
Young . . . like a kid and happy.

At this point I asked Roy to be aware of any message from his
Higher Self that would be beneficial for him concerning his relationship with Patricia.

Roy: "See it for what it is." I feel like I have to stay with
Patricia. I'm starting to pull away from her like I did
before.

Sam: What do you need to do to resolve these experiences,
so they don't control your present behavior?

Roy: To feel I'm good. In this life, a little voice tells me I've
got an angle to everything. I do, not just to be good,
but I have an ulterior motive. It would never let me
do anything good without taking it away from me.
Robbing me all the time of satisfaction.

After the session ended, Roy and I talked about honesty, values, love, and his future with Patricia. He felt eager to get back to
her, but I knew they would both benefit from more work. Definite
changes in their behavior with each other needed to occur and be
nurtured, if this relationship were to continue. That didn't happen.

Later on, I did hear from Patricia. She told me that after the
past-life regressions they slowly drifted further apart and were no
longer seeing each other. It seemed as if their being together in the
present lifetime had been based on their desire for each other in
the past, and not so much on who they had become now. She

thought that ending the relationship was for the best. Although it was certainly tougher for her financially, she wanted to get on with her life.

The fact that Patricia flashed on the lifetime that Roy was to encounter in his session when she saw herself in the saloon-type, "Jack the Ripper" number is still intriguing. As a past-life therapist I feel that it would have been fascinating to have covered that same life with her, but Patricia's subconscious had taken her instead to the past life that she had needed to explore.

XVII

No Way Home

All nature is but art unknown to thee,
all chance, direction which thou cannot see.
— Alexander Pope

Randall Holloway needed to know why he felt plagued by a pattern of trying to leave and not being able to do so. He had moved into town from his family's home a couple of hours away. Yet, instead of feeling free, he felt that the town's energy had woven a web of ensnarement that left him at times desperate to leave and always feeling trapped. On several occasions he had left, only to return in a very short time feeling defeated. The need to leave constantly resided uppermost in his mind, but for some unknown reason he feared leaving, and so he stayed, much to his chagrin, as if he were somehow obligated to stay here for the rest of his life, not too far from home.

In the cause lifetime, Randall saw himself as a young man in his late twenties, tall and thin, dressed in black boots, with black pants tucked into his boots. He wore a white shirt, black vest with a black string tie, and a black hat. He enjoyed coming into town to visit the taverns and play cards. It made him feel like a man on his own, when in fact he had been the man of the house, taking care of his sister and mother since his father had left many years earlier. He loved them very much, but also felt them to be a burden that should not be his responsibility. He described the home-stead as a log cabin on some land about a two-hour carriage ride out of town. His mother feared that one day he would be like his father and never come back.

This time he did stay longer than he had intended to stay. Usually he would stay for a couple of days, but this time he was having a good time and didn't want to leave. He identified with the women on the riverboat, where he also liked to play cards. Randall felt that they were like him, stuck doing something they didn't like doing. He felt as if he were married with a child and had never gotten to be a kid.

Randall knew that his mother, and especially his sister, would like to come into town more, but he didn't want his friends to see that side of him, the tenderness that he felt for his family. People saw him as tough and that helped him with his own self-image. He did feel, however, that he had wasted his life. He knew that he could win at playing cards, which did help out at home, yet he also thought about all the money he had spent, lost, and drunk up. Still, he didn't want people to be dependent on him for their happiness, something that also happened frequently in his present life.

When he finally decided to get on home, he felt guilty about having been gone so long. As he rode down a dirt road in the middle of a sunny afternoon, it began to get dark off in the distance beyond the trees. The wind picked up, announcing an on-coming storm. He began thinking that he really should have left the day before. It started to rain, but the storm hadn't really hit yet.

As he approached a bridge, he heard a roar, the sound of roar-ing water, but at the time Randall didn't recognize it as such. With the storm getting closer he grew intent on hurrying across the bridge, as he felt an urgency to get home. As soon as he began crossing the bridge, the water hit in a flash flood without warning. He had no time to reach the other side. Upset with himself, he realized it was now too late to turn around. He still thought he might be okay, but became emotional, feeling that his horse didn't stand a chance hooked up to the carriage. In these desperate moments, he bore the guilt of the death of his horse. As the rampaging water hit, sweeping the carriage out from under him, he jumped up in a futile effort to keep his head above the tumultuous onslaught.

Randall couldn't breathe as he found himself swept swiftly along by the unrelinquishing muddy water, his body being broken and scraped as it catapulted into rocks and debris. Traveling rapidly downstream, he became aware of his body being twisted at weird angles. This caused a feeling of great emotion and panic, as he wondered who would take care of his mother and sister. No longer fighting the ravaging water, Randall felt warm, as his now numb body continued to be pushed along. Soon he lay face up in the muddy water on grass, his body all broken, and still, unable to move. Randall found himself above his body looking out over the land and feeling sad because he was going to miss his body.

Randall's last conscious thought before making his transition was that if he hadn't gone to town he would still have been okay to take care of his mom and sister. He felt that he had abandoned his family for a drink, and that thought left him feeling guilty. This dying thought had governed his present life. Any time he did leave, he found himself unable to stay away. Against his will he felt drawn to make his way back home. Getting back home had been something he could not do in this particular past life.

Often now, too, he found himself in a situation where he took care of people who ought to be taking care of themselves, and in doing so shortchanged himself. He found himself doing this even though he didn't want to feel responsible to, or for, other people. This behavior not only repeated the old pattern of taking care of his mother and sister, but also served as a kind of atonement that Randall had subconsciously set himself up to perform in the present, for his failure to be there to care for people in the past.

Randall had always experienced an active dream state but had decided as a teenager to stop letting his dreams bother him. Significantly, one of several recurring dreams found him in open, choppy water, feeling suffocated. Dreams serve as an avenue to our subconscious, peeling back the layers, giving us peeks of insightful design, helping us to open doors to a greater understanding of self.

For weeks after Randall's regression, he continued to experience further realizations that had nothing to do with his presenting issue. One of his insights related to one of Randall's biggest fears—drowning. He did not fear clear, still water, as in a swimming pool, but had always been terrified of muddy, choppy, quickly-moving water, or water that, like the ocean, tugged at his body. For some previously unknown reason, Randall had carried a memory of the taste of muddy water. Also, he had reacted to movie scenes that depicted people in dire straits in water—always he would feel a sense of panic in his throat and find himself unable to breathe. Further, Randall had suffered from breathing problems in his present life. Now he felt that he knew the origins of all of these responses.

Another interesting insight concerned his having always been drawn to weak, sickly animals. He would bring them home to care for them, only to have them die. He believed that he did this in order to set himself up to reexperience the guilt and loss of having caused his horse to drown. Any time a big animal stumbled or fell, it horrified him.

This regression proved to be very helpful for Randall. He found himself able to take the displaced, unresolved feelings of the past, put them back where they came from, understand them and deal with them. He later told me that his regression had had immediate results. His life-long urge to flee had disappeared. Randall continued to live in the vicinity of home, in the same town, realizing he now had the freedom to leave and would, when the time was right.

XVIII

Mommie Dearest

> *I shall follow the path*
> *to wherever my destiny*
> *and my mission for Truth*
> *shall take me.*
> — Kahlil Gibran

Lydia Graves was an educated and intelligent seventy-three-year-old woman who had always been curious about past-life regression. Well-versed in the Edgar Cayce material, she knew someone whose relative had been cured by following the suggestions in a Cayce reading. She didn't really have anything specific to work on, but just wanted to have the experience. I explained to her that it was important to have a reason to do the work, that it is not something to be done out of curiosity.

As we conversed, it did not take long to find us needing to decide which issue would be most beneficial to address. As a natural recourse, we decided to let the subconscious mind take us to the past life from which Lydia would gain the most understanding.

Lydia spoke of having weak lungs and suffering frequent pneumonia, the first time being when she had been only ten months old. Often in past-life regression work the age at which something traumatic occurs in the past will also prove to be a significant time in the present. Another important episode occurred at age nineteen when she tried to break up with the man her mother wanted her to marry. Lydia wanted to be with a man she had met and fallen in love with. Her mother's pick wanted to continue seeing Lydia throughout the winter break from college, so they could attend all their scheduled parties and social functions. She agreed to this arrangement, against the wishes of the man she loved.

After the holidays, she suffered pneumonia so badly that she missed the entire second semester of her sophomore year. She had made herself sick as a way out of all the confusion. Lydia had not been able to stand up for herself against her mother's wishes. As a result, she never wanted to ever get out of bed again. Maternal manipulation caused her to marry her mother's choice for her, a man she did not love, and to break up with the man she did love. When she told the man she loved that she would marry someone else, he was devastated and she never saw him again.

It was not uncommon for Lydia to suffer pneumonia three to four times a year. She had based many of her life decisions on her poor health. Because of her low energy she never had the confidence to do a great many things. All of her life she had needed lots of rest. When asked how she felt about her poor health, she responded by saying, "It is just a cross you have to bear."

When Lydia had been fourteen years old, much to her chagrin her father had died. Lydia didn't even like her mother and could not understand why she had allowed this woman to run her life. Lydia somehow felt she was hurting everybody else, but ended up hurting herself the most. She knew before the marriage that it would be a disaster, but blindly she thought she could make it work. After crying through the first six weeks of the marriage, and then staying in the marriage for thirty-three years, Lydia finally divorced. She has since learned that she can't make everybody happy.

Working through some initial resistance, Lydia entered the past life through a huge paneled oak door into an enormous room with tall windows that let in lots of light. She described the draperies as heavy and the room as richly paneled, with a huge carved stone fireplace on one wall. The room was very fancy, with extremely high ceilings and quite a lot of molding, and a tapestry on one wall. Lydia felt *very* good in this room. She was ten years old and lost in the memories of when she had been happy, laughing and playing with her father. She didn't want to leave the room, to leave the happiness she had known there.

Again after much resistance, Lydia finally moved to the incident responsible for her wanting to stay in that "happy room." She looked out a window at a cart. At this point, Lydia in the present gasped, "Oh, my God, it's the French Revolution!" She recognized the cart as one used to take people to the guillotine. The little girl watched in absolute horror as her father, the key to her happiness, was forcibly taken away by soldiers who wore uniforms with gold buttons. She felt that she wanted to scream and couldn't. In abject resignation, she said she would be all right, that "you have to face what you have to face." (This was the same attitude taken in the present life in regard to her poor health, which she referred to as "a cross you have to bear.")

After her father had been taken away, she had been left standing in the courtyard, totally unraveled, her hysterical mother crying and screaming, completely wrapped up in her own emotions. All of the servants scurried about trying to help her mother. Appalled herself at what had transpired, and desperately needing comfort, the little girl found herself ignored and uncared for. She had no brothers or sisters, no one to whom she could turn for solace. The light of her life had been snatched from her and she was alone.

In her dismay, she felt so very sad, because she knew she would not ever see him again. When asked how that made her feel, she replied that she would "just have to grow up in a hurry and manage." Everybody would look after her mother and she would have to, also. She was only ten years old and no one ever comforted or consoled her, just left her alone to wander from room to room in this huge, opulent house where she lived. Her thoughts were simply, "What do I do now?" Every day she spent by herself, which she had been accustomed to doing, but now without her dear father, she had no one.

Lydia found this lifetime so uncomfortable and so painful that she resisted continuing. Therefore, we moved forward in time to age sixteen, where she found herself so alone and so sad that she did not want to stay in that life. She just wanted out. An apparition wandering the house would have received more attention. This had been her lot in life since her father had been taken away.

On one particular day, she went into her mother's bedroom to find her mother sitting in front of a dressing table, admiring herself in a hand mirror. Lots of servants fussed over her, as they scampered about. Her mother wore a fancy blue satin dress and a powdered wig, but she didn't seem sad anymore. She planned to go out with friends. Lydia stated that she did not seem that important to her mother. Her mother barely noticed her, and on this day, that was it—all that she could bear. Lydia left the room feeling terribly lonely and despondent.

After Lydia experienced this interminable bleakness, I asked her to go back to a happy time. Immediately she found herself in the "happy room." In this room so warm and full of light, she felt wonderful. She and her father were playing. He was dressed in cream satin knee breeches and a matching cutaway coat, with white stockings, satin shoes with a buckle, and a white wig. He seemed so happy to be with her. Gleefully, they played a game of blind man's bluff, while servants enjoyed watching them play.

Upon reluctantly leaving that scene, Lydia said she would like to get this life over. It felt much too painful. If she could not stay in that room, she just didn't want to be there. Lydia then asked to move forward to the day of her death. The intensity of her desire to remove herself from memories of this life as quickly as possible caused Lydia to move abruptly into recollection of another life and time as a very old hump-backed lady with a cane. But with a little prompting Lydia admitted that this old woman did not belong to that little girl. Lydia had simply jumped into memories of another life, any life, because this one had been so very dreadful that she would do anything to get out of it.

And indeed she did. Lydia did not live to be an old woman in the French lifetime. She drowned herself at age nineteen, in a pool of water with a willow tree hanging over it, out on the expansive grounds of her family's estate. As she had stood on a small arched bridge looking down into the water, she had hoped that this would be a way out. Finally, she could be free. "I won't have to do this anymore" became her final thought as she eased herself gently down into the water. Her body floated under the bridge, as she viewed it from above.

Once on the other side, Lydia found herself glad to be out of that life even if it had meant killing herself. Upon realizing that she had committed suicide in that life, Lydia's hands covered her face and she wept . . . and coughed—a smothering, choking cough. Nineteen had been the same age that she had married in her present life, the same age at which she had given in to her mother for good. In her present life, Lydia had been exposed to several people who took their own lives. She now realized why she could so easily understand them and their decision.

Lydia's major realizations from this French lifetime proved to be as rich as the lifetime itself was opulent in its wealth. First, and perhaps foremost, is the fact that drowning fills the lungs with water. Since Lydia had been ten months old she had been trying to fill her lungs with water, using pneumonia as the avenue. While she drowned in her earlier lifetime, she had experienced a terrific burning sensation in her chest, a sensation identical to the one she felt in the present whenever she came down with pneumonia or any respiratory problem.

Her chest really began to hurt as she remembered the water searing her lungs. Then she began to cough a choking cough that continued for some time. I offered Lydia a drink of water, which turned out to be the very last thing she would have wanted under the circumstances.

In both the French lifetime and her present one, Lydia saw the mother as the same entity. In both lifetimes the mother had been absent in the role of nurturer. In the present, her black nanny had filled the void. In the past, there was no one. In both life-times, Lydia had felt responsible for her mother and at the same time would do anything to get away from her. In the present lifetime, she had escaped by marrying, but she had married the person her mother had wanted her to marry. In the present, when she and her husband had moved back to the same town in which her mother resided, Lydia felt that she could have taken her life again. Instead she developed severe allergies (obviously allergies to her mother).

"How strange," Lydia mused, "that I have been carrying these memories around and letting them influence my decisions in this life. But it certainly explains so many things. I'm sure my conscious decision to do everything my mother wanted me to do in this life has been a direct result of this and other past lives. At the time of that decision, when I was nineteen, I determined not to ever *really talk* to my mother again. I must have let this hatred of her carry over in my attitude toward my children, in that I have never felt that my own children could ever truly love me, that they must feel the same resentment toward me that I felt toward my mother. This feeling was always there, but I could never pinpoint it, or even consciously admit it. That burden has been lifted."

Lydia said that one of the most interesting things about this past life had been the way that it all fit together, in a natural manner, not contrived. She knew that she hadn't made it up. It certainly would not be anything that she ever wanted or expected. "And most assuredly," she stated, "the physical reactions were rock-bottom reality! And still are!"

For instance, when Lydia later started to read the notes of our session she became violently sick to her stomach and had to stop. After that, when we spoke on the phone, she felt cold chills while discussing the session. This overwhelming connection between then and now proved to be an amazing revelation to her. She realized that those horrible feelings from the past life were the same as what she had felt in the present, when she had been nineteen years old and didn't have the courage to be her own person. "I would have done anything to have gotten out of that life. It's truly bothersome to know that I have done it again in this life. Only this time, I literally committed *emotional* suicide." After Lydia's decision to let her mother control her life, she had built a wall around herself, a wall that she did not break down until she reached her thirties.

Always Lydia had felt that for some reason her mother had been ashamed of her. In the present life, at the age of sixteen Lydia had attended a dinner party with her mother, when a woman had come up and patted her on the head and said, "You are an attractive child, honey, but you'll never be the beauty your mother was." This incident occurred at the same age as Lydia had been in the past, when she had watched her mother getting all dressed up. In the past life her mother had been a beauty and a flirt, while Lydia had remained shy, bookish, and introverted. She had not been unattractive, but certainly she dressed much more simply than had her mother. She had remained an unhappy and lonely child who couldn't measure up. Her failure to be able to please people had become more than she could bear in that life, as well as in this one. After having made this realization Lydia said, "Oh man, that's a ringer."

In her present life, Lydia realized she had tried too hard to please others and had sacrificed herself in the doing. She said that was stupid. After a bit of musing, she pondered, "Maybe I walked out on it before, and in this life I had to see it through. But when I really needed to get out, I used pneumonia." (This illness is very similar to drowning.) In her present life, it is not to be overlooked that her father had died from bronchial pneumonia. Also, as in the past life, she had lost her father at a young age, and in both lifetimes she had adored her father.

One thing from Lydia's childhood that had always puzzled her until her regression was her reaction to a conversation her mother and two of her mother's friends once had about death, heaven, sin, and so on, when Lydia was about four years old. Lydia had spoken up and said that she was not afraid of dying. They had all turned to her and asked her questions regarding her statement. She had continued to state flatly that she was certainly not afraid of dying, while she had felt very emotional as she thought, "It's the living that scares me." One of the ladies then patted Lydia on the head. Meanwhile, her mother commented, "She's such a strange child."

A few weeks after our session, Lydia found pictures of a room that was seventeenth-century French, with the huge stone fireplace, large tapestry on the wall and similar furniture. Having the same ambiance, it looked very much like her "happy room." However, the room in the French house of her past-life recollection had been larger, with larger windows and classical façade. The house would have been considered an older house during the time of the French Revolution in the latter part of the eighteenth century. The way her parents had dressed also resembled dress of that period. She even discovered the exact same blue of her mother's satin dress in some draperies that had belonged to Marie Antoinette, as well as in some paintings of the period.

After this regression, I couldn't help thinking how truly intriguing it would have been to have worked with Lydia much earlier in her life. What a blessing it would have been to have broken the pattern of illness and her mother's smothering hold on her at a younger age, when Lydia could have more richly lived the rewards of her resolution and freedom, and saved herself from years of illness and heartache. However, since there are no accidents in life, perhaps the arduous path that Lydia took to these realizations provided a needed lesson that she definitely learned, and a journey never to need repeating.

XIX

The Four of Us

*The way of redemption
leads neither to the left
nor to the right
but into one's own heart,
and there alone is God,
and there, freedom.*
— Herman Hesse

Perhaps we are all bisexual. Perhaps there are several determinant factors, not the least of which is genetic. How many chromosomes of Y does it take to make a "man"? What if there are a few less than the "norm," that then mix with just enough X to make a blend that is female in makeup but male in body? Then, of course, there's the environment. What are you exposed to as a young child? Maybe your babysitter dressed you up in cute little dresses and painted your fingernails pink to go with your blonde curls, even though you were a boy. Maybe you liked it. Certainly, karma has to enter into the overall picture. What lessons are needed? Perhaps you need to learn the lesson of tolerance, or an acceptance of self. What experiences does the soul need to move it further along its evolutionary path?

Maybe we have locked ourselves within too confined a border, too limited a space. Maybe we are male in some things and female in others. We all know a girl who is considered a "tomboy," or a boy who is called a "sissy." For the most part, our society accepts these people, but often theirs is a painful journey. It's also okay now for a woman to wear the pants in the family, so to speak, and for the man to be the primary childcare person in a marriage. Role reversal is a sign of the times.

Only when we get into sexual waters do people get weird. What's the difference? Well, there are those quotes from the Bible that say it is an abomination. Then again, that is the same book that says, in I Corinthians, Chapter 11, "The head of every man is Christ; and the head of the woman is the man; and the head of Christ is God." A man prays to God with his head uncovered. A woman must have hers covered, else she dishonors herself. It goes on to say in verse 7, "For a man indeed ought not to cover his head, forasmuch as he is the image and glory of God: but the woman is the glory of the man." "Bull!" I say. Guess this has to do with the nuns covering their heads and the priests not? Or is it the double standard that still shamefully exists today that makes women worth less than men? In some cultures, women are forced into marriages, burned alive with the husband's dead body, covered from head to toe in black, not allowed to own land, or preach from the pulpit, and the list goes on.

My point here is that we don't always know who actually wrote and *translated* this book, nor what their personal, or political, agendas were. Mistranslations are a known fact. Certain books of the Bible have been removed. Others have been edited to fit the propaganda of the time. Personally, I know God is not a god of wrath, as certain parts of the Bible indicate, but One of Love. What we do know is that we are all created equal, in the beginning. Karmically speaking, our choices have created an inequality, since we each have our own record of our deeds for which we must take responsibility. But, in the beginning . . .

Maybe it's time to break the barriers of prejudice and intolerance and realize that one day a person may feel more male and another day more female. Maybe we don't have to be caged into predetermined forms of actions, but can instead allow ourselves to be present in the moment. There may be a person of your own sex whom you meet in your life, and your feelings for that person may run so deep that you need more than friendship when you seek to express those feelings. Maybe showing your love in a sensual, physical way is a fuller expression. But that doesn't mean you are necessarily gay or straight, automatically a member of a select group. You see the problem is the labeling that occurs—gay, straight, bi, purple, two-tone. Perhaps we are all three, or four, or five—more one than another in certain circumstances. We have to reach a point where it does not matter.

So many of us live our lives fearing that who we really are, or what our feelings really are, might slip out one day and destroy us. I think the real problem is that we have tried to put people in little boxes that define who supposedly they are. Such labeling fails to take into consideration the fact that we are forever changing. We all know that we may feel one way about a particular matter one day, and at a later point we have a different perspective. Is one right and another wrong? Or must we take into account time, place, and situation?

Perhaps it is time to consider that we are sexual beings who have the ability to express our sexuality in myriad ways. As long as no one is being harmed, and both parties are willing participants, why should it matter? Perhaps then people could actually feel free to stop *defining themselves by their sexuality*, and rather take into consideration the whole being. Now wouldn't that be refreshing!

Take the case of Thomas Billings. His presenting problem was that he wanted to reach some understanding of the homosexual tendency of his nature, and how it could or could not exist in his present situation.

Thomas was a man in his early fifties who had tried to play by the rules. During his youth, certain things had happened to him that continued to haunt him. One was a boyhood game of horse one summer in the gym, when he was about eleven years of age. The winner got to pull on all the losers' penises.

The other experience occurred during the time that he spent in the hospital with rheumatic fever, when he was about thirteen years old. He remained sick for two to three weeks in a contagious ward. The doctor, making his rounds with about four or five other people, examined different parts of Thomas and also massaged his penis. Thomas was awake at the time. The doctor asked Thomas if that felt good, to which Thomas replied truthfully that it did. The others giggled and smiled. Thomas didn't understand. His penis got hard. Again the doctor asked Thomas if it felt good, if Thomas liked it, to which he replied that yes he did. The group then left. Thomas was in a great deal of pain due to his illness. His joints hurt and he had to take four or five aspirin every four hours.

About a day later, the doctor came back by himself and repeated his earlier actions. He came in, said hi, stood there, and asked Thomas how he was doing. He then examined Thomas, once again moving his hand onto Thomas's penis, again asking him if it felt good, to which Thomas again said yes. The doctor then put his other hand on his own penis. After that he left and never came back.

Thomas stated that he didn't know why the doctor had pushed his own penis down. He did know that the doctor's touching him felt good, and that he actually wanted the doctor to do it. When Thomas returned home from the hospital, the experience bothered him, so he told his father what this doctor had done. His father replied, "The doctor was probably just doing his job." Thomas's father did nothing, his parents not being the type of people to question authority, certainly not the authority of a doctor.

However, Thomas remained feeling confused and guilty because the doctor's touching had felt good. But there was no one to explain to him what had happened. Nothing else was ever said about it, and soon thereafter his dad died. His father's death was a major blow to Thomas as we shall see.

It goes without saying that the doctor's actions had been inappropriate and criminal. So many instances exist of people in the role of caregivers who take advantage of those who are helpless to help themselves. And, as in Thomas's case, the actions of these people do untold damage.

On three occasions in his twenties Thomas visited a gay bar, but he couldn't do anything. One of those times he actually went home with a man, but had to leave because the situation made him vomit. Those who are so intolerant of alternative lifestyles never take into consideration the kind of pain and torment that many people suffer as they try to discover who they really are. A little kindness and understanding would go a long, long way.

So Thomas put his homosexual feelings behind him, married and had five children. After over twenty years of marriage, Thomas's wife announced that she was gay. He thought it was terrible. Being raised a Catholic he thought marriage should be a permanent commitment. He moved out and went to a couple of gay bars himself, but couldn't follow through. If drunk he could dance, but that was it. In counseling, his counselor told him he was bisexual.

Thomas stated that if he found himself sitting across from a man, he often would have thoughts that he wanted to kiss him. It would be a spontaneous thought, but one that he couldn't act on. Thomas, instead, married a second time and still found himself dealing with some of the same control issues presented in his first marriage.

We would deal with other issues over time, but in this initial session he needed to gain understanding of his homosexual leanings.

Transpersonal hypnotherapy is a wonderful tool to use in accessing those parts of ourselves that cause behavior that is not in our best interests. If, as I explain to my clients, we think of ourselves, of our personality, as a circle, or pie, then each part of ourselves, each piece of the whole, represents a subpersonality. For instance, there is the part of us that loves to dance, or read, or hike, or hates the color orange, or becomes fearful in a particular situation, or overeats as a form of protection. That part of us behaves in a certain way because of something that happened somewhere along the way that now continues to influence our behavior.

Suppose a person started overeating as a young girl because she knew her father was abusing her older, thin sister, and he constantly referred to overweight people as disgusting. Upon hearing that statement, a part of this young girl made a decision to become overweight as a form of protection. Perhaps the father died when she was twenty-one and had never molested her because he found her so disgusting. But she still continued her pattern of overeating several years later, even though her reason to do so was no longer valid.

Through transpersonal hypnotherapy, we are able to dialogue with the subpersonality that is responsible for a behavior, thus gaining insight into why it is behaving the way it is and what it can do to change its behavior. If this subpersonality is indeed a part of you, it is more than willing to take on another job description, if it becomes convinced that it is in your best interests to do so. Neither I, nor my client, can come up with a better job or role for this subpersonality to play than the subpersonality itself can. Sometimes work is needed to help the subpersonality to understand its role in the greater scheme of things, and to assure the subpersonality that it would still be needed and would remain a part of the whole. Often its behavior had begun during a time when that behavior had been helpful or necessary, but once that situation had been resolved, the subpersonality continued its behavior. That behavior over time can become the problem.

In transpersonal hypnotherapy we are able to work with the subconscious, as well as the superconscious, dimensions of the mind. This means going beyond the personal conscious level of knowing into the transpersonal level, into working with one's Higher Self, and into that state of all knowingness and wholeness wherein we find one's true essence. The work of Transpersonal Hypnotherapy is to actualize this dimension of self by identifying and releasing the false programming carried in the subconscious and conscious mind. It is this old pattern that obscures who, in essence, we really are. We need to draw that essence into fuller expression by accessing the Higher Self, the Transpersonal Self, while we are in a deeply relaxed or an altered state of consciousness. In this state of being we can access the origin, or cause, of any self-limiting pattern, from any time frame, including childhood, birth, prenatal, or past life.

Thomas's work represented a classic case in which subpersonalities were definite and defined, but they operated at cross-purposes to himself, and at times to each other. When I asked to speak to the cause of Thomas's homosexual tendencies, a soft gentle, very feminine voice answered, "I'm here." The voice belonged to Sally. I encouraged her to come forward and make herself known, telling her that she had been given the space to express herself. This is what Sally had to say.

Sally: I'm secret. I can't come out much. (Hesitantly.) I like to come out.

Sam: What holds you back?

Sally: Shame keeps me back . . . rejection, by people around me.

Sam: What else?

Sally: Fear . . . the unknown . . . what I will look like if I express myself.

Sam: What would you look like if you had the chance to express yourself?

Sally: Ahhh . . . female clothes . . . soft, loose . . . red, blue . . . rainbow colors. I'd be thin, long hair . . . black hair. A prominent nose, sensuous mouth, pointed chin, nice shoulders, thin arms and fingers . . . nails. Breasts . . . not too big, a nice size. Stomach small, hips proportioned. Smooth, thin legs and feet. Nice looking.

It was obvious that this description of how Sally would look if she could come out of hiding was a fantasy that Thomas had held for a long time.

Sam: How would you feel?

Sally: I'd feel sexual.

Sam: How do you feel toward Thomas?

Sally: He's in the way.

Sam: How do you function in Thomas's life?

Sally: I disrupt things . . . cause confusion.

Sam: What is your positive intent for doing what you do?

Sally: I want to come out. I want to be intimate . . . with other men . . . somebody who is tender and nice. It confuses Thomas. It makes him feel guilty . . . scares him.

Sam: What are the negative consequences of doing what you do?

Sally: I hurt him with his wife. I make him feel like he's lying about who he is. . . . I think he's nice. . . . He's not able to handle it.

Sam: What is the deeper need that you are trying to fulfill that has motivated this behavior?

Sally: To become complete . . . having a relationship . . . being me.

Sam: How would this affect Thomas?

Sally: It would destroy Thomas. . . . I don't want to do that.

Sam: What is an alternative way to meet that need?

Sally: To be me at certain times. Times when no one would know . . . seems secret and dirty. . . . It wouldn't work.

Sam: Thomas, how do you feel about this?

Thomas: I obviously have a feminine side. I want to let it out without it destroying me, and without it hurting others.

Sam: Who would get hurt?

Thomas: Kathy, my wife. My kids might not understand. They don't like it, but try to accept their mother's homosexuality. But, one of our sons won't speak to her anymore.

Sam: Is there anything you would like to say to Sally?

Thomas: I don't hate you. I just want to find a way to integrate you.

Sam: Sally, is there anything else you would like to express at this point in time?

Sally: No.

I thanked Sally and asked her to step aside while I asked if any other subpersonalities, any other part of Thomas, played a role in this situation. If so, I asked that Thomas just let it emerge and give it a chance to reveal itself to him without any judgment from him, allowing it to use his voice and nothing else.

Sam: What is the general feeling that emanates from it?
Thomas: I don't know.
Sam: We're asking you to make yourself known. This is
             your opportunity to express your feelings, your needs.
             Are you there?

A very different, flip but definite female voice emerged and said yes. I asked with whom I was speaking and the voice replied, "Bobby." Bobby sounded vivacious and full of life. More than anything else in the world she wanted to have fun!

Sam: Bobby, how do you feel about Thomas?
Bobby: He's confused. He's in the way.
Sam: How do you function in Thomas's life?
Bobby: (After a pause.) I'm not used to talking . . . I'm used
             to dancing, fluttering around . . . I'm some kind of
             dancer . . . a dance hall girl. I'm adventuresome,
             spontaneous, flirty.
Sam: How would you describe yourself?
Bobby: Blonde, rosy cheeks, sexy, alive . . . ready for fun.
             Don't get much fun.
Sam: What is your idea of fun?
Bobby: Dancing, making love, drinking. (It is interesting to
             note that Thomas had been in AA for over ten years,
             which had definitely drained Bobby's fun.)
Sam: What is your positive intent for behaving in this way?
Bobby: Come out and have fun! Being loved, being desired.
             Thomas doesn't get enough. He's got to earn it.
Sam: How does he earn it?
Bobby: By being good, being more masculine . . . Causes

anger . . . the more masculine, the more dominating he becomes, the more he causes anger in himself and others.

One of Thomas's issues was his anger. It had hurt him in his job and in his personal relationships. We would deal with this anger and its origin in our later work.

Sam: What are the negative consequences of your behavior for Thomas?

Bobby: He'd be lost. He'd have to give up everything. . . . He'd have more fun . . . for a while. He needs to be living for himself, for me. Just to have fun. He needs to get a whole new life. Probably lose a lot. Worth it for a while, but he'd have a hard time. He'd go for some of it. If he'd just let his dominant side (to Bobby this is his feminine nature), come out and take him where it takes him. He needs to know it's okay, not wrong to have a feminine side. He needs to accept it. Be more open, more fun, more thrill seeking, more alive!

Sam: How do you see him accomplishing this?

Bobby: He could do those things and be who he is. He's a guy trying to do the right thing. He needs to enjoy without worrying if he will succeed. Be open, not so judgmental. Dance, flirt . . . do both . . . probably both. Don't judge it. Just do it!

Sam: What is the deeper need that you are trying to fulfill that has motivated this behavior?

Bobby: I want to be *loved* and have fun. . . . I want to love . . . *become full*. I want to be alive!! I want all of it. He can do that. Expand a little bit, not worry. Just do with the good spirit of not hurting anybody.

Sam: What is an alternative way to meet this need of being loved and becoming full?

Bobby: He needs to take some risks. Get out of his rut. He

needs to give up his judgmental attitude of homo-
sexuals. He has this in him, too, so he needs to be
more compassionate. (What Bobby asked would not
be so easy for Thomas, a Catholic who had carried his
guilt for most of his life.)

Sam: Thomas, how do you feel about this?

Thomas: She's brought out the need to have fun, not judge,
          and find a healthy release for it. I'm just half of what I
          am now.

Sam: What would a healthy release be?

Thomas: Having some place where I could wear women's
          clothes. Alone at first . . . then with someone. Going
          out would be the last thing.

Sam: Bobby, is there anything else you would like to say
          for now?

Bobby: No, that's it.

At this juncture in the session, I asked if there was any part of
Thomas that had a problem with this. Naturally, the judgmental
one now got his chance. We learned as the session continued that
his name was Lloyd. I gave Lloyd permission to express himself.
Lloyd had a thoroughly deep, very masculine voice.

Lloyd: I'm masculine, strong, know what I want. I want him
          to be strong, male, successful, make money, get over
          all this stuff.

Sam: Why do you feel he needs to get over all this stuff?

Lloyd: He's causing shame. He needs to just be more manly.
          Fight it. I feel like I'm losing my grip on him.

Sam: How does this make you feel?

Lloyd: Makes me feel angry . . . but, he's not happy.

Sam: How do you feel toward Thomas?

Lloyd: I respect him. He's a little wimpy at times. He needs
          to get more assertive. Needs to get on. Start standing
          up to people. Get on, or quit his job and get a better
          one. Thomas needs to work harder. I was raised that

way, that people work hard. . . . He's talking about behavior that's not acceptable. I don't want to be a part of it. Be tough on me. But, he's not making it. Means well . . . If he has to, I want him to do what he needs to do.

Sam: How do you function in Thomas's life?

Lloyd: As the driving force. I pull him up when he's down. But . . . I can't support him in all this. I'm not strong enough. I'm just part of the package.

Sam: What is your positive intent for doing what you do?

Lloyd: To help him be happy, successful. Be of help to others in a manly way.

Sam: What are the negative consequences of your actions?

Lloyd: I dominate, take over. I dominate when I feel fearful. It alienates others. I become defensive; makes others defensive. I don't allow him to grow. The anger that is expressed is too big for the situation.

This anger had been a problem in both work and his relationships. Thomas would blow sky high when the situation did not warrant it. This overreaction had at times been costly.

Sam: What is the deeper need you are trying to fulfill that motivates this behavior?

Lloyd: I want to feel safe.

Sam: Is there an alternative, more positive way for you to feel safe?

Lloyd: I've got to expand, just like he does. . . . I've got to be willing. This doesn't work.

Sam: Lloyd, imagine yourself experiencing that behavior. What is that like for you?

Lloyd: Experiencing expansion . . . It'd be fearful. I'd be on edge, nervous, suspicious probably. It would be a stretch. I'd have to let go of the reins, take a lesser role. . . . I could do that, if it's the best thing for Thomas.

Sam: What are your feelings about all that Lloyd has
            brought forward?

Thomas: I think the intent is good . . . but bottom line . . . I
            know I'll follow his way. Be alone, a loner. I feel he
            has my best interests at heart. He's been through a
            lot.

After asking Lloyd if he had anything else to add at this time,
I asked all three subpersonalities to participate in a mediation,
wherein they each could ask the other what each one needed from
the other, and invite each one to share what he or she would need
from the other in the way of making a change, or changes.

Lloyd said to Bobby that what he needed from her was for her
to realize that he didn't want to be gentle. He wanted her to be
careful, not to destroy him in the process. But, he also said that he
didn't want her to stop, because she had something "we" need.

Bobby said she would help Lloyd and Thomas to have fun,
and advised Lloyd that they all have Thomas's best interests at
heart. "We're all in this thing together."

Sally needed Lloyd to be gentle, to know that she was a part
of Thomas. "Be gentle, Lloyd, it'll be all right. Sounds exciting."

To Bobby, Sally said that she looked forward to this, felt excited.
"I'm ready. I've waited a long time for this. I'm ready for the fun."

Sam: Well, Thomas, what do you have to say about all this?

Thomas: I've learned whole new sides of me. . . . I feel closer to
            the identity of Sally. I want that part of me to come
            out. . . . I appreciate Lloyd's generosity. . . . I'm
            curious about Bobby. I'm excited about this. I've
            carried this around a long time. I am a good person. I
            just need to find a way.

This became an appropriate time to ask for the guidance of
Thomas's Inner Guide. We did this by calling for an animal to come
to Thomas that would lead him to his Inner Guide. The animal mani-
fested as a horse, brown with a white spot on its forehead and black

mane and tail. It was a young horse. Thomas followed him as it led him to where his Inner Guide waited for him. Thomas felt the presence of his Inner Guide and put out his hand. A soft woman's hand, warm and soft, took his. This energy emanated trusting and peaceful energy, a goodness, a wisdom. She was middle-aged with silver-grey hair and blue eyes. Dressed like an American Indian woman, she appeared very friendly and smiled at Thomas.

I now instructed Thomas to ask her if she was his true Inner Guide, and to receive her response. She continued to smile and said yes she was. I now asked Thomas to project a mental beam of light to that person and notice what happened. As he did so, the energy around her body glowed. It grew bright and radiated out from her. She felt comfortable and trusting to him.

Now I asked Thomas to experience his Inner Guide and how she felt toward him. He said that she felt loving and understanding, amused and confident. He proceeded to ask her what change or changes he now needed to make.

IG: *Just relax.* It will be all right. In time it will be fine.
           Go easy. Accept yourself and your feelings. Change
           will come.
Thomas: Is this a good journey I'm going on?
IG: It's your journey and one you must go down.
Thomas: Will you help me in this change? Guide me and
           protect me?
IG: I'll be with you the whole way.
Thomas: I'm ready for the journey.
IG: We'll go together.
Thomas: It's nice to know that I'm not doing this on my own.
           (She smiled.) In the morning, when I see the sun, I'll
           remember that she's there.

I now asked Thomas, his Inner Guide, and his three subpersonalities to join one another in ascending a beautiful golden column of light, feeling themselves all working together to Thomas's highest good.

Thomas's Inner Guide now addressed his three subpersonalities.

IG: I want you all to work together to make this man
          whole and you will become whole.

Sam: What is Sally's reaction to all this?

Thomas: She's smiling, she's happy, at peace with her body
          and herself. She's excited. She's dancing, throwing her
          arms up. She's happy.

Sam: What about Bobby?

Thomas   She's glowing and smiling and almost crying from
          happiness.

Sam: And Lloyd?

Thomas: He has a big grin on his face. He can't believe it. He's
          excited. He's on for the ride.

Sam: And how is your Inner Guide reacting to all this?

Thomas: She has a glow about her and a peace . . . an all-
          knowing smile.

Sam: And what about you, Thomas?

Thomas: I'm happy . . . smiling . . . amazed! Looking at these
          people and realizing they're all me. I'm feeling free
          and happy, so happy.

Sam: Great. Now I want you to ask Sally what she wants
          from you and let her share her response with me.

Thomas: Sally, what do you want from me?

Sally: I want you to let me exist in you. To let me be part of
          you, so I can be there and we can be happy together.
          Let me work in you and express myself. . . . Love me.

Sam: Now ask her what she needs from you.

Thomas: Sally, what do you need from me?

Sally: Just respect Thomas, and be gentle. Just *be yourself.*

Sam: Now do the same thing with Bobby.

Thomas: What do you want from me, Bobby?

Bobby: I want you to be open to fun, excitement, experimen-
          tation, living. Let Sally exist. Be open to that side of
          you.

Thomas: What do you need from me?

Bobby: Open and trust the change. Let me be me.

Sam: Now do the same with Lloyd.

Thomas: What do you want from me, Lloyd?

Lloyd: I just want you to be mindful of me. Don't shock me into this. Expand me gently.

Thomas: What do you need from me?

Lloyd: Remember that I'm a good part of you, too. Don't abandon me. (Here Lloyd grew emotional.) I'm scared.

Thomas: We're both scared. I need you as much as I need these people. You're not going anywhere.

Sam: Okay, now tell each of them what you want from them.

Thomas: I want you, Lloyd, to just let go of the reins. Don't run away on me. Sally, I want you to feel free to be yourself. And Bobby, I want you to do what you need to do to help me. Just be gentle and don't hurt anybody in the process.

Sam: Good. Now, Thomas, ask your Inner Guide to just be there and remember to use her wisdom in all this. All right, now I want you to envision a time in the not too distant future when you are feeling good about yourself, when you are feeling whole, and are bathed in acceptance, all of the parts of yourself working together for the common good.

I now gave Thomas a little time to complete this process. I then asked him how he felt.

Thomas: I feel myself mellowing, not worried so much about work, relationships; trying to envision a way to express feminine side.

Sam: Okay, let's do that now.

Thomas now allowed himself to envision the experience of being in feminine clothes and being with someone of his own sex in a positive, loving situation, feeling good about himself at the completion.

I now asked Thomas, his Inner Guide, and his three subpersonalities to join hands forming a circle of loving, healing light, inviting Sally, Bobby, and Lloyd to balance their energies with one another, and within Thomas, taking as much time as needed to complete the process. I then made positive suggestions to reinforce the work we had done. Lastly, I connected Thomas with his Higher Self so as to receive any message that would be most beneficial at this time. His Higher Self told Thomas to trust himself and expand, adding that there was another lifetime that would be helpful to explore. This we did in our next session.

In closing, I reiterated to Thomas that he would go forward from this day knowing that he creates his own reality. I reminded him that he had asked for guidance and help to trust himself, to expand and to enjoy life, truly accepting all parts of himself, knowing that they functioned as one, well, together, working for his highest good, to express all that he is.

By the time of our next session, Thomas had bought some feminine intimate clothing. He found their purchase to be an intimidating process. However, actually putting them on gave him a freeing sensation. He now felt more certain that he wanted to stay married, although he no longer wanted to live his life "with most of who I am having been put in a bag." He felt that he wanted to try expressing the softer feminine side of himself in his sexual relationship with his wife. He realized that anything that made him feel fear, that made him feel inadequate, he refused to own. He wanted to get rid of it by projecting it onto other people's behavior.

In this session, Thomas determined that the time had come to stop living in fear, to stop living with a sense of impending doom. He knew that the time had come to move on, but seemingly he couldn't. He was so afraid of the feminine. He still felt the need to be in control of everything. In his work he could not control decisions others above him made that he knew would not be in the best interests of the company's growth, but his position did

not let his opinions be heard. So, his great deal of frustration mani-
fested as anger. More than anything Thomas felt strongly that he
now had to deal with his *lack of trust,* a lack of trust that he would
be okay, that things would work out, that the Universe would
provide. To him Murphy's law made more sense. Whatever could
go wrong would. We began a past-life regression.

As Thomas stepped through the light at the end of the tunnel, he perceived his feet as covered with soft leather moccasins.
He stood outside, on a path, wearing leather pants and a loose
canvas pullover shirt. He said that he felt like an Indian, male,
with long hair lying on his shoulders. He stood alone.

Sam: What are you feeling?

Thomas: I feel excitement. I'm going to do something. I'm
           hunting for something.

Sam: Do you have anything in your hands?

Thomas: Yes, I'm carrying a tomahawk.

Sam: Now, be aware of what you are doing.

Thomas: I'm running from people.

Sam: Who are you running from?

Thomas: From soldiers, people with guns.

Sam: How does this make you feel?

Thomas: I feel frightened. I've got to get away.

Sam: What's happening?

Thomas: They're shooting at me . . . I'm running . . . ducking
           down, trying to get to the water, to a canoe to get
           away. . . . I'm in the canoe. They're shooting. I think
           I get shot. Fall into the water. I'm in pain and drown-
           ing. I'm going down the river, like rapids. Trying to
           hold on to the rocks. They're catching up with me
           and they're shooting at me. They shoot me . . . kill
           me. I get hit in back of head, arm, and when I roll
           over, the chest.

Sam: What is your last conscious thought?

Thomas: It's over. It's a relief. I didn't get away. They've got me
           and it's over.

Sam:	Move back to the beginning, before you were on the path.
Thomas:	We. were in a battle. . . . We were overwhelmed.
Sam:	Where does this happen?
Thomas:	In our village. We were swarmed down on. Only ten or so of us. They shot everybody. We don't have guns.
Sam:	Who swarms the village?
Thomas:	British soldiers.
Sam:	How do, you feel toward them?
Thomas:	They are inhuman, ruthless cowards. . . . They have rifles. . . . I had a wife and daughter. They were killed in the village. My daughter is only five years old. She was just sitting out playing with a couple of kids . . . and she just got shot. Then, my wife came running over to her and she got shot. . . . All got shot quick. . . . We must have been running from them before. We're camped in a wooded area in a valley. Normally, we live near water.
Sam:	Who are "we"?
Thomas:	We are Wyandottes.
Sam:	Where do your people live?
Thomas:	We live in Ohio, Pennsylvania, upper New York. . . .
Sam:	What are you feeling about what's happened?
Thomas:	I feel like we've been hunted down.
Sam:	How does this make you feel?
Thomas:	My reaction is to get away. Fight them another day. I feel outrage . . . fear . . . anger . . . helplessness.
Sam:	Let's go back to what happens when you reach the canoe.
Thomas:	I get shot in the right shoulder as I push off and start paddling. It hurts. I've got to get away. . . . I can't die like this. *I've got to get even.* (This attitude of needing to get even had carried over into his relationships, especially at work.) Makes me feel hopeless.
Sam:	If the hopelessness could speak, what would it say?
Thomas:	Why let me die in this way? Why let them die in this

way? Let me live longer to get even with these animals. . . . What does it all mean? Why were we
hunted down like dogs? . . . It just happens. . . .
Why be alive and have that happen . . . end like that?

Now, I asked Thomas to move right on through his death
experience to the other side, stepping into the light that is his
Higher Self and becoming aware of the attachments he still carried
to this previous life. The attachments were anger, hopelessness,
despair, the idea that somebody was out to get him, a sense of loss,
outrage, fear of the unknown, as well as fear of what was coming,
and a fear of people. We dealt with each of them in turn.

Sam: Where does this anger come from?
Thomas: Anger that this could happen. That there is a God
           that would let it happen. My family and I didn't
           deserve this. To be killed like dogs, hunted down.
           They took what I wanted—my loves. Then, they
           snuffed out my own life. Where was the God that was
           looking out for me? Why didn't You give me some
           warning so I could have done something? Whose side
           were You on? (Thomas expressed a great deal of anger
           now, filled with emotion.) I don't want to be any part
           of anything that lets that happen. I'd like to kill the
           people that killed me.
Sam: Where is this anger now?
Thomas: It's buried, because when it comes out, it's harmful
           and mean . . . way out of proportion. It's out of
           control.
Sam: Is this the anger that erupts in the present in your
           work and personal relationships?
Thomas: Yeah, it's the same.
Sam: Let the anger out now. Give it a voice.
Thomas: (Intense anger now explodes from Thomas.) Get
           away! Get away!! Don't shoot! I'll kill you!!! God, why
           did you let this happen? I'll kill you dogs. Hunted

down like a dog. I'll come back and kill you. You destroyed me and my family!! I want nothing to do with you, God!!!!!

Thomas screamed this last part, bringing up tears and the sadness behind the anger—the sadness at losing everything . . . *of being abandoned by God.* He felt terrible, lonely, and lost. This was much the same way that he had felt when his father died and when his wife went away on business trips, that he was once again being abandoned.

Sam: What about the hopelessness?

Thomas: In the present, I always feel like somebody is going to get me. What is close to me is going to get taken away. I don't measure up, because if I did I could have saved my family, my people. It was a situation with no way out.

This feeling of not measuring up in the present, because of an inability to have saved loved ones in the past, is a common theme running through past-life regression work.

Sam: What about the despair, the sense of loss?

Thomas: It comes up all the time as the insecurity I feel about my job . . . the constant turmoil in my marriages, the arguments . . . the confusion. I had to raise myself from the time I was fourteen when my dad died. I wasn't capable of raising myself.

Sam: And the sense of outrage?

Thomas: When that doctor was molesting me, the others with him were giggling, as if I were completely insignificant . . . the way my dad's death was treated like a social event. No one ever tried to talk to me, to see how I was doing.

Sam: What about the fear?

Thomas: I fear what's coming. Never occurs to me that it

might be good. I have a fear of people. I don't trust them. I fear the loss of my job. I fear that I don't measure up . . . that I'll be alone. I fear people . . . the power that they have . . . soldiers with guns.

Sam: What else do you now realize?

Thomas: I've always been against authority; those above me, I have a problem with. Most people I've ever worked with would say that I'm a difficult person. I don't trust them. We don't always have the same agenda . . . I don't need them. It's all about a lack of trust. God deserted us in the village. God deserted me when my father died. God deserted me when I had to leave my young son behind when our marriage broke up. She ended the marriage, yet I was the one that had to leave.

All of his statements revolved around trust, or a lack thereof. Thomas found himself able to make the connections to this Indian past life, understanding now where the anger, the hopelessness, the impending doom and all the rest of his emotions had come from.

In our next session, Thomas and I worked to reinforce the positive steps he had taken as a result of this regression. His relationships with others had improved. He no longer created the problems. His attitude had changed. He grew more aware of who he was, and he began to learn to accept the fact that God is there for him.

Thomas said that he was now dealing with his issues. He now looked at people for what was right with them instead of what was wrong. He found himself to be less judgmental and more understanding. No matter what might happen, he had learned to be open to what was in front of him.

When the old tapes of *got to get even* or *they've got me* would start, he began to remind himself that being in control was not necessary, just *being* was. Being true to himself in the situation at hand, and truly expressing what he felt, took precedence. He understood he could now do so without using language destructive to himself and others. Thomas learned to trust that whatever happens will be okay.

What was so pleasurable for me was that I got to see the subtle transformation taking place in Thomas. He was becoming more and more self-assured as time went by. He was more positive and, quite naturally, he was becoming more spiritual. He was taking responsibility when it was his "stuff" and learning to detach when the "stuff" coming his way had nothing to do with him.

In this next session, we decided to access a lifetime that would give us insight into Thomas's need to have more confidence in both himself and his future. But before we started the regression, we met with his Inner Guide to ask her what changes Thomas needed to make in his life, or in his behavior, in order to express more fully all that he could be.

IG:	Be more open to what's in front of you. Be more accepting. Keep doing what you're doing and just enjoy the day. Explore who you are. Trust your own goodness. Have fun.
Thomas:	In area of gay . . . whatever you call it . . . how do I deal with that?
IG:	Just be calm and peaceful with it. Let it reveal itself as it will. Continue to do what you're doing. You'll know.
Thomas:	In my job, what do I do for my future?
IG:	Learn what you need to learn today. Talk to people you trust. Keep aware of your needs. Be open and take *chances*.
Thomas:	In area of wife, what do I do?
IG:	Build her up and praise her and love the woman she is, and you'll get more in return.
Thomas:	How about my kids?
IG:	Accept them where they are. Put yourself in their shoes and listen more. Think of them more often.
Thomas:	Thinking of the kids makes me a little sad. I think

what they need is what I need. The key to all of us becoming whole is that we have to give to each other. They need to see that I love them a little more often. Somehow I have to let go of the idea of money when it comes to them. Let go of idea of what it's going to cost me. Enjoy them. Listen to their problems. Don't try to solve them. If I can help, then do so.

Next, we dropped in on Sally, Bobby, and Lloyd to see how they were faring.

Sally: I'm feeling neglected. I think Thomas has forgotten. He's doing better, but I think he's moving away from us. I help him to be more comfortable with himself. I don't react, just let things happen. My positive intention is to help him to lighten up a little. Good for me that he doesn't go too quick. Keep in the process.

Bobby: I'm bored! I feel like I'm being left in the cupboard. He needs to have some fun, like a dancing class. (Here, Thomas suggested going away with his wife for Valentine's Day, which perked Bobby up.) I can be patient for a while. My function is to probably not stir it up. My positive intent is that he'll open up more if he continues, and I'll be able to blend in, instead of taking him down a road he can't go. I'll lighten up. Take the joy in each day. Thomas won't forget.

Lloyd: No problems here. I support Thomas by trying to keep him out of the battles. Eliminate his being too critical and too demanding. It's actually a lot better. I will continue.

Obviously, things had begun working out more to Lloyd's liking than to what the girls wanted. But they all had Thomas's best interests at heart and remained willing to continue because they all recognized Thomas's progress. Now we could move into the cause lifetime regarding Thomas's lack of confidence in himself and his future.

Thomas: It's the painted desert just like in the Western movies. I'm in the cavalry, on a horse, wearing boots, coveralls on legs, blue uniform. Sitting still. I'm alone.

Sam: How do you feel about being alone?

Thomas: There's a loneliness, a danger. I'm a scout, looking for Indians. I'm about five miles away from my own people.

Sam: What's the next significant thing that happens?

Thomas: I see Indians on the horizon. They look like they're ready to do some damage. I need to get back and warn my people. I turn around and start riding hard. They're coming pretty good. . . . I'm riding hard . . . long way to go . . . My life is in danger . . . so is everybody else's.

Sam: What's happening now?

Thomas: Some Indians appear in front of me. They capture me. I don't know why they don't kill me. They're holding me. I'm still sitting on my horse. Normally, they just kill people. They're Apaches. . . . They have guns. (This surprises Thomas.) They encircle me . . . hold me off. The rest of them went on by. . . . They're going to get the cavalry.

Sam: How does that make you feel?

Thomas: I feel like I failed to warn them. . . . I feel frightened. . . . What's going to happen to me?

Sam: What does happen?

Thomas: They get me down off my horse. Put rope around my shoulders and just drag me along the ground. They're going fast. I'm conscious. . . . It's hurting . . . could kill me . . . pain in my head. Every part of my body . . . all of the dust . . . Just getting hurt more . . . weaker and weaker. One of them comes along and shoots an arrow in my back. Another comes along and chops my head with a tomahawk, in front. Cuts head open . . . pound it in. . . . Takes a knife and scalps me. The other one retrieves the arrow and they leave me. . . . It's a horrible way to die.

Sam: What are your feelings during all of this?

Thomas: When being dragged, I feel, my God, this is how it's going to end. When I get the arrow . . . the pain of it . . . hurts like hell. There's no way out of this. The ultimate is when they pound in my head and leave me as an animal. I'm in my twenties. I'm going to die. Feelings are mostly *fear.* What a horrible way to die. Shock. Being a scout, there's always the possibility. But when it happens, it's so final. The pain is so great . . . of being dragged on the ground. Shocked.

Sam: Let's move through the death experience and totally out of the body to the Other Side. What are you experiencing?

Thomas: It was quick. No forewarning. Life was snuffed out quickly. When it happened was no way to be prepared for it. Thank God there's a life after. It's peaceful here. Can leave that corpse and move on. It just is what it was. It's not the end.

Sam: Now, let's move up the column of golden light to your Higher Self, becoming aware of your attachments to this past life.

Thomas: The fear of the unknown, that somehow I could control events before they happen . . . I feel responsible.

Sam: Okay, first, what about the fear of the unknown?

Thomas: Been in places when thought was safe and have rug pulled out from under me. Sort through what was mine and what isn't. Shake your faith in having any control over anything. They tend to mark you (Here Thomas referred to situations where he found the rug pulled out, as in this past life.) so when you feel it,

	you know you are in trouble . . . last thing you ever want to see again.
Sam:	And what about feeling responsible?
Thomas:	I failed to warn them . . . I'm not measuring up in present life.
Sam:	I want you to leave that feeling of failure in the past, but first be aware of any connection to the present.
Thomas:	The big one is when I go on job interviews, I tell my weaknesses, not my strengths.
Sam:	Good. Now leave it in the past.
Thomas:	I'm going to dump it in the grave with the trooper, when somebody finds body and buries it . . . or vultures eat him, eat all that, too.
Sam:	What about the feeling of no way out?
Thomas:	Still gets in the way. I have to not give it any power. Live as if today and tomorrow are okay. Good judgment in work. View work in good way. I don't need to put me in the equation every time. Be more objective in evaluating what I do. It's not life or death in this deal. Absolutely more than two options . . . always a way out. Can broaden my horizons by figuring out other options. Any situation I stay in is of my own choosing. . . . Now just be responsible for what I do.

With the help of this regression, Thomas gained much insight into how he had let the death in this past life dictate the way he handled situations in the present. He had expected to fail, expected to be held responsible, even when the problem had not been his fault. He had not allowed himself ownership of what he did well. Now, he saw himself in full acceptance of the reality that he could move through life without having the rug pulled out from under him. He now came to terms with the shame and failure he had carried concerning the failure of his first marriage and the loss of his first job. Looking at both situations clearly, he now saw that the marriage had problems from the beginning and that he had done the best he could in that job. The direction the company had chosen to take had been one he couldn't do. Thomas now left the shame and failure of those two present-life occurrences back in the past with the trooper. Interestingly, Thomas always referred to the scout as the "trooper."

Our next past-life regression came out of Thomas's question, "Why do I set myself up so I'm not okay? There's an inner conviction that I'm okay. My shoes are good."

This time as Thomas entered the regression a gray wall blocked his way. It presented itself because Thomas resisted looking at what he would find behind it. The resistance had to do with his accepting the fact that he had been there at this time in history. Working through the resistance, Thomas found himself in sandals, wearing a brown robe.

Thomas: The earth is bare, dirt road. It's daytime, a cold day. I'm alone. I'm in the country, kind of hilly. It's a gray day, dark. Time when Jesus was on the Earth. I'm walking . . . walking to Calvary. There's some kind of answer there. I'm going to the crucifixion. I don't know why.

Sam: What are you feeling?

Thomas: The gloom and despair of that moment . . . lack of hope . . . the feeling of being alone and abandoned . . . If I'm believing I'm truly alone and without hope, I don't have a clue what to do.

Sam: What are you doing?

Thomas: I'm crying. . . . I'm crying because I'm lost. There's no hope.

Sam: What is the reason there is no hope?

Thomas: Apparently, whomever I put my faith in is gone. Apparently, I'm not enough. . . . Getting the idea that the Spirit is within me . . . that's the gift I got. I had to cry and feel totally beaten to see another way. Whatever was to be given is inside me. That was what I was to get from the experience, instead of being sad and defeated.

Sam: How are you feeling now?

Thomas: I feel light, feel myself rising up, feeling alive and free.
          I've been given the gift to live. Makes me feel good.
          Makes me feel happy and enthusiastic. Gives me
          energy. Even death can't stop that gift. I've been given
          the light to go on—to live. I had to shed the old life
          by crying and feeling this loss. All this happened at
          Calvary. He's dead on the cross and it's dark and
          rainy. It's just ugly. I'm just alone. Don't see anyone I
          know. There must be people there. I'm a follower of
          Jesus.

We now moved back in time to the first time he saw Jesus.

Thomas: It's the Sermon on the Mount. There's a light around
          him, and a new way. I feel enlightened, drawn to
          him, changed . . . probably confused. I'm male . . .
          twenty or so years old. I go up to be closer to Him, to
          get to know Him. I do get closer. He looks at me with
          love and understanding . . . just His glance . . . I just
          feel different. I feel like I've been touched. I want to
          become part of whatever it is. I follow Him. I become
          a follower and hang with Him. I feel whole, feel good.
          He says, "Come sit beside me, Philip." He continues
          to teach to whomever is around. I feel honored. I feel
          special.

Sam: What kind of work do you do?

Thomas: I'm a fisherman.

Sam: Move forward now to a significant time in your life.

Thomas: Out on a boat. There was a storm. It was frightening.
          He just stood up and told it to stop and it did. "Be
          gentle." The sea was calm and the sky was clear and
          everything became peaceful. Guess I was in awe of
          Him. I just knew he was more than a man. Made me
          feel that this Man was important. I needed to do
          what He told me.

Sam: What did he tell you?

Thomas: He said, "Trust me. Help other people. Listen to my
            words. Follow me." Which I was already doing.
            Following Him. We went ashore, sat around the fire.
            He talked some more. There was a Holiness there, a
            life-changing experience that was just going to go on
            and on. We did go on. When He died that just
            destroyed it, because He was everything. Later, in the
            weeping, the Spirit came upon me and whatever He
            had was in me, and that was the gift He gave me. I
            was no longer afraid. I could go out and talk to the
            people and spread His words and look at them
            differently. They needed to be loved. To bring some-
            thing to their lives that they didn't have . . . to
            awaken the Spirit within them. Feel good doing this
            work. . . . Others with me. Feel alive, worthwhile.
            Good comes from it.

I now asked Thomas to move forward to his death.

Thomas: I'm about twenty-six, twenty-seven years old. I'm
            outside. It's the same kind of death—crucifixion. But,
            I'm not afraid, because they can't kill the Spirit.

Sam: Why were you crucified?

Thomas: Happened because spreading His word, causing
            unrest . . . change. Apparently, when you change the
            norm you are in trouble.

Sam: Were you crucified alone or were others with you?

Thomas: Two others died with me.

Sam: What are your dying thoughts?

Thomas: Anticipation of where I was going . . . to be with
            Jesus. The Spirit is alive. The conviction is inside.
            They can't kill it. See me being turned on by the
            Spirit and what they do doesn't matter.

Sam: Now move through the death experience to the Other
            Side. What are you aware of?

Thomas: Bright, happy, joyous . . . free and open. No worries.
           No need to worry.

Sam: Connect now with your Higher Self and with its
           help, make the realizations you need to now be aware
           of.

Thomas: Problem with my present life is that there is no inner
           fire, no enthusiasm. Been beaten down over a long
           period of time, losing sight of just what I'm looking
           for. People I've come into contact with have their own
           value system . . . not mine, and in process of dealing
           with them I have adopted theirs, which slowly
           destroys me, or renders me ineffective. I have to be
           true to who I am. My value system is such that I need
           to be willing to walk that walk, disappoint whomever,
           and help a lot of people. I can't always give people
           what they want, not in my best interests. There's no
           point in focusing on the negative. There's nothing to
           be derived in that. Need to change what needs to be
           changed inside me. I need to be more honest with
           who I am. If I don't share common goal, then say so. I
           need to get involved in things where I'm helping
           people, instead of concentrating so much on making
           money; or help people as I'm doing my job. I need to
           trust things will work out. Trusting has not been in
           my life for a long time. It started when my dad died.
           I felt abandoned, fearful and overwhelmed. Mother
           didn't allow herself to be emotionally supportive for
           me. Later on, I had to give her love so she could
           finally give me some, and she couldn't do a whole lot
           of that either.

Sam: What is keeping you from realizing in the present
           that truth that the Spirit is within—the gift you were
           given as Philip?

Thomas: Experiences up to now reinforce the lack of trust . . .
           the negative aspects of life. I must be trying to hold
           on to something, instead of having it always leave.

My father, mother, marriages, relationships, kids, jobs, I try to hold on to them so I don't feel that loss, like I did when Jesus died. I haven't had much inner conviction of myself. The abandonment of Jesus and my father left a void. The force of the feelings of hopelessness when Jesus died reignited with the death of my father.

Sam: Transfer the feelings of Spirit entering you that you felt then as Philip into the fourteen-year-old boy you were when your father died. When you had no one to comfort you, no one to turn to, no one to trust, allow those wondrous feelings of Spirit to merge into your total beingness, letting you know that you have all you need to face whatever comes. It all resides within *yourself.*

In later sessions, Thomas worked to build up his self-esteem, coming to know deep within himself that it was okay to simply be who he was—to be Thomas. He knew he was on his own journey. It was no one else's. He was no longer denying his own power. He knew his job was not who he was. He had reached the point in his life where he could accept his own Divinity, that he was a part of God. The guilt and shame he carried from the past had now been left in the past. He was free to be. He now dealt much more easily and confidently with whatever came up each day in his life, trusting himself and the Universe to provide all he needed. He knew it would be an ongoing process.

Closing

In Chekhov's presence
everyone felt in himself
a desire to be simpler,
more truthful,
more one's self.
— Maxim Gorky

Enter joyously into the work of *knowing the self.* This journey may lead you into past lives, or down another path that you may need to travel. Heed whatever speaks to you. Mark your steps, wherever they may take you, to free yourself of the fear that holds you bound as a bud on the stem of life, a bud that never fully opens to the sun.

There are power places across the planet, in countries all over the world. Some are better known than others, even famous. Some are known by the very few. Others have yet to be discovered. The most important one may be the earth under your feet, the earth in your own garden.

Be still wherever you are and know that you are God. Then there is truly no separation. Earth, you, and God are One and the vibration that this realization sets into motion opens the channel, the kundalini dances, and you are on fire. It is Transmutation Time—time to move beyond this plane of existence.

We, as a humanity, are moving into a higher vibration. All of the past, all of our lives, all of our choices lead us to this moment. The shift in consciousness is now. It is an awakening to the Self.

Dare to be the Rose of Self, opening to reveal the Light of the "*I Am*" within.

We are approaching an archway of Light. Only those who bear Light, who are the Lightbearers, can pass through. We serve as the bridge, the bridge to the life we were destined to live—simply be who you are and take your place—in the life of the One Humanity.

Signs of recognition are all around us, and within us, reinforcing the forward momentum of our choices. Symbols abound. A spiritual hunger exists within humanity, and it is a hunger that will not be abated. Insights are startling us awake. Intuition is opening the door of revelation. The gathering is about upon the Earth.

Listen to the still small voice of your True Self—heed the intuitive promptings of your Higher Self. Enter into the Circle of Light. We are all here now. The wondrous dance has begun. Don't be late. Don't hesitate. Leave your fear behind. Take your place in the Garden of Light, in the seat of your soul. Dance. . . . Stars are beneath your feet. . . .

About the Author

Samantha Doane-Bates, BA, CHT has been a metaphysician for
over twenty-nine years. She is a certified Transpersonal Clinical
Hypnotherapist, board certified Past-Life Regression Therapist, and
professional astrologer. Samantha has taught classes, lectured, conducted workshops and seminars in this country and in Sweden.
She is a professional faculty member of the International Association for Regression Research and Therapies, has been a faculty
member of the American Federation of Astrologers, has served as
President and a member of the Board of Directors of Aquarius
Workshops, and is a member of the American Council of Hypno-
tist Examiners. After living in Los Angeles for twenty years,
Samantha now resides in Lexington, Kentucky, where she has a
private practice. She can be reached at *www.samanthadoane-
bates.com.*